Birds
at Your Feeder

Birds at Your Feeder

A Guide to Feeding Habits, Behavior,
Distribution, and Abundance

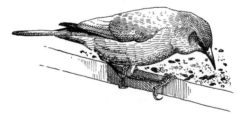

Erica H. Dunn and Diane L. Tessaglia-Hymes

Illustrations by Peter Burke

Abundance maps by Jeffrey Price

Summarizing data from Project FeederWatch, a continent-wide
survey sponsored by Cornell Laboratory of Ornithology, Bird Studies Canada,
National Audubon Society, and the Canadian Nature Federation

W. W. Norton & Company • New York • London

Copyright © 1999 by Erica H. Dunn

All rights reserved
Printed in the United States of America
First published as a Norton paperback 2001

For information about permission to reproduce selections from this book,
write to Permissions, W. W. Norton & Company, Inc., 500 Fifth Avenue,
New York, NY 10110.

The text of this book is composed in Weidemann Book, with the display set in
Caxton Light.
Design and composition by Dana Sloan
Manufacturing by Quebecor Printing, Fairfield, Inc.

Library of Congress Cataloging-in-Publication Data

Dunn, Erica H.
Birds at your feeder : a guide to feeding habits, behavior, distribution, and
abundance / Erica H. Dunn and Diane L. Tessaglia-Hymes ; illustrations by
Peter Burke ; abundance maps by Jeffrey Price ; sponsored by
Cornell Laboratory of Ornithology ... [et al.].
p.   cm.
Includes bibliographical references (p.   ) and index.
ISBN 0-393-04737-7
1. Birds—North America. 2. Birds—Feeding and feeds—North America.
I. Tessaglia-Hymes, Diane L.   II. Cornell University. Laboratory of
Ornithology.   III. Title.
QL681.D87   1999
598'.097—dc21   98-35661
                                                            CIP

ISBN 0-393-32231-9 pbk.

W. W. Norton & Company, Inc., 500 Fifth Avenue, New York, N.Y. 10110
www.wwnorton.com

W. W. Norton & Company Ltd., Castle House, 75/76 Wells Street, London W1T 3QT

1 2 3 4 5 6 7 8 9 0

In memory of William H. Drury Jr., 1921–1992
Teacher, mentor, and valued friend
and
To Greg Butcher in appreciation for
guidance, support, and friendship

This book summarizes results from Project FeederWatch, a continent-wide survey of bird feeders sponsored by the following organizations.

The Cornell Laboratory of Ornithology (CLO) is a membership institute dedicated to the study, appreciation, and conservation of birds worldwide. CLO maintains programs in academic research, public education, and citizen science to foster understanding about nature and the importance of earth's biological diversity. CLO and Cornell University together provide an international center for training both amateurs and professionals in the ecology, evolutionary biology, and conservation of birds. The lab is the data center for Project FeederWatch.

Bird Studies Canada conducts and promotes studies of birds and communicates results to the public, with an emphasis on studies that increase understanding of avian distribution, abundance, and population changes and their underlying causes as well as studies that support conservation of Canadian birds and their habitats. BSC has a long tradition of involving volunteer naturalists in scientific studies. It founded the immediate forerunner of Project FeederWatch and continues to administer FeederWatch in Canada.

The National Audubon Society's mission is to conserve and restore natural ecosystems, focusing on birds and other wildlife for the benefit of humanity and the earth's biological diversity. Among its many educational and research ventures, NAS is a partner in sponsoring Project FeederWatch.

The Canadian Nature Federation is Canada's national voice for the protection of nature, its diversity and the processes that sustain it. CNF promotes Project FeederWatch as part of its environmental education activities.

Acknowledgments

This book would never have come about without the enthusiastic and dedicated support of the thousands of feeder owners enrolled in Project FeederWatch. Participants often tell us that their enjoyment of winter bird feeding is enhanced by taking part in FeederWatch, and we sincerely hope that this book will further add to their appreciation of the birds they love to watch.

The authors' employers, the Canadian Wildlife Service and the Cornell Laboratory of Ornithology respectively, contributed much-appreciated time for us to complete this book. Other CLO staff also made significant contributions. Margaret Barker ensured that the program expanded and continued to run smoothly, while Colleen Dittman and Inga Wells spent untold hours opening envelopes and editing data. Roger Slothower's help in automating production of percentage maps was invaluable. Paul Prior and Jon McCracken of Bird Studies Canada read the entire manuscript and made numerous suggestions that greatly improved the final product, as did Gale Evva Gelfand. Peter Hussell helped make graphs. Finally, we wish to thank the dozens of corporate sponsors who have given generous support to Project FeederWatch over the years.

Table of Contents

Birds
at Your Feeder

Introduction

◆

Nearly one-third of the entire North American population over age sixteen is involved in bird feeding—close to the *combined* total for participation in hunting and fishing (about 10% and 20% of adults, respectively). Not only is the bird-food industry large, it is still growing, increasingly emphasizing specialty products for attracting or discouraging specific bird species.

Despite this wide interest in bird feeding, and although birds are among the best-studied organisms on earth, remarkably little research has been focused on birds using feeders. Until now we have not even had good information on exactly which species of birds visit feeders in various parts of North America—let alone how frequently they visit or in what numbers.

This book aims to fill some of the basic information gaps and show how bird feeding fits into the winter survival strategies of our feeder clientele. We have summarized many of the fascinating nuggets of information that can be found in the scientific literature about our common feeder birds, such as how many acorns a Blue Jay can store each fall or why Dark-eyed Juncos flick their outer white tail feathers. We also cover some of the scientific data on characteristics of people who feed birds and what foods they offer. And there is a comprehensive discussion of the known positive and negative effects of bird feeding on bird populations.

This book, then, goes a step or two beyond the "how-to" of bird feeding, a subject on which many good books are already available. The core of this volume is a series of species accounts, offering authoritative information on the biology of common feeder birds that is relevant to what you see in your own backyard. Each of these accounts has maps showing distribution and abundance of birds at feeders. The data for these maps and much else in this book come from Project FeederWatch, an ongoing cooperative survey that attracts over 10,000 participants annually (to join, see Appendix

I). Since 1987 volunteer FeederWatchers from all parts of North America have recorded the birds at their feeders at weekly intervals from November to April. Many of the results from this remarkable project are being published here for the first time.

A Profile of Bird Feeding

◆

When a hungry bird decides to dine out at a fast-food establishment, where should it go, and what is it likely to find there? Just as a restaurant guide for humans summarizes information on proprietors, the physical settings of dining rooms, and the menus, so should we be able to describe these same characteristics for bird feeders. In practice, however, it is not at all easy to find out who feeds birds. If you send out a questionnaire, the people most likely to reply are those most keen on bird feeding, so results are biased. The only way to get a truly representative picture is to interview a random sample of respondents.

Both the United States and Canadian governments have undertaken such surveys on people's attitudes to wildlife, and the results are very similar for the two countries. In 1980–81, about 20% of all North American adults purchased seed specifically to give to birds, and later surveys showed that this figure had risen to about one-third of the populace. Americans alone served up over a billion pounds of seed in 1985. Many additional people offered miscellaneous foods, such as kitchen scraps.

Men and women share equally in the enjoyment of feeding animals, in contrast to other wildlife activities often undertaken predominantly by men, such as hunting. Not surprisingly, the people who are most likely to feed birds are those with leisure time (including many retirees) and those who own homes (giving them a yard in which to put up feeders).

Given this profile of the average bird-feeding restaurateur, what is the expected physical setting an avian customer can expect when it drops in to dine? A survey of feeder owners among the members of the Wisconsin Ornithological Society indicated that about 40% lived in rural areas and about 40% in suburbia. Less than one-fifth lived in urban centers. Similar figures came from a 1996 survey of six thousand Project FeederWatch participants spread all across North America. The majority, including many of the urban dwellers, lived within a mile of a stream or pond and a woodlot. Nearly every FeederWatch yard was planted with both deciduous and coniferous trees and shrubs—but remember that FeederWatchers are committed naturalists who may be more fond of yard plantings than the average homeowner.

Most people in the general population feed birds only in winter, but FeederWatchers usually offer food year-round. In the 1996 survey the most popular types of feeders were hanging seed dispensers (used by 90% of participants in Project FeederWatch), suet holders (83%) and raised platforms for seeds (68%). Over half of participants on the West Coast had hummingbird feeders. Plain (unsugared) water was rarely offered where freezing occurs, but in arid regions like the American Southwest, 90% of FeederWatchers provided water regularly. Most participants operated numerous feeders of several different designs, typically seven in total, although one enthusiastic individual operated thirty-eight feeders. Note once again that these figures are from a committed subset of feeder owners; one or two feeders per home is much more likely to be the norm.

Lastly, we take a look at the menus typically available at avian restaurants. "Mixed seed" is a near ubiquitous offering, provided by casual as well as serious feeders of birds. The average Project Feeder-Watch participant commonly offers three foods in addition to mixed seed: suet, black-oil sunflower, and niger (thistle). Niger and suet are more frequently found on menus in the East, while black-oil sunflower is a northern specialty. The average FeederWatcher runs through more than 300 pounds of seed each winter and 20 pounds of suet and fat-based bird "puddings."

A survey of specialty foods offered by participants in Project FeederWatch uncovered an amazing array, of which only the most common sorts are listed in Table 1. The "miscellaneous" foods of Table 1 included such seeds as milo (offered at 2% of feeders), barley, canola, oats, canary seed, and wheat (each available at 1% of sites). A few feeders were laid out with a veritable bird banquet, including gourmet-quality nuts (walnuts, almonds, pecans, pine nuts), mealworms (usually purchased but sometimes home-grown), and even earthworms or grubs collected from gardens. Other foods occasionally offered included cheese, alfalfa pellets, goat chow, grape jelly, salt licks—even dead rodents. Some FeederWatchers put out nonedible

Table 1

Common feeder foods

People with a strong interest in bird feeding often provide foods other than seed mixtures. Here are the ones presented most commonly by FeederWatch participants.

Food	Percent of sites (out of more than 6,000) at which this food was offered in 1996
Black-oil sunflower seed	72
Niger seed	62
Suet/fat	54
Water	51
Bird "puddings"	32
Cracked corn	20
Baked goods	19
Striped sunflower seed	14
Hulled peanuts	14
Whole corn	14
Fruit	13
Hulled sunflower	12
Millet	11
Sugar water	10
Peanut butter mixes	10
Peanuts in shell	10
Eggshells	9
Safflower seed	8
Grit	7
Table scraps	6
Popcorn (already popped)	5
Meat scraps	4
Pet food	4
Peanut hearts	3
Other foods (see text)	7

items to attract birds, such as the grit listed in Table 1 and (in spring-time) materials for nest building.

Birds in search of a fast-food restaurant, then, should easily be able to find one in any settled area of North America, at least during the winter (many bird buffets close for the summer). Well-treed residential neighborhoods constitute the avian strip malls where feeders are most likely to be found. Once a bird has located a feeder, it can be fairly certain of finding sunflower seeds, cracked corn, and other small seeds; but higher-class establishments may offer a far wider selection on their menus, including beverages and sweets. However, like gourmet restaurants for humans, sites like these are harder to find.

Key references: Brittingham and Temple 1989, 1992b, Filion et al. 1985, 1993, Shaw and Mangun 1984, U.S. Fish and Wildlife Service 1988, U.S. Dept. of the Interior et al. 1997.

Feeder Clientele

◆

The previous chapter considered what is available to birds on the lookout for a bird-feeder dining establishment. Here the topic is a market analysis for the restaurant proprietors—feeder owners. Who are their potential customers, and what do their clients prefer to eat?

Naturally the most common feeder species are birds that eat seeds, and these make up only a limited proportion of the seven hundred-plus bird species of North America. Jays, chickadees, nuthatches, and finches all find feeder foods acceptable substitutes for the tree seeds that make up part of their normal diets. Weed-seed consumers, such as sparrows, are also readily attracted; however, not every seed-eating species will necessarily visit feeders. The most common visitors are those that thrive in mixed agricultural and residential landscapes. Species that like wide-open country often find feeders less congenial, and this is probably the reason that blackbirds are relatively uncommon in backyards (although some feeder owners find them distressingly numerous).

Unlike food preferences and habitat considerations, social behavior does not appear to be important in determining whether or not a species is a "feeder species." A few regular visitors are fiercely territorial, such as mockingbirds; some spend the winter in loosely territorial flocks, chickadees among them; while others live in foot-loose wandering flocks, including Pine Siskins.

Quite a few birds with little or no interest in seeds can also be attracted to feeders if you take the trouble to provide appropriate foods. Suet is relished by such species as woodpeckers because their normal fare includes fat-rich beetle larvae, and hummingbirds are, of course, attracted to sugar water, which mimics their natural diet of flower nectar. Fruit eaters may visit to consume dried or fresh fruit that has either been purchased or gathered from wild sources in season and frozen for later use—although few people will want to collect the poison ivy berries that are an avian favorite. Many insect-eating species will sample small bits of crumbled suet, and FeederWatch participants have reported hawks and eagles carrying off chunks of beef heart or rabbit carcasses that were put out for their benefit. Even herons and egrets can be induced to visit feeders by offering fish (either dead or alive). One feeder owner with more esoteric interests hauled two dead horses home from her local veterinarian, put them out in the back pasture—and attracted seventy-five Turkey Vultures.

In total, over 350 bird species have been reported by participants in Project FeederWatch to take food from feeders. Only about ninety of these visit regularly enough to merit detailed accounts in the pages ahead. Approximately 180 more are casual visitors, with a few records turned in each year. The most regular of these are listed in Table 2. Another dozen or so are escaped cage birds or domestic poultry, ranging from budgerigars, lovebirds, exotic finches, and a variety of large parrots to peacocks and ornamental pheasants. Finally, about sixty wild species have been recorded by FeederWatchers only once or twice over the life of the project. These are usually migratory stragglers, sick birds, or vagrants desperate for a source of nourishment whether the food source is appropriate or not. Some of these rare sightings are of common birds that are only rare as feeder visitors, and a few are likely to have resulted from misidentification, but many are genuine rarities that have been confirmed by local birding experts, such as the well-documented records from FeederWatchers of a Brambling in the state of Washington and a Rustic Bunting in British Columbia.

Of course, out of the large number of species that occasionally come to feeders, only a relatively small number turn up at any one location. As shown in Figure 1, most sites are visited by only ten to

---

Table 2
Wild species recorded regularly but uncommonly at feeders

These species were reported visiting at least 10 feeders in 1994 (out of nearly 6,000 with data from Project FeederWatch sites). The list includes some insectivorous and predatory birds that may have been attracted by water or potential prey rather than by foods offered in the feeders themselves.

Great Blue Heron	Nuttall's Woodpecker
Turkey Vulture	Black Phoebe
Canada Goose	Eastern Phoebe

Wood Duck
American Black Duck
Mallard
Bald Eagle
Northern Harrier
Northern Goshawk
Red-shouldered Hawk
Red-tailed Hawk
American Kestrel
Merlin
Peregrine Falcon
Ruffed Grouse
Wild Turkey
Northern Bobwhite
Killdeer
Ring-billed Gull
Herring Gull
Ringed Turtle-Dove
White-winged Dove
Common Ground-Dove
Greater Roadrunner
Eastern Screech-Owl
Great Horned Owl
Northern Pygmy-Owl
Barred Owl
Costa's Hummingbird
Allen's Hummingbird
Red-headed Woodpecker
Acorn Woodpecker
Gila Woodpecker
Red-naped Sapsucker
Red-breasted Sapsucker
Ladder-backed Woodpecker
Nuttall's Woodpecker
Black Phoebe
Eastern Phoebe
Say's Phoebe
Loggerhead Shrike
Northern Shrike

Hutton's Vireo
Clark's Nutcracker
Horned Lark
Bridled Titmouse
Verdin
House Wren
Winter Wren
Golden-crowned Kinglet
Blue-gray Gnatcatcher
Western Bluebird
Mountain Bluebird
Townsend's Solitaire
Wood Thrush
Gray Catbird
California Thrasher
Orange-crowned Warbler
Townsend's Warbler
Yellow-throated Warbler
Black-and-white Warbler
Abert's Towhee
Rufous-crowned Sparrow
Lark Sparrow
Black-throated Sparrow
Savannah Sparrow
Lincoln's Sparrow
Swamp Sparrow
Snow Bunting
Rose-breasted Grosbeak
Black-headed Grosbeak
Indigo Bunting
Western Meadowlark
Rusty Blackbird
Boat-tailed Grackle
Hooded Oriole
Baltimore Oriole
Red Crossbill
White-winged Crossbill
Eurasian Tree Sparrow

Fig. 1: Most North American birdfeeders are visited by 11–25 species each winter.

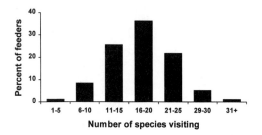

twenty-five species over the course of an entire winter. The variation among feeders can be related to the size of the winter avifauna in different regions. For example, the typical Alaskan feeder hosts only eight species, and northern feeders in general attract fewer species than sites farther south. Within any one region, however, there is still a lot of variation in the number of species visiting, depending on neighborhood habitat, feeder surroundings, numbers of feeders, and types of food offered. One FeederWatcher in California handily outdistanced the regional average of eighteen species by attracting fifty-one during a single winter.

Although bird feeders are usually put out with the intention of attracting birds, other animals are only too happy to take advantage of a free food source. Hummingbird feeders draw insects, for example, often to the annoyance of human proprietors. A surprising number of mammals have been recorded at feeders, too (Table 3), not even counting the domestic varieties that have been reported, including horses, burros, and Brahma bulls—among other types of cattle. The most frequent wild mammal visitor is, of course, the gray squirrel, reported by just under half of FeederWatch observers in western regions and by nearly 80% in the east. These squirrels frequently face a barrage of obstacles specifically designed to impede their access, but other mammals, such as deer, are usually more welcome. Some feeder owners try hard to attract them by putting out hay or salt licks, but normally the attraction is inadvertent. Surprised FeederWatchers have learned that vegetarian moose are fond of sunflower seeds and that meat-eating weasels, raccoons, and bears are not above swiping a suet basket. (While most people take these latter incidents in stride, it is hard to ignore a black bear that has become a repeat offender, and the only recourse in such cases is to stop offering suet altogether.) A few predators are attracted by the birds and mammals using the feeders rather than by the feeders themselves. The mountain lion noted in Table 3, for example, was attracted by deer that were eating bird seed.

Table 3

Mammals reported visiting feeders

Predators were usually attracted by other feeder visitors, rather than by birdseed. (Data from Project FeederWatch.)

Opossum
Armadillo
Gray (Desert) Shrew
Short-tailed Shrew
Star-nosed Mole
Eastern Mole
unidentified bat
Coyote
Gray (Timber) Wolf
Red Fox
Gray Fox
Swift Fox
Black Bear
Raccoon
Ring-tailed Cat
Marten
Fisher
Short-tailed Weasel (Ermine)
Least Weasel
Mink
River Otter
Striped Skunk
Hog-nosed Skunk
Badger
Mountain Lion (Cougar, Panther)
Bobcat
Woodchuck
California Ground Squirrel
Rock Squirrel
Round-tailed Ground Squirrel

Thirteen-lined Ground Squirrel
Golden-mantled Squirrel
Yuma Antelope Squirrel
White-tailed Antelope Squirrel
Eastern Chipmunk
Townsend's Chipmunk
Cliff Chipmunk
Merriam's Chipmunk
Least Chipmunk
Western Gray Squirrel
Tassél-eared (Abert, Kaibab) Squirrel
Eastern Gray Squirrel
Eastern Fox Squirrel
Apache Fox Squirrel
Red Squirrel
Chickaree (Douglas' Squirrel)
Southern Flying Squirrel
Northern Flying Squirrel
Pocket Gopher
San Diego Pocket Mouse
Stephens' Kangaroo Rat
Pacific Kangaroo Rat
Beaver
Cactus Mouse
California Mouse
Deer Mouse
White-footed Mouse
Eastern Woodrat
Dusky-footed Woodrat

(table cont. page 12)

Hispid Cotton Rat

Southern Bog Lemming

Boreal Red-backed Vole

Meadow Vole

Muskrat

Woodland Jumping Mouse

Brown (Norway) Rat

House Mouse

Porcupine

Nutria

Pika

Snowshoe (Varying) Hare

Black-tailed Jack Rabbit

Eastern Cottontail

New England Cottontail

Desert Cottontail

Mountain Cottontail

Brush Rabbit

Marsh Rabbit

Peccary (Javelina)

Elk (Wapiti)

Mule (Black-tailed) Deer

White-tailed Deer

Moose

Having identified the customer base for our bird-feeding efforts, our next question concerns the foods that will most appeal to the feeder visitors we want to attract. As noted in the previous chapter, nearly all feeder owners put out "mixed bird seed" (usually including cracked corn, sunflower, and smaller seeds, such as millet, oats, barley, or milo), and many will offer unadulterated sunflower and suet, as well. But are these foods really the most effective attractants?

Surprisingly little research has been done on food preferences of birds at feeders, aside from one classic study by Aelrod Geis in the 1970s. Although results from that study are widely used as a guide, Geis tested relatively few foods and in only one geographic location. More recently we have learned that there can be regional differences in culinary tastes. A continent-wide controlled test conducted by the Cornell Laboratory of Ornithology documented preferences of ground-feeding birds for millet, black-oil sunflower, or red milo. Results from nearly five thousand test sites showed that milo was more likely to be eaten in Southwestern or West Coast portions of the United States than elsewhere in North America. To learn more about the foods that birds eat at feeders, Project Feeder-Watch undertook a special study in 1991–92, and results from that inquiry are summarized in the species accounts. The accounts also include information on natural foods, perhaps indicating potential for new commercial bird foods, such as grass seed, insect pupae, or dried berries.

Bird Feeders and Bird Populations

◆

Restaurateurs want to know about public-health issues concerning their business, and so do feeder owners. Every person who regularly feeds birds occasionally wonders about possible negative effects. Might birds become dependent on feeders and lose their natural foraging skills? Do feeders lure birds to areas where predation and disease are more likely than in the wild? Or does bird feeding only serve to increase the abundance of pest species that could have a negative impact on rarer songbirds?

There is no evidence that birds develop a feeder addiction to the extent that they fail to migrate as they should. The odd vagrant that turns up at a feeder in winter when it should be in Mexico is probably there because of injury, illness, or a flaw in internal migratory controls. Although feeders may help some of these individuals survive, most stragglers do not make it through the winter because they are physiologically ill-equipped to survive a northern winter. Therefore, the habit of failing to migrate has little chance of spreading through the population.

On the other hand, it is possible that feeders have contributed to recent northward range expansions in certain resident or near-resident species, including the Northern Cardinal and Tufted Titmouse. If so, then these species (which can obviously survive cold weather) must have been unable in prefeeder days to find enough natural food. If we were suddenly to cease all bird feeding, any artificial range expansions that depended on bird feeding alone (as opposed to climate amelioration or habitat change) would shift southward again very quickly through natural selection. However, the chances of such sudden and widespread cessation of bird feeding are very small.

People who are worried about closing down their feeders for a midwinter holiday can be quite confident that flocking species will be able to find substitute food supplies because they are used to covering a lot of ground in a day. However, if a feeder constitutes the main source of food in a strongly territorial bird's home area, that individual may suffer when a feeder closes down. In such cases you may want to ask a neighbor to keep your feeders filled.

Another health-and-safety concern is whether resident birds might develop a long-term dependency on bird feeders, "forgetting" natural foraging techniques. Experiments with Black-capped Chickadees showed that this did not occur. When feeders were removed for a winter from a site where they had long been available, overwinter survival of the suddenly deprived chickadees was the same as for a population that had never experienced feeders.

In another study on Black-capped Chickadees, survival rates were tracked in woodlots that were similar except for differing availability of feeders. In this case, chickadee flocks without feeder access survived the winter less well than chickadees with supplemental food—but only in winters with prolonged and severe cold snaps. This suggests that bird feeding in areas with a relatively mild winter climate may have no effect on population size. Moreover, the study showed no difference in density of chickadees breeding in the two study areas in the spring following the experiments. If "extra" birds that survived because of winter bird feeding bred at all, they must have dispersed to other, perhaps less suitable, areas, possibly negating any gains made in chickadee numbers over the winter. Overall, then, the impact of bird feeding on chickadee populations appears to be small, although there may be a net benefit.

Other studies have also generated results that can be difficult to interpret. For example, birds often move out of natural habitat in severe weather and into suburban areas that are rich in bird feeders. In some species the few individuals that do not move back home in spring and remain to nest have poor reproductive success—but no one knows how much this offsets the gains from improved overwinter survival.

Each of the research projects described here required intensive effort over a period of years, so data does not accumulate quickly. And even when we have solid, clear results, any documented effect of bird feeding might apply only to the species studied or a particular geographic location. We can get around these limitations of single-species studies by looking at continent-wide population trends in feeder birds. If feeder species have increased or decreased as a group in directions that differ from trends in other bird populations, this would constitute strong circumstantial evidence that feeders have played a role. In a test of this, population trends were obtained from North America's flagship avian monitoring program, the Breeding Bird Survey, for the most widespread feeder species (the thirty-five species reported by participants in Project FeederWatch as visiting at least 50% of feeders in the core of their winter range).

If nothing in particular is happening to bird populations, we would expect about half the species to be increasing and half to be declining, simply by chance. (Population trends of zero are quite rare.) The figures for the thirty-five widespread feeder species did not differ statistically from the expected fifty-fifty ratio. This was also true when analysis was restricted to the twenty-eight species with statistically significant trends (those for which population change was strong enough that we can be quite sure they were not chance results).

All the feeder species with significant population trends are listed in Table 4. It is apparent that the more woodland-dependent birds, such as nuthatches, woodpeckers, and chickadees, are on the increase side of the ledger, while most of the "pest" species are among the decliners, including nest robbers (Blue Jay, Common Grackle, Black-billed Magpie), nest-site competitors (House Sparrow, European Starling) and a nest parasite (Brown-headed Cowbird). The declining species include many scrub and grassland species—groups that are known to be declining in much of North America whether they visit feeders regularly or not. This analysis, then, suggests that bird feeding is not having a broad-scale negative impact on bird populations.

There is also evidence that bird feeding does not cause mortality to rise above natural levels through exposing birds to unusual danger from window collisions, disease, or predation. This evidence came from a study in which participants in Project FeederWatch recorded any deaths observed in their yards over an entire winter, providing details on causes and surrounding circumstances.

In that study, "window strikes" accounted for more deaths near feeders than any other factor (close to half of the two thousand-plus deaths reported). We estimated that between one and ten birds per building might be killed annually by striking windows in North America, a figure that probably represents less than a percent or two of all birds alive each fall but nonetheless important enough a problem that homeowners with regular window-strike problems should take corrective measures.

Predation was the second most important cause of death in the Project FeederWatch study, implicated in about one-third of cases. Sharp-shinned and Cooper's Hawks were the culprits in about half of the predation events actually witnessed, and cats in 30%. However, bird-eating hawks must consume one to three prey items daily to satisfy their energy needs, and most FeederWatchers who witnessed predation saw only one or two cases over the whole winter.

Table 4

Feeder species with significant population changes, 1966–1996.

Data from North America's Breeding Bird Survey.

Percent of Feeders Visited	Increasing Populations	Decreasing Populations
>75%	Red-bellied Woodpecker Hairy Woodpecker Western Scrub-Jay Black-capped Chickadee Tufted Titmouse White-breasted Nuthatch Carolina Wren House Finch	Mourning Dove Blue Jay Carolina Chickadee European Starling Dark-eyed Junco American Goldfinch House Sparrow
50–75%	American Crow Red-breasted Nuthatch Spotted Towhee	Northern Flicker Black-billed Magpie Northern Mockingbird Eastern Towhee Song Sparrow White-throated Sparrow White-crowned Sparrow Brown-headed Cowbird Common Grackle Purple Finch

We therefore concluded that the majority of hawks use feeders opportunistically, not as a primary food source.

In European studies, up to 30% of juvenile titmice were killed by Sparrowhawks in the nesting season, and bird-eating hawks at a migration stopover site ate an estimated 10% of all finches passing through in a single autumn. Compared to this level of risk, bird feeders are positively safe havens. Indeed, work on two species of titmice in Europe showed that individuals visiting feeders were less prone to predation by Pygmy Owls than those wintering in areas lacking feeders, partly because birds at feeders were quieter (attracting less attention to themselves), and they could also spend more of their time watching out for predators instead of searching for food.

The FeederWatch study documented only one bird death at every two feeders over the course of the winter, from any cause. There is, of course, no doubt that many dead birds were not found or reported. Nonetheless, natural mortality rates in songbirds are about 35 to 50% annually, which would lead us to predict at least four to five bird deaths over a winter at an average FeederWatch home. Actual figures were a tenth of that prediction. Even if under-reporting was a severe problem, therefore, it appears that feeders do not draw birds into an environment that is *more* dangerous than the one they face in the wild.

These analyses suggest that bird feeding has not had a blanket effect on populations of all feeder species. More subtle effects may exist, of course, perhaps varying among species (positive for some, negative for others). However, it will take detailed studies on individual species to demonstrate such effects. In the meantime, you can continue to feed birds with a clear conscience. All current evidence suggests you are not unduly upsetting natural ecological systems.

Key references: Askins 1993, Brittingham and Temple 1988, 1992a, Cowie and Hinsley 1987, Desrochers et al. 1988, Dunn 1993, Dunn and Tessaglia 1994, Geis 1980, Graber and Graber 1983a, Jannsson et al. 1981, Källender 1981, Lindstrom 1989, Orell 1989, Perrins and Birkhead 1980, Sauer et al. 1997, Stiles 1984, Terres 1981, van Balen 1980, Wilson 1994.

Species Accounts: Introduction

◆

The species accounts that follow give detailed information on the birds that are most widespread at North American bird feeders. You can get a great deal out of this book by simply reviewing the maps showing distribution and abundance at feeders, but if you have a particular interest in one species, you can delve deeper to learn more.

For each species, the text summarizes winter ecology, aimed at increasing your appreciation and understanding of bird behavior that you may witness in your backyard. A section follows on "Feeder-Watch Findings," with comments on food preferences at feeders and other results from Project FeederWatch. Additional information is presented in charts and maps.

The original data presented here were collected by thousands of volunteer FeederWatchers, who since 1987 have recorded the numbers of birds at feeders all across North America, observing for two-day periods every second week from November to April. (Dates of observation are staggered randomly among observers, so we actually have data from each week of the winter.) Results tell us which species come to feeders regularly, how often they visit, and where they occur most abundantly; we can track changes in these values through each winter season and from year to year.

Project FeederWatch divides the continent into regions for certain analyses (Figure 2). Species covered by the accounts are those that normally visit 10% or more of the feeders during winter within at least one of those regions. This definition of what is a "common" feeder species arbitrarily excludes some that are very limited in distribution. For example, Costa's Hummingbirds are regular visitors to feeders; but because their mainly Mexican winter range barely extends into the southwestern United States, they do not visit enough feeders in our coverage area to merit an account here.

"FeederWatch Findings" gives comments on the charts and maps and makes note of any differences among rural, suburban, and urban habitats that are statistically significant. (Differences in

Fig. 2: This book covers species that visit 10% or more of feeders in one of the
FeederWatch regions shown here.

proportion of feeders visited by habitat were tested with Chi square,
while habitat differences in abundance and percent of weeks visited
were detected using Duncan's multiple-range tests, weighted to empha-
size data from the regions where most feeders were visited.)

Food choices documented by a special Project FeederWatch
study are also listed under "FeederWatch Findings." "Favorite feeder
foods" are those that were selected by a species on more than a third
of its visits to feeders, while food items in italics were chosen on
more than two-thirds of visits. "Infrequent choices" were selected on
fewer than a third of visits. Sites were included in analysis of food
choice only if a food was offered regularly throughout the winter and
there had been at least five observations of food choice for the species
in question. Results are based on data from ten or more feeders unless
reference is made to small samples.

Many foods were offered too infrequently for us to find out how
attractive they really are, and our study did not control for feeder
design, which clearly can affect food choices. (For example, ground-
feeding quail cannot eat seed from a hanging tube feeder.) Moreover,
many of the foods "selected" by birds may in fact have been chosen

only because more preferred foods were not offered. Despite these caveats the food-choice summaries in this book provide an excellent guide to the types of feeder foods that each species will accept—published for the first time in the case of some less common feeder species.

Next in the species accounts come four charts that depict results from 1994 (results vary little from year to year). The upper-left bar chart shows the percentage of feeders reporting different levels of abundance. (*Abundance* is the maximum number recorded each week that the species was present, averaged over the year.) Consult this chart to find out how your own feeder counts compare to others across the continent, and look at the maps to see how you stack up against others in your region. For example, you might host few birds relative to others in North America as a whole (as shown by the chart), but may attract more than is typical for your region (illustrated by the abundance map).

The upper-right chart illustrates seasonal changes in abundance. Patterns vary among species, and we note some of the interesting features of these differences under "FeederWatch Findings."

The second bar graph (lower left) shows the percentage of feeders across the continent that reported the species present on few vs. many count periods each winter (there are ten two-week count periods from November through April). The more these graphs are skewed to the right, the more faithful a species is at visiting feeders through the entire winter.

The final chart (lower right) illustrates seasonal variation in percentage of feeders visited. Often this chart can help with interpretation of the previous one. For example, the seasonal pattern shows whether a species that visits only a few times a year does so because it is only present during migration.

Distribution of FeederWatch participants is not even across the continent but varies with human population density (Figure 3). We did not want results in the charts to be heavily weighted by the large mass of data from the eastern United States, so all figures for abundance and percent of feeders visited were calculated separately for each state or province (or, in a few cases, combinations of adjacent small states). These averages were then averaged again to derive the continental values depicted in the graphs. Although the basic units of calculation were not areas of equal size, our procedure did go some way to reducing regional bias.

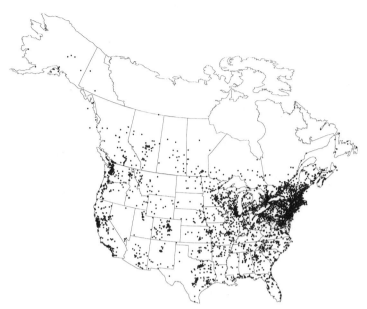

Fig. 3:   Distribution of FeederWatch participants.

The maps in each account summarize FeederWatch results for 1992–1994. The majority of species change little in distribution and abundance between years, and by using data from three years we were able to include more sites than if we had chosen a single year. However, a few "boom and bust" species are widespread one year and nearly absent the next. The text for these species discusses the range of variation possible.

The first (upper) map in each account illustrates geographic variation in the percent of feeders visited by the species at least once between November and April. This map tells you immediately whether a species is a frequent feeder visitor in your area or a less common one. As an aid to interpretation, we show the locations of feeders that were *not* visited by a species (in grey), whereas white areas show regions with little or no FeederWatch coverage.

To prepare these maps, we first calculated the percent of feeders visited within each United States zip code or Canadian postal code area (dropping any postal zone with fewer than five feeders so that percentage calculations would not be skewed by low numbers). We then used a method known as *kriging* to extrapolate results 200km beyond the center of each postal zone, averaging values with those from overlapping 200km circles to provide a smoothed picture of the percent of feeders visited in a region. The resulting map depicts local averages but does not extrapolate across regions where there are few feeders, so gaps in coverage are clearly illustrated.

The second (lower) map in each account illustrates abundance, defined as the average peak count when the species is present. For example, a feeder with a maximum count of two juncos in one week, six in another week, and none at all during the rest of the winter would have an average maximum count of four for the year (as would a feeder that reported four each week for the entire winter). You can use this map to compare the attractiveness of your own feeder to others in your region. Remember, though, that FeederWatchers operate more feeders than the average person so mapped abundance is probably on the high side for more typical feeder owners.

The abundance-mapping procedure also used kriging to smooth data, but included results from all feeders no matter how sparsely distributed. Instead, abundance at each feeder was averaged with abundance at feeders closest to it (no matter how far away), although giving greater weight to nearby sites. Resulting maps show estimates of the most likely abundance values for areas from which we have no data. This works well where gaps in coverage are not large, but extrapolations across large areas with no data can sometimes give misleading estimates. Abundance maps can be compared with the percentage maps to aid interpretation, and specific anomalies are noted under the "FeederWatch Findings" section of each account. Because data are especially sparse in Alaska, the Yukon, and the Northwest Territories, we represent average abundance for species occurring in those regions with an icon (in the shape of the state of Alaska).

The scales for shading abundance maps were selected to provide additional information. The lowest category of abundance shown on the map applies to approximately half of all feeders visited by the species. An additional quarter of all North American FeederWatchers reported the second level of abundance, 15% reported the third highest level, and the highest abundance category of all includes sightings from only 10% of sites.

Often birds turn up at feeders outside their normal haunts, and these appear on maps as isolated patches of shading distant from other records. We have edited the maps to delete obvious errors but have retained outliers for species that are known to turn up occasionally in unusual locations. Note that the dates of FeederWatch coverage include part of the migration season for many species, so the maps in this book should not be regarded as showing winter range.

Sharp-shinned Hawk

Accipiter striatus

It is a bit ironic that the first species appearing in this book is a predator, attracted to bird feeders not by the food you put out but by other birds. (The reason it appears first is due to its taxonomic sequence.) Small birds are the primary food of Sharp-shinned Hawks, although reptiles, insects, and small mammals add a small fraction (about 5%) to the diet.

Feeder owners may be lucky enough to observe the hunting behavior that has earned this hawk the nickname "bushwhacker." Sharp-shins often make short flights skimming closely over or around bushes or treetops, surprising potential victims and perhaps flushing them from cover. Another of the hawk's techniques is to hide within dense cover, then dash out to attack unwary prey.

The hunting Sharp-shinned Hawk can display an impressive agility. Victims are grabbed from feeder perches, in midair, or even as they rebound off windows. It sometimes looks as if Sharp-shins are deliberately driving victims into windows to kill them, but impacts are more likely the result of panic flights. Indeed, Sharp-shins themselves are sometimes killed in such chases. If the target prey manages to reach cover, a sharpie may run up on foot, extend a leg into the vegetation, and haul the erstwhile escapee from its inadequate haven.

In a study of predation at bird feeders by Project FeederWatch volunteers, the vast majority of Sharp-shinned Hawk victims were found to belong to only seven species (see "Favorite Feeder Foods"). Female Sharp-shins selected somewhat larger prey species, in keeping with their larger size relative to males, but both sexes favored prey just about the size of the most common feeder visitors: species that are widespread and that forage on the ground in flocks. Predation was especially high at feeders with the greatest levels of bird traffic. Sharp-shinned Hawks caused over a third of the predation deaths reported in the FeederWatch study, and because a single hawk must eat approximately a bird a day, one predator settling into your neighborhood for the winter could make quite a dent in your feeder population. Nonetheless, the vast majority of observers reported only one or two cases of Sharp-shin predation over the entire winter. While many instances doubtless went unobserved, most Sharp-shins seemed to make only occasional, opportunistic forays at feeders where birds were most visible and active, attacking whatever was most accessible. If you are bothered by a hawk that takes up regular residence in your yard, try stopping all bird feeding for a week or two. When the handy lunch counter in your backyard is closed, the hawk may decide to move elsewhere.

In former years Sharp-shinned Hawks were persecuted by farmers and hunters, who considered them vermin. These small predators can't handle a chicken, but perhaps they picked off the odd chick, and doubtless they were lumped together with larger predators that caused more severe problems. DDT may have lowered hawk numbers, too, both through direct toxicity and reduction of the songbird populations on which these predators depend. Now, with greater protection, Sharp-shinned Hawks appear to be doing well.

Key references: Dunn and Tessaglia 1994, Gaddis 1980, Klem 1981, Palmer 1988, Reynolds and Meslow 1984, Storer 1966.

FeederWatch Findings

There is little regional variation in the abundance of the Sharp-shinned Hawk because nearly every visit is by a single bird. Reports are slightly more frequent from suburban and urban feeders than from rural sites, perhaps reflecting the extra visibility of prey flocks (and of hawks) in more manicured settings. Only about 10% of feeders report Sharp-shinned Hawks present for more than half the winter season. Despite infrequent visits, they are reported at least once per winter from a surprising proportion of feeders—over a third in some regions. They are seen most often during early winter, when northern-nesting birds are moving through the United States as migrants.

Favorite feeder foods: Mourning Dove, Blue Jay, European Starling, Dark-eyed Junco, Pine Siskin, House Finch, House Sparrow.

Infrequent choices: FeederWatchers reported twenty-one additional prey species, similar in size to those listed above.

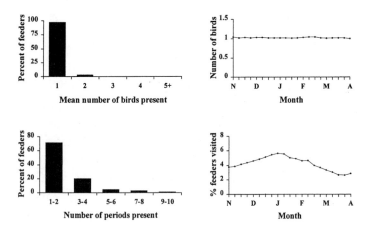

Sharp-shinned Hawk: percent of feeders visited

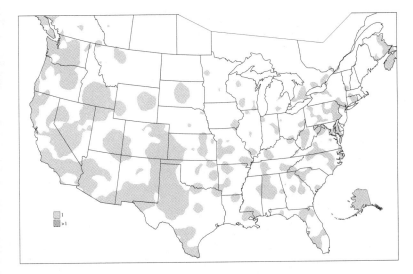

0
<30
30–60
61–90
>90

Abundance at feeders

1
>1

Cooper's Hawk
Accipiter cooperii

Cooper's Hawks, though larger than Sharp-shins, can easily be confused with that species—especially if glimpsed only momentarily during an attack on the birds at your feeder. Female Cooper's are fairly recognizable because they are so much bigger than males (and Sharp-shins)—the size difference between the sexes in Cooper's Hawks is among the greatest for any of the worlds' raptors—but male Cooper's Hawks and female Sharp-shins are close in size.

A study of predation at feeders by Project FeederWatch volunteers showed that on average, Cooper's Hawks selected larger prey than Sharp-shins did, and Mourning Doves were a favorite meal. Numerous studies of food habits have shown that a typical prey item for a Cooper's Hawk weighs about 5 ounces, so a roughly 4-ounce Mourning Dove makes a most tempting target.

Cooper's Hawks could potentially have a major effect on feeder populations because each one must eat a Mourning Dove (or the approximate equivalent) every day or two to fill its energy requirements. However, up to half the diet is made up of other animals, including mammals, reptiles, amphibians, and the odd insect. By contrast, Sharp-shins eat small birds almost exclusively. This dietary difference was reflected in the results of the FeederWatch study, which recorded less than half as many predation incidents by Cooper's Hawks as by Sharp-shinned Hawks.

Cooper's Hawk hunting tactics are similar to those described for Sharp-shins, except that Cooper's are more likely to search for prey from a hidden perch than they are to "bushwhack." They also prefer hunting in low, shrubby areas instead of the treetops favored by Sharpies.

After a flapping approach, a Cooper's Hawk may glide for several yards, then suddenly swing the feet and pelvis forward with exquisite timing so that the talons strike the victim with maximum impact. When the feet strike, they are moving 15% faster than the pelvis, slamming into the prey at a speed of over 10 yards per second. The talons then grip and relax repeatedly in response to prey movement. The hawk may sit for up to ten minutes over its victim before eating it or carrying the corpse away. At other times the meal will start before the victim is completely dead—a behavior particularly likely to cause distress in human viewers. The usual feeding sequence involves plucking the victim's breast feathers, then eating the head, followed by viscera, and finally the muscle. A hungry hawk leaves little behind except a pile of body feathers and a pair of wings.

After a meal the hawk has little time to relax before the next hunt because only about a third of all attacks on wild prey are successful. A preference for easier victims may have been the reason that Cooper's Hawks occasionally attacked poultry back in the days when backyard chicken coops were common. Shooting by farmers may have contributed to the midcentury population decline of this species, but Cooper's Hawks appear to have since recovered.

Key references: Bent 1937, Dunn and Tessaglia 1994, Goslow 1971, Kenward 1978, Palmer 1988, Reynolds and Meslow 1984, Rosenfield and Bielefeldt 1993.

FeederWatch Findings

Cooper's Hawks are more than twice as likely to be reported at suburban feeders as at rural or urban sites. Like Sharp-shinned Hawks, they are seen at over a quarter of feeders in some areas but only rarely visit them regularly. Most sightings are of lone individuals. Feeders are most likely to be visited in the middle of the winter.

Favorite feeder foods: Species making up 5% or more of kills at FeederWatch sites in a special one-year study: Mourning Dove (especially), European Starling, Dark-eyed Junco, House Sparrow.

Infrequent choices: Eighteen other species of similar size to those listed above.

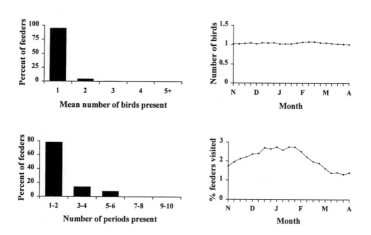

Cooper's Hawk: percent of feeders visited

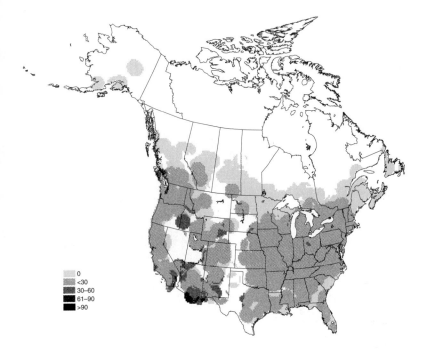

0
<30
30–60
61–90
>90

Abundance at feeders

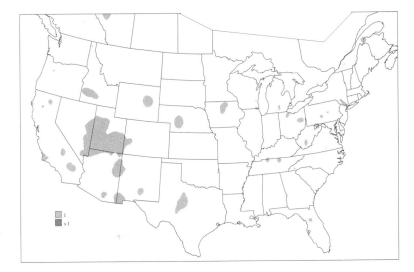

1
>1

Ring-necked Pheasant

Phasianus colchicus

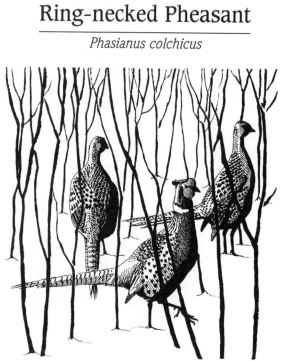

The Ring-necked Pheasant seems so much a part of the North American bird fauna that we sometimes forget it was introduced. This native of China had a long history of association with man and agriculture in Asia and Europe prior to its introduction into Oregon in 1881. Pheasants spread rapidly from there, augmented by continued releases elsewhere, and quickly attained a coast-to-coast distribution.

Pheasants gather into flocks for the winter in areas that provide a combination of good food supply and abundant shelter. The sexes segregate into separate winter flocks, each of which has a strong dominance hierarchy. Within a large flock there may be smaller groups that forage or roost together, but these are fluid associations comprised of different individuals on different days. The advent of spring precipitates the breakup of flocks and the beginning of territorial behavior. Usually the dominant male selects the territory close to where he spent the winter, while other males are forced to disperse farther afield. You will certainly be aware of it if a pheasant sets up shop near your home, as his raucous, deep-throated squawk is hard to ignore (especially in the wee hours of the morning). The polygynous males acquire harems, usually of just a few females, although up to eighteen have been reported, and one captive male managed to attract fifty.

Pheasants are not terribly common at feeders, probably because they favor agricultural habitats that are a form of giant bird feeder in themselves. If pheasants do visit, you should be able to observe signs of their social behavior: males and females visiting separately in winter, single males with several females visiting in spring, and occasional altercations between individuals that illustrate why the dominance hierarchy is called a "pecking order."

Pheasants are, of course, ground feeders, typically feeding on waste grain, but they are fond of sunflower seed if they can get it. Fruit-bearing bushes are evidently the source of a special treat, turning the normally dignified pheasant into an ungainly clown as it jumps for out-of-reach berries. Feeding is especially intense early in the morning and late in the day, but once the pheasant's capacious crop is filled, a bird can retreat to shelter for long periods of relaxation.

While large bird species typically live a lot longer than small ones, there are not as many geriatric pheasants as one might expect. Normally one-third die each winter and up to two-thirds can die when there are long periods of very cold weather. Lack of food is evidently not the main cause; healthy pheasants have been known to survive for surprisingly long periods without food. Instead, exposure and heavy predation appear to cause most deaths. Pheasants are also rather stupid about crossing roads and frequently figure as traffic fatalities. Although one pheasant was reported to have lived seven years, most individuals in the wild probably do not last that long.

Key references: Bent 1932, Collias and Tabler 1951, Farris et al. 1977, Roselaar 1980.

FeederWatch Findings

Ring-necked Pheasants are most likely to visit feeders in the northern United States and the Maritime provinces of Canada. They are more than twice as often reported at rural feeders as at urban ones, with suburban sites falling in between. Where pheasants do attend feeders, they usually do so infrequently, although 20% of visited sites (many of them in the Maritimes) have pheasants coming by all winter. Numbers remain quite steady throughout the winter.

Favorite feeder foods: *Cracked corn,* mixed seed, black-oil sunflower. (Small samples indicate that *wheat,* millet, hulled sunflower, and whole corn are also favored foods).

Infrequent choices: Striped sunflower, water. (Safflower and barley may also be accepted.)

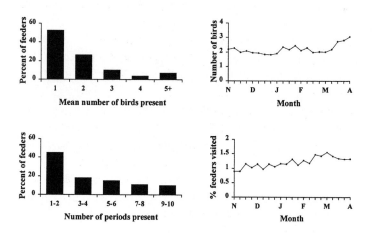

Ring-necked Pheasant: percent of feeders visited

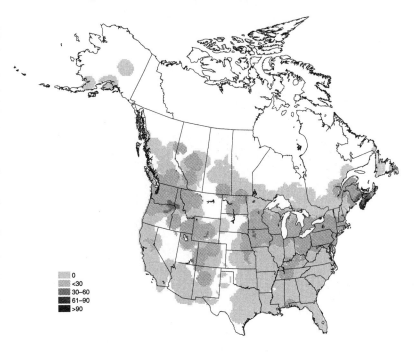

Abundance at feeders

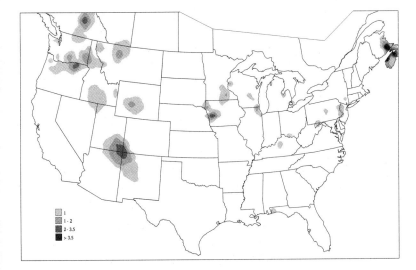

California Quail

Callipepla californica

There could hardly be a finer sight at a bird feeder than several dozen California Quail arriving on foot, their jaunty black head plumes reminiscent of ceremoniously dressed horses at Buckingham Palace. As many as three hundred quail may converge at once, although flocks of twenty to fifty are more the norm.

California Quail were so common in the last century that thousands were shot by market hunters for California restaurants. Farmers nonetheless recognized quail as useful for eating weed seeds and insects and would often sprinkle grain on the snow near their fields to encourage a local quail population. Today quail come readily to suburban areas to scout out feeders or forage on lawns, halting traffic as they hike across roadways.

Winter flocks, or "coveys," are made up of local families that join together for the season. Each covey tends to roost as a unit but may break into smaller foraging groups in the daytime. Coveys rarely interact, maintaining distances up to half a mile, with strange birds being recognized and excluded unless the invader is very persistent at joining the flock.

Covey formation probably reduces predation. Careful observers of feeders may see additional behaviors that help foil predators; for example, one bird serves as a sentinel while the remainder of the flock feeds. The contact calls used to keep flock members together are difficult for predators (or humans) to locate exactly, whereas alarm calls meant to advertise the location of a predator can be precisely pinpointed by the listener.

Antipredator behaviors are, of course, prudent for a small ground feeder that would rather sprint than fly, but they do not provide complete protection. Quail coveys in suburban areas suffer more predation than do birds in wilder areas, especially from cats. Despite this, California Quail are less dependent on brushy cover than most of their close relatives. Even in suburbia, some quail can survive as long as there is an acre or two of rough ground and at least some heavy shrubbery to afford protective cover.

Attractants to quail include just about any seed scattered on the ground. To help protect the birds from predators, try putting food on an elevated surface. (Quail at one location fed regularly from a deck that was nearly 20 feet above ground level.) Dry seed is not an adequate year-round diet, however, and sprouting greens are required foodstuffs both in winter and spring. Legumes are especially popular, and a covey of quail can quickly denude a garden of emerging peas and beans. So important are these foods that shortages of lush green shoots may cause population decline in drought years even when there is plenty of drinking water available.

Key references: Bent 1932, Botsford et al. 1988, Dennis 1988, Emlen 1939, Genelly 1955, Howard and Emlen 1942, Leopold 1977, Williams 1969.

FeederWatch Findings

This species exhibits large habitat differences in feeder abundance. It is twice as numerous at rural sites as in more built-up settings, even though nearly as many suburban sites are visited as rural ones. (Few urban feeders report quail.) About a quarter of sites hosting these quail report them only occasionally, but half entertain this species throughout the winter. Flock sizes diminish gradually from midwinter to spring—at the same time as percent of feeders visited increases—suggesting the birds are spreading out. The apparent lack of birds in Nevada (see maps) results from a gap in FeederWatch coverage—California Quail are actually quite abundant there.

Favorite feeder foods: *Mixed seed, millet, cracked corn,* and (according to small samples) wheat.

Infrequent choices: Black-oil sunflower, water. (Small samples show quail may also eat canary seed, milo, niger, and oats.)

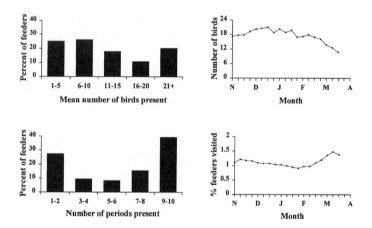

California Quail: percent of feeders visited

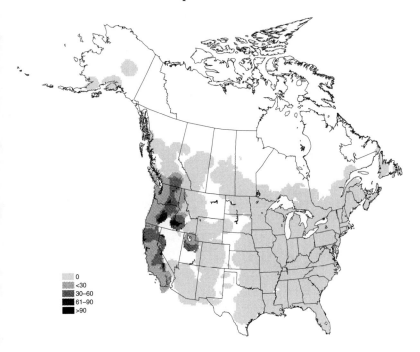

- 0
- <30
- 30–60
- 61–90
- >90

Abundance at feeders

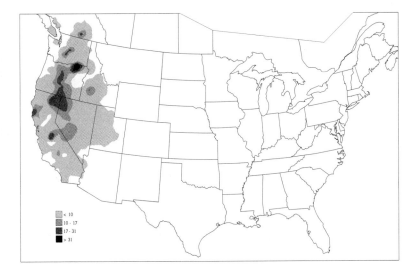

- < 10
- 10 - 17
- 17 - 31
- > 31

Gambel's Quail

Callipepla gambelii

Westerners are the only people who regularly see quail at feeders, and what a treat they get. While Gambel's and the closely related California Quail are the only quail widespread enough at feeders to merit an account here, Scaled, Montezuma, and Mountain Quail also visit yards. By contrast, the sole eastern quail species, Northern Bobwhite, is not a feeder habitué.

Gambel's Quail has a long history of association with man— and not always a happy one for the quail. Hunted as food by Indians and market hunters, these plumed birds were also sought for the striking decorations their topknots could provide. Today these quail are not considered a prime game species because they prefer not to fly unless forced. Hunters must crash through thorny brush to locate a covey and then fire at birds that are often making a speedy escape on foot. Despite being hunted, Gambel's Quail have also benefited from association with man. Early in the century this species began to frequent small farmsteads scattered along river bottoms, becoming quite tame and sometimes pilfering poultry food. Nowadays these quail are similarly attracted to bird feeders.

Gambel's Quail used to be referred to as the Desert Quail, which nicely sums up its Sonoran habitat and preference for brushy areas, especially mesquite. Hot weather is evidently not a severe problem, as these quail can survive in Death Valley where temperatures reach 135°F. As long as there is enough groundwater to support succulent greens, Gambel's Quail need never take a drink—although populations of both California and Gambel's Quail do decrease in drought years. Cold appears to pose greater difficulties than does heat because these quail do best where the mean January temperature stays above freezing.

Winter flocks, or "coveys", of Gambel's Quail are made up of several local families and perhaps a few nonbreeding adults, usually numbering five to fifteen birds in total but up to two hundred in some cases. The coveys are fairly sedentary, moving less than 1,000 feet per day, although a much larger area is covered over the course of the whole winter. In spring the birds spread out for the breeding season. Young males move the farthest, while experienced pairs nest within the area where they spent the winter.

Seeds of mesquite, desert vetch, and other desert plants are the main natural foods of Gambel's Quail, but these birds also eat leaves and shoots. At feeders they accept most small seeds scattered on the ground and will readily drink from a source of water. Most visits to yards take place in the several hours just after dawn and before dusk, when the quail fill their crops and carry away a supply of food to see them through the midday heat or to have as a bedtime snack before retiring for the night.

When Gambel's Quail come to visit, an advance scout may cautiously enter your yard to check it out before giving the "all-clear" call to the rest of the flock, which then troops into the yard with forward-tilted plumes bobbing. One bird often stands guard as others feed. If you are close, you can hear the low conversation of quail constantly giving their rising *took* contact calls. Mild alarms are frequent, with *chip-chip-chip* calls drawing other quail to investigate the cause of concern. A frightened flock will usually run for cover. House cats probably make serious inroads on quail numbers in residential areas, while other enemies include hawks, owls, foxes, and coyotes.

Key references: Bent 1932, Dennis 1991, Ellis and Stokes 1966, Gullion 1960, 1962, Johnsgard 1973.

FeederWatch Findings

Gambel's Quail is somewhat overlooked as a feeder species because it has such a restricted range, yet it visits nearly half of feeders in Arizona. Moreover, numbers of quail at feeders within their range can be high—averaging over thirty birds at rural sites (declining as spring approaches). Flock sizes appear much smaller in more urban settings, but our sample sizes there are quite low. Although numbers are highest at rural sites, the chances of seeing these quail at all is greater at suburban feeders. Feeders that attract quail are likely to have them visiting all winter long.

Favorite feeder foods: *Mixed seed,* water. Small samples indicate other favored foods include millet and *cracked corn,* while whole corn, milo, and baked goods may also be accepted.

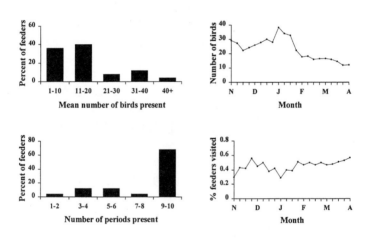

Gambel's Quail: percent of feeders visited

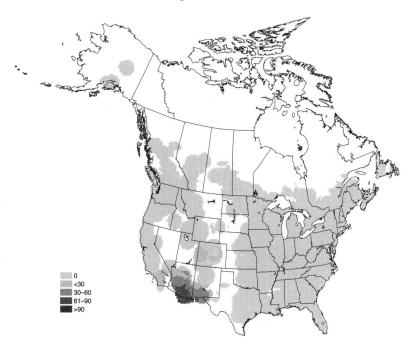

0
<30
30–60
61–90
>90

Abundance at feeders

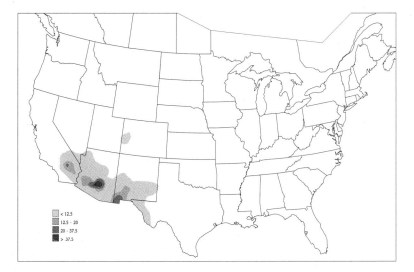

< 12.5
12.5 - 20
20 - 37.5
> 37.5

Rock Dove

Columba livia

"Rock Dove" is the proper name for the domestic pigeon. Given this bird's reputation as a scrounger for handouts in parks, it is perhaps surprising that pigeons are relatively uncommon at feeders. One reason is that their greatest abundance is in cities, where few people maintain feeders. Moreover, the wary pigeon is happiest feeding with large flocks in wide-open areas where predators are easily visible. Most feeder owners have smaller, more heavily vegetated yards than this species cares for.

Where pigeons do attend feeders, they frequently make pests of themselves. Flocks of twenty to fifty are typical, and the jostling of these large birds may drive other species away. Plus, droppings are particularly voluminous, related to the pigeon's habit of swallowing seeds whole rather than husking them first. You can limit pigeon numbers by offering sunflower seeds only or by putting grain in tube feeders and other types with small perches.

We have only ourselves to thank for the close relationship of

Rock Doves to human populations. Domesticated as long as five thousand years ago, pigeons were introduced to North America by the first settlers and moved west with them. By 1796 they had even reached Hawaii. Ancestral pigeons were apparently associated with fertility goddesses of the eastern Mediterranean region, and today's wild Rock Doves are descendants of dovecote pigeons bred for centuries to be prolific breeders. You can see the distinctive courtship flight at any time of year—in which pairs soar with wings held in a V pattern—because experienced adults may nest six or more times annually. Even youngsters can breed three times before they are a year old. On the other hand, up to two-thirds of pigeons may not attempt to breed at all in a given year, and overall reproductive success is low. Less than a third of eggs produce squabs, and about half of the young die before the age of two months.

While large numbers of Rock Doves may visit a feeding site regularly, they do not do so as a cohesive flock. Some come only in the morning, others only in the afternoon, and some only every week or two. Regular visitors are occasionally supplemented by more casual drop-ins. Several behaviors help decrease competition in the flock and increase foraging efficiency. For example, the birds are highly individualistic in their food preferences, each one selecting a certain seed type within the available mix. Moreover, larger individuals are dominant to smaller ones, thereby gaining first access to food without any argument.

Pigeons are frequent subjects of learning studies, and results show them to be about on a par with white rats in ability to remember where good and poor food sources are. This helps the birds to avoid wasteful searches of areas that previously were bare and prompts occasional rechecks of sites where there was once a bonanza. Rock Doves readily learn to identify particular humans who can be counted on for handouts.

Key references: Giraldeau and Lefebvre 1985, Johnston 1992, Johnston and Johnson 1990, Lefebvre 1985, Murton et al. 1972, Roberts 1988, Williams and Fleischer 1989.

FeederWatch Findings

Urban feeders are twice as likely to host Rock Doves as suburban locations, and the latter are in turn twice as likely to have them as rural sites. Frequency of visit through the winter follows the same pattern: Rural sites report these birds sporadically, while urban sites attract them all season. Flock size, however, remains constant across all habitats (declining slightly from December onward).

Favorite feeder foods: *Cracked corn, mixed seed,* sunflower (all types), baked goods.

Infrequent choices: Millet, safflower, whole corn, niger, hulled peanuts, water. (Small samples show pigeons also accept milo, peanut hearts, pet food, and popped corn.)

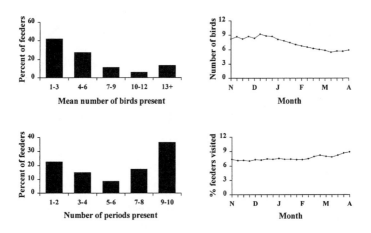

Rock Dove: percent of feeders visited

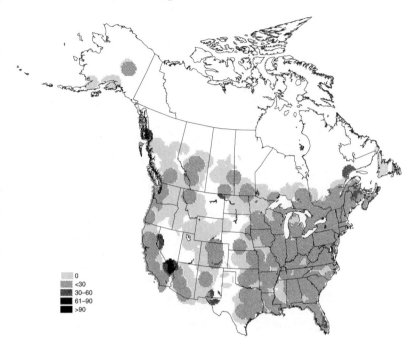

0
<30
30–60
61–90
>90

Abundance at feeders

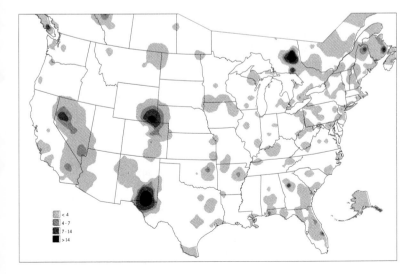

< 4
4 - 7
7 - 14
> 14

47

Band-tailed Pigeon

Columba fasciata

The robust Band-tailed Pigeon looks similar to the slightly small-er city pigeon but differs from it markedly in food habits and behav-ior. It is essentially a woodland species that feeds especially on fruit and nuts. Acorns are a favored food, but while most acorn eaters shuck the nuts first, the weak-billed Band-tailed Pigeon simply swal-lows them whole. Their diet also includes such fruit as elderberry, mulberry, and mistletoe, and perhaps surprisingly, these pigeons also consume the pollen of hemlock trees. The grains so beloved of other North American doves are not ignored totally, however, and the Band-tail will sample them at feeders. While Rock Doves are often considered pests at feeders, Band-tails are usually more wel-come. Flocks are relatively peaceful and depart after a bout of feed-ing, leaving the field open for other visitors.

Besides attracting Band-tails with grain, grit, or water, you can try offering crushed eggshell as a source of calcium for producing eggs. Although the Band-tail is not as prolific as certain other pigeon species, it can breed at any time of year (whenever there is sufficient food in the local area) and lay up to three clutches annually. The chick—usually a singleton but occasionally joined by a sibling—is initially fed entirely on "crop milk," a fat-rich secretion of the parent's crop that allows child rearing at those times of year when there are no insects or other baby foods available.

Band-tailed Pigeons are strong flyers, beating their wings two hundred to three hundred times a minute and achieving speeds up to 75 mph. Flying strength is important for a bird that must roam widely to locate concentrations of fruits or acorns. These pigeons will often commute to higher altitude areas for nighttime roosting, making daily trips downslope to forage. Band-tails are also partially migratory, withdrawing from the northern parts of their range in fall to take up residence from California to Mexico in winter.

Band-tailed Pigeons often feed in flocks, and you may see them foraging in fields, leap-frogging over one another so that the flock appears to roll along like a kind of wave. Studies of a variety of pigeon species have shown that flocking reduces risk of predation and increases feeding efficiency: The larger the flock, the earlier an approaching predator is detected, allowing birds to eat more efficiently because they can spend less of their time being vigilant.

Other adaptions to reducing predation are anatomical. A pigeon's crop is four to five times more capacious than its stomach, so a bird can collect a large supply of food in a short time and then retire to a predator-free site to digest at leisure. And because Band-tails and other doves can drink by sucking water through their strawlike bills—most other birds have to tip back their heads to swallow—this, too, may allow pigeons to fill up rapidly and get away quickly from water holes where predators often lie in wait.

At one time Band-tailed Pigeons were nearly extirpated by hunters, as their relatively large size makes them a tempting target. Regulation of hunting has allowed population recovery.

Key references: Gutiérrez et al. 1975, Kautz and Braun 1981, March and Sadlier 1972, Martin et al. 1951, Phelan 1987, Siegfried and Underhill 1975, Skutch 1991.

FeederWatch Findings

The Band-tailed Pigeon visits feeders in flocks of up to twenty individuals, with largest numbers present in midwinter. Thereafter numbers per feeder decline while the number of feeders visited rises, probably reflecting migratory movements back toward breeding areas. About a third of feeders where these pigeons occur report them only a few time a year, but it is not uncommon to host them throughout the winter. On the maps, records in the Southwest (outside California) are primarily of migrants, as pigeons breeding in that area generally winter in Mexico.

Favorite feeder foods: *Cracked corn,* mixed seed, black-oil sunflower, water, and (based on small samples) millet and hulled sunflower.

Infrequent choices: Small samples indicate that striped sunflower, hulled peanuts, peanut hearts, whole corn, and milo may also be acceptable foods.

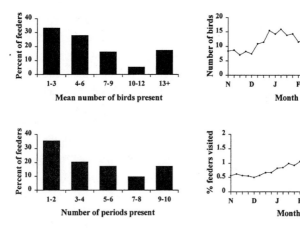

Band-tailed Pigeon: percent of feeders visited

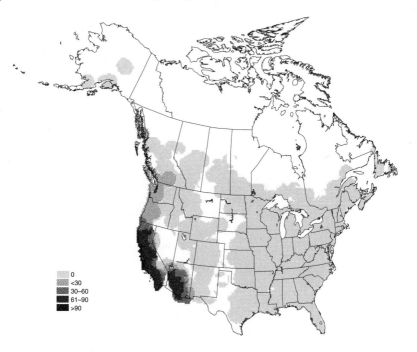

0
<30
30–60
61–90
>90

Abundance at feeders

< 4.5
4.5 - 8.5
8.5 - 17
> 17

Mourning Dove

Zenaida macroura

Doves are a symbol in many cultures for innocence and gentleness, while their cooing calls suggest sadness (thus the name "Mourning" Dove for this species). This peaceful reputation is largely undeserved, though, as male doves are highly aggressive during the reproductive cycle and may remain testy even in the more gregarious phases of winter flocking.

Mourning Doves form winter flocks in November and December, the flocks averaging about fifty birds but ranging from a few to several hundred. As is true of many gregarious species, a dominance hierarchy imposes a degree of internal organization on the flock. However, Mourning Dove males are not automatically dominant to females—unlike the dominance relationships in many other species.

While paired birds stay together throughout the winter if both survive, hunting pressure and natural mortality often prevent this from happening. Indeed, more Mourning Doves are shot in North America than all other migratory gamebirds combined—about 70 million a year. Nonhunting mortality is thought to be four to five times the hunting losses, so overall about one-half to three-quarters of all Mourning Doves die annually.

Winter flocks spend their days in favorite fields eating grain or small seeds. Despite liking corn and millet, Mourning Doves also eat seeds much tinier than we would think of putting in our feeders: One patient scientist counted 17,200 grass seeds in a single Mourning Dove stomach. Deep snow will cause flocks to move to farms and grain-storage sites or to more urbanized areas where feeders are common, but once the snow thins out again, they usually return to more open habitat. Light snow causes less disruption to foraging patterns, as it can easily be whisked aside with a swipe of the bill.

Regardless of snow conditions, cold weather alone may pose problems for Mourning Doves. A majority of the birds spending the winter in Ontario were found to have lost one or more toes to frost-bite. While most of the doves that breed in Canada migrate south in winter, studies show that more and more are staying north. Some say this is due to greater supplies of waste grain in fields, while others feel that bird feeding is a factor.

When it comes to hot weather, Mourning Doves are much better adapted. Although unable to sweat (no birds can), they pant a lot as a means of losing heat through evaporative cooling. This in turn requires water—lots of it. Daily water intake quadruples when temperatures rise from room temperature to 100°F so these doves are absent from hot areas that are also very arid. Dependence on water can be dangerous because predators learn to hang about isolated water holes to pick off birds coming to drink, but Mourning Doves have evolved a countermove that reduces their vulnerability. In less than one minute, a dove can suck up more than three times its daily water requirement, reducing the time it must spend near water sources. Another beat-the-heat trick of a Mourning Dove is to allow its body temperature to rise above air temperature so that heat is lost passively to the surrounding air. A dove can get as hot as 113°F without ill effect, whereas most other warm-blooded animals reaching that temperature would be either severely debilitated or dead.

Key references: Armstrong and Noakes 1983, Davison and Sullivan 1963, Dennis 1981, 1991, Geis 1980, Hennessy and Van Camp 1963, Leopold and Dedon 1983, Mirachi and Baskett 1994, Shuman et al. 1988, Skutch 1991.

FeederWatch Findings

The Mourning Dove is one of the most common birds at feeders, visiting virtually all sites in some regions, whether urban, suburban, or rural. Although typically present at feeders through the entire winter, numbers of doves at each site decline by about half as the season progresses.

Favorite feeder foods: *Mixed seed, cracked corn,* millet, canary seed, black-oil and hulled sunflower, water.

Infrequent choices: Striped sunflower, safflower, whole corn, milo, wheat, niger, oats, peanuts (hulled or hearts), dried fruit, baked goods, popped corn. (Small samples show doves occasionally eating canola and barley, as well.)

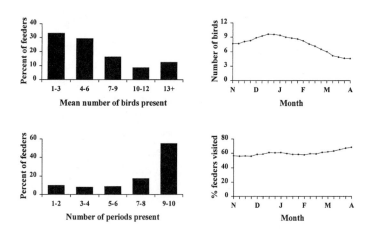

Mourning Dove: percent of feeders visited

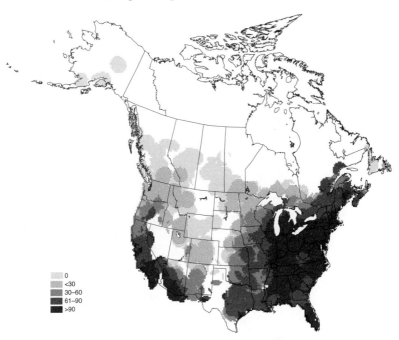

0
<30
30–60
61–90
>90

Abundance at feeders

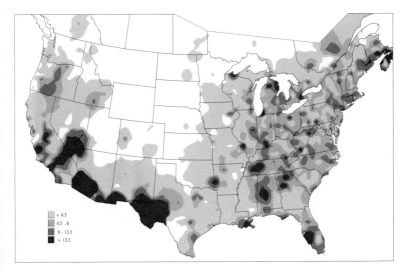

< 4.5
4.5 .8
8 - 13.5
> 13.5

Inca Dove

Columbina inca

Inca Doves are associated with the arid Southwest, but they reside mainly in towns, loitering about where humans provide sources of food and water. It has been estimated that in certain areas and at certain times of year, fully one-half of all Inca Dove food may come from bird feeders. Water sources are equally important, as the doves must drink about 15% of their weight each day to survive the heat. These doves can also be found hunting for food alongside domestic poultry, walking with their heads erect, nodding with each step, and often brushing aside loose soil with their bills to expose buried weed and grass seeds.

Like most of the pigeon family, Inca Doves breed throughout much of the year and only stop to catch their breaths in midwinter. Feeder owners may observe the courting behavior typical of all doves, in which the male parades before the female with tail fanned wide, bowing and cooing. Rival males sometimes get into ferocious fights, belying their innocent appearance (and the use of doves as symbols for peace and purity of heart).

Inca Doves are gregarious at all seasons but especially during midwinter, when reproductive activities shut down. Flocks of ten to fifty birds forage or loaf together, tending to coalesce into larger flocks in late afternoon. Every half hour or so there is a round of calling throughout the flock—which may serve to hold the group together but can drive human listeners crazy. The monotonous, two-syllable call is often said to sound like "no hope," and it is repeated ad nauseam.

One of the side effects of the strong flocking tendency of Inca Doves is a susceptibility to salmonellosis. This disease is spread through exposure to contaminated droppings and is also fairly common in other flocking species that visit feeders, such as finches.

Inca Doves do rather poorly in cold weather and may die if temperatures drop below 21°F. If you watch Inca Doves that are feeling chilly, you may be treated to a circus performance: Between bouts of feeding, several birds line up to huddle closely, usually in an open area where they can keep a sharp eye out for predators. When five or more birds are taking part, some climb on top of the others to form layers or a minipyramid. The maximum number of participants reported to date is twelve, in three layers. Every five minutes or so the birds on the outside of the bottom layer fly to the top, precipitating a redistribution into a new formation. This behavior has only been observed in the daytime. It is probably colder at night, but a pyramid of doves might be especially attractive to nocturnal predators, and those predators could not be easily spotted in the dark. Instead, doves roost solitarily and cope with cold nights by going into torpor—a state of reduced metabolism that saves energy. This physiological response to cold is known to occur in hummingbirds, too, which can also run out of energy quickly in cold conditions.

Key references: Dennis 1991, Mueller 1992, Robertson and Schnapf 1987.

FeederWatch Findings

The Inca Dove is a localized specialty, visiting nearly 50% of feeders in Texas. The gap in West Texas on the distribution map indicates lack of FeederWatch sites in that area rather than a lack of doves. Rural locations are less than half as likely to be visited as feeders in more built-up areas. Most feeders that host these doves have them as visitors all season long. Flock size at feeders declines slightly as spring approaches.

Frequent feeder foods: *Mixed seed*, water (and probably *millet* and *cracked corn*).

Infrequent choices: Black-oil sunflower, niger (and based on small samples, striped sunflower and whole corn).

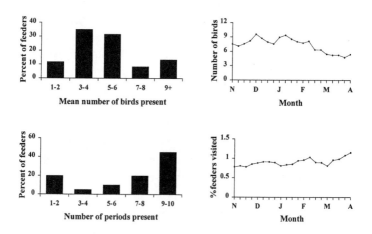

Inca Dove: percent of feeders visited

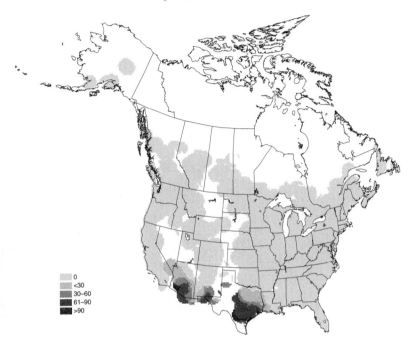

Abundance at feeders

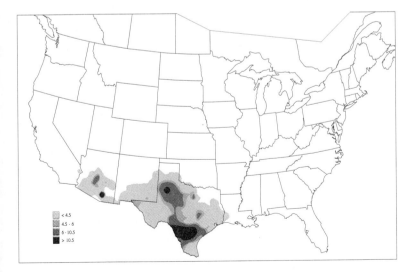

Ruby-throated Hummingbird

Archilochus colubris

The tiny buzz bombs known as hummingbirds are very different from other birds attracted to feeders. Not only do they drink sugar water and ignore seeds, but everything from tongue construction to flight mode is uniquely adapted for feeding on nectar. This does not prevent hummers from eating insects, though, which are an important source of protein in their diet. Because hummingbirds are not built primarily for insect catching, they usually take the easy way out and concentrate on nabbing resting insects that are encountered by chance. These may include bugs trapped in sticky sap or nectar, and on occasion hummers even pilfer insects caught in spiders' webs.

The Ruby-throat has the broadest breeding distribution of any North American hummingbird and is the only one common in the eastern half of the continent. Because it migrates to Central America for the winter, Ruby-throat sightings at feeders are mostly confined to the summer or migration seasons.

If you are lucky enough to host Ruby-throats during the nesting season, you may witness the male's aerial flight display, meant to impress a female sitting nearby. The male flies back and forth in a shallow arc, described by bird bander Marguerite Baumgartner as "swinging on an invisible pendulum with the speed of a bullet and the precision of an automaton."

Following the breeding season, males quickly lose their interest in family matters and begin migrating several weeks earlier than the females and immatures. If hummingbirds visit your feeders all day long, they are probably still residents; but if you see them only in early morning and late afternoon, they are probably migrating because migratory flights take place in midday. Over a period of about a month, a series of migrants may use your feeders without your realizing they are different individuals.

Despite their seeming fragility, Ruby-throated Hummingbirds are hardy enough to migrate across the Gulf of Mexico in a single hop. Nonetheless, because they nest much farther north than most other hummingbird species, they are vulnerable to poor weather in spring. The problem to be faced is evidently one of food shortage rather than of cold per se, as illustrated by one Ruby-throat's ability to survive two Wisconsin snowstorms—and temperatures of 12°F—with the aid of a bird feeder.

One means of finding food in early spring is to associate with Yellow-bellied Sapsuckers. Ruby-throats often rely on tree sap from sapsucker wells in the weeks before flowers begin to bloom. In early spring, tree sap consists of about 16 to 20% sugar—just the concentration preferred by hummingbirds. One researcher found that in six cases, nests of Ruby-throats were within 1000 feet of a tree frequented by sapsuckers, and all six incubating females fed almost exclusively at the sap wells that those woodpeckers had drilled.

Another adaptation to food finding is an impressive ability of hummingbirds to remember locations of food sources from day to day over a very wide area. Spring migrants occasionally astonish feeder owners by hovering expectantly over the spots where feeders or flowers were available a year previously.

Hovering involves seventy-five-plus wing beats a second (yes, *second*), which of course is energetically expensive, so ready sources of food are essential. Ruby-throats can save energy by going into nocturnal torpor, a state of reduced metabolic activity akin to a one-night hibernation. This can get the birds through a short-term food shortage, but feeders can contribute to survival when natural food supplies are low for longer periods.

Key references: Baumgartner 1980, Bent 1940, Hiebert 1991, Kodric-Brown and Brown 1978, Lukes 1980, Miller and Miller 1971, Miller and Nero 1983, Parrish 1988, Southwick and Southwick 1980, Willimont et al. 1988.

FeederWatch Findings

For the most part, the map shows locations of Ruby-throated Hummingbirds in the early stages of spring migration. If the Feeder-Watch survey were to continue past April, it would show feeder visits throughout the eastern United States. Most sites host one territorial Ruby-throat at a time, although more may visit in bad weather or if there are multiple feeders present.

Frequent feeder foods: *Sugar water.*

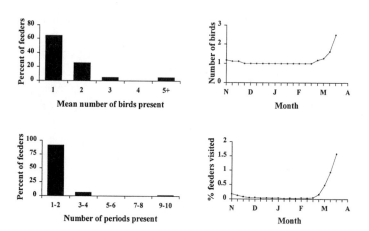

Ruby-throated Hummingbird: percent of feeders visited

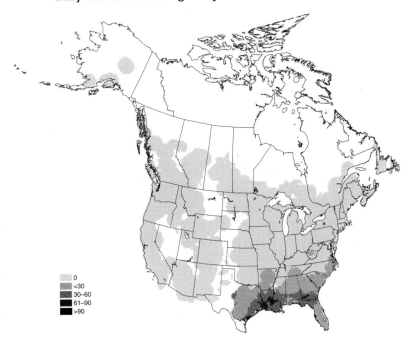

0
<30
30–60
61–90
>90

Abundance at feeders

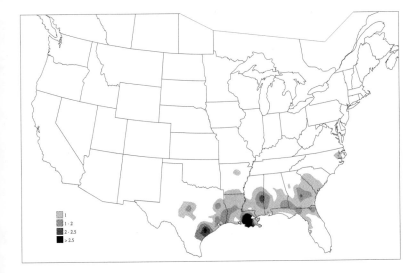

1
1 - 2
2 - 2.5
> 2.5

Black-chinned Hummingbird

Archilochus alexandri

The Black-chin is one of the more widespread hummingbirds in western North America but only during the breeding season. Most "winter" sightings are of migrants on their way to or from Mexico, although a few do overwinter in the American Southwest. Perhaps this is the reason there is little published information on the winter ecology of Black-chinned Hummingbirds, and this account concentrates instead on lore that applies to hummingbirds in general (see other hummingbird accounts for more).

Hummingbirds are often described as tiny jewels because of the brilliant iridescence of their feathers, which flash color or not according to the angle of light. Most bird colors result from pigmentation, but in hummers it is the microscopic construction of feathers that is responsible.

Hummingbirds are marvelously coadapted with their food plants. At least thirty-one plant species in North America have evolved modifications specifically to cater to hummingbirds—principally, a copious production of nectar and a blooming cycle that corresponds to periods of maximum hummingbird abundance on either the birds' breeding range or migration routes. The benefit to the plants is that each hummingbird visitor gets dusted with pollen to carry to the next flower—key links in a very efficient pollinization system. Many other animals also like nectar, however, and this pollination strategy works well only if the plant can exclude nectar-robbing species that take advantage of the food but are not good pollinators. Thus, hummingbird-adapted plants often have long tubular flowers whose nectar is available only to the long-beaked hummingbirds. The nectar of hummingbird-pollinated flowers is rich in sucrose and glucose, which hummingbirds prefer, whereas other flowers produce more of the fructose favored by insect pollinators.

Hummingbirds have evolved right along with their food plants. Their extensible tongues have two long grooves from front to back in just the right dimensions to draw up liquids by capillary action, provided the solution is about 20% sugar—which is precisely the concentration produced by bird-pollinated flowers. (The one-to-four sugar solution ratio suggested for feeders is 23% sugar). Hummingbirds may also lick up nectar, flicking the tongue out and in rapidly and wiping the nectar into the mouth as the tongue moves outward again. This less-efficient feeding method is required when sugar concentrations are much higher than 20% but works well at feeders where the pool of sugar water is much deeper than it is in flowers.

Despite common belief, hummingbirds do not have an innate preference for red. Instead, this color happens to contrast well with a background of green foliage, making flowers readily visible. The association between red flowers and food must be learned by each hummingbird. In fact, these birds are easily trained to take food from feeders of other colors. Training trials have also demonstrated that Black-chinned and certain other hummingbirds can see some ultraviolet light, which suggests that the "colors" they see may be quite different from what our own eyes perceive.

Hummingbird food resources are ephemeral and unpredictable, so investigative behavior and learning ability may be crucial ingredients to hummingbird survival strategies. For example, newly opened flowers produce more nectar than older ones, and both Black-chinned and Ruby-throated Hummingbirds are known to visit these preferentially. To test the learning abilities of hummingbirds, one experimenter artificially added nectar to older flowers with a syringe. The birds quickly discovered this sudden rejuvenation and readily switched to older blooms for the duration of the experiment.

Black-chinned Hummingbirds can be quite successful at defending territories with few nectar sources, and they are able to extract more energy out of the flowers than species such as Anna's Hummingbirds, which prefer areas of dense blooms. They can also defend feeders as long as there are not too many competitors about. Once several Black-chins start using a feeder, there will be a breakdown of monopoly by a single bird despite high levels of aggressive behavior.

Key references: Austin 1975, Bertin 1982, Ewald and Bransfield 1987, George 1980, Goldsmith 1980, Kingsolver and Daniel 1983, Miller 1985, Miller et al. 1985, Stiles 1976, Roberts 1995, Rusch et al. 1996.

FeederWatch Findings

Black-chinned Hummingbirds are seen on the FeederWatch survey primarily as spring migrants, but some feeders in the southern United States host them all winter. The apparent gap in distribution in West Texas results from lack of FeederWatch coverage there. Black-chins are recorded at twice as many suburban and rural feeders as at urban sites.

Frequent feeder foods: Small samples indicate *sugar water* is visited regularly, and plain water is taken on occasion, as well.

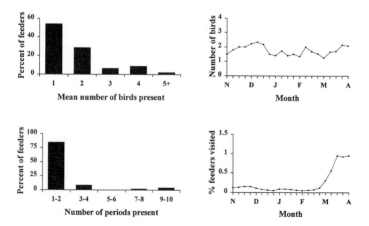

Black-chinned Hummingbird: percent of feeders visited

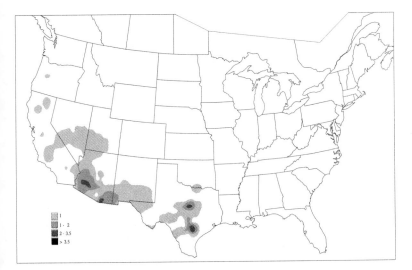

Abundance at feeders

Anna's Hummingbird

Calypte anna

This is the only hummingbird species whose entire range, both summer and winter, is largely contained within the United States, mostly in California. It is also the only North American species without an extensive migration. Nonetheless, limited banding suggests turnover in the individuals present at a given feeder, and there is some midwinter movement from west to east. Postbreeding movements may take birds northward into Canada and Alaska, perhaps to take advantage of the later flowering seasons there.

Most native California plants do not bloom in the winter, and Anna's Hummingbirds have adapted by becoming more insectivorous and less dependent on nectar than other hummingbird species. Indeed, given sugar water alone, Anna's Hummingbirds lose weight, and their estimated protein needs require them to eat the equivalent of thirty-eight tiny flies each day. These hummers can be seen hawking for minuscule flying insects, gleaning from tree trunks, or even picking food from spider webs (sometimes becoming entangled themselves). They are known to feed on tree sap at Acorn Woodpecker workings but do not rely on sap as a regular source of food in the way that Rufous and Ruby-throated Hummingbirds seem to do.

There is now an abundance cf exotic, winter-flowering vegetation in California, which may help explain why the range of Anna's Hummingbirds has expanded since the 1930s. Feeders, too, have probably played a role. Cold snaps can decimate Anna's Hummingbird populations, not because of inability on their part to survive the cold but by the wilting of the flowers and the killing of the insects on which the birds rely. At such times hummingbird defense of limited food resources can become ferocious. During one freeze, a male Anna's was seen to kill another, using its bill as a spear. You can help birds through such emergencies by providing extra feeders; even simply serving sugar water in any small dish for a few days.

Perhaps because Anna's Hummingbirds are less dependent on nectar than other North American species, they usually are not very aggressive in defending territories that have few flowers. However, when patches of flowers are dense, Anna's will defend territories as pugnaciously as any other species. Males evidently guard feeders, as well, judging from the fact that females visit feeders less often than the more assertive males.

Feeder owners may notice an increase in hummingbird traffic late in the day as the birds "tank up" for the night. You can increase the traffic further by also providing plain water that hummers will use both for drinking and bathing. They avoid deep water but will bathe in shallow pools or dishes, or even take a shower in your sprinkler. With patience you can train hummingbirds to perch on your hands, but sometimes no training is required. One observer in British Columbia described venturing outdoors in his pajamas to tend feeders during a sudden cold spell—and having to literally cool his heels when a hummer landed on his finger to take lengthy sips from the feeder.

Triggered by the onset of winter rains, Anna's Hummingbirds nest from December to June, so you can witness courtship and spot youngsters in months when much of North America is blanketed in snow. The male's spectacular courtship flight takes him vertically upward, nearly beyond sight; then he descends precipitously, only to swoop sideways at the last moment to describe a J shape right under the nose of a perching female.

Key references: Ewald and Bransfield 1987, Harris-Haller and Harris 1991, Kattan and Murcia 1985, Phillips 1975, Russell 1996, Stallcup 1991.

FeederWatch Findings

Anna's Hummingbird visits nearly 80% of feeders in California, often for most of the winter. Suburban sites are most likely to be visited; rural feeders, the least. Nevertheless, abundance is twice as high at those rural sites. As with other hummingbirds that defend food sources, greater abundance may be related to having multiple feeders in one's yard.

Frequent feeder foods: *Sugar water.*

Infrequent choices: Suet, plain water, mixed seed. (In the latter case, probably eating tiny fragments only.)

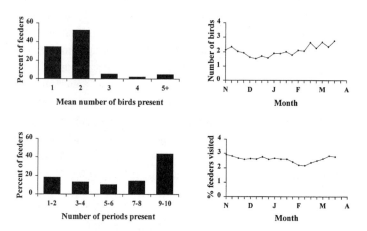

Anna's Hummingbird: percent of feeders visited

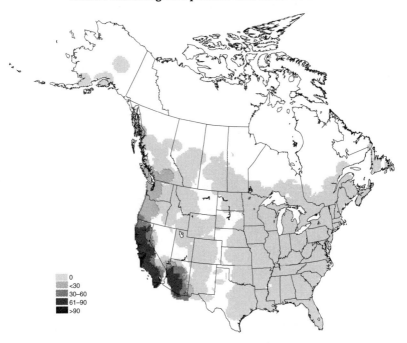

0
<30
30–60
61–90
>90

Abundance at feeders

1
1 - 2
2 - 2.5
> 2.5

Rufous Hummingbird

Selasphorus rufus

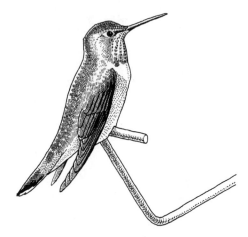

Rufous Hummingbirds nest farther north than any other hummingbird species. They must undertake a long migration from the nesting areas (which extend from northern California to southern parts of the Yukon) to their winter home centered in Mexico—the longest migration of any bird when the distance is converted to number of body lengths flown. In the United States, feeder owners south of Oregon see this species only during migration, except at a few wintering sites in extreme southern parts of the country. The species is apparently overwintering more often in the southeastern United States than in the past.

Like several other western hummingbird species, Rufous Hummingbirds migrate in an elliptical route. In spring they usually hug the West Coast to avoid late-winter storms in the still-snowy mountains, but some may head farther inland—buzzing astonished hikers on high-altitude glaciers. These birds breed early, so "fall" migration can begin as early as late June. In this season males moving south along the Rocky Mountains utilize mountain flowers that bloom in profusion just after snowmelt. Females and immatures follow a few weeks later, visiting higher elevations that were still snow covered when the males passed by. They establish temporary territories in mountain meadows for up to two weeks to build up fuel for the next migratory hop.

Rufous Hummingbirds are particularly known for their pugnacious personality and strong territorial defense, but there are times when defense of a nectar resource might backfire, as when an especially attractive food source requires all of a bird's time to fend off intruders. The energetic expense of maintaining a territory might also be prohibitive if food plants are far apart. Theorists (who sometimes base academic careers on thinking about such things) predict that territorial behavior should break down under conditions like the ones just described. Hummingbirds have in fact been the subject of considerable experimental study, since territorial and non-territorial species often coexist. Food supplies can easily be manipulated, and many ingenious experiments have been conducted by cutting off flowers, adding nectar to others with syringes, and even installing fake flowers with nectar flow that can be controlled by the experimenter. For the most part, hummingbirds act as theory says they should, modifying their territorial and food-hunting behavior according to prevailing conditions in a way that allows them to extract the most food in the most energy-efficient manner.

Energy efficiency is an important consideration for hummingbirds, as they burn calories at a prodigious rate (Rufous Hummingbirds beat their wings forty-four times a second). They are particularly adapted to use oxygen at a high rate, having evolved special blood and muscle characteristics, large hearts (in proportion to body size), and one of the most metabolically active livers known. Some of the muscle adaptations may only be possible for a small animal, which the Rufous hummer certainly is. It tips the scales at only about one-eighth of an ounce, or a little less than the weight of a quarter.

Rufous Hummingbirds, like Ruby-throats, will follow sapsuckers and defend sap wells against other hummers. Although California has fifty species of flowers used by hummingbirds, British Columbia has only about ten and Alaska only five, so the association between sapsuckers and Rufous Hummingbirds may assure an important food source that contributes to the ability of these tiny birds to nest so far north so early in the spring. Another important factor is a relatively high incidence of insects in the diet. And finally, Rufous

Hummingbirds can conserve energy by roosting at lower (warmer) elevations than where they spend the day or by going into torpor at nighttime. But even these adaptations may not be enough when cold snaps wipe out natural food supplies, and at such times bird feeders may be important to hummingbird survival.

Key references: Calder 1993, Ewald 1985, Gass et al. 1976, Gass and Lertzman 1980, Hill et al. 1998, Kodric-Brown and Brown 1978, Phillips 1975, Sutherland et al. 1982, Tooze and Gass 1985.

FeederWatch Findings

Like the Ruby-throated and Black-chinned Hummingbirds, the Rufous Hummingbird is seen on FeederWatch counts mainly as a spring migrant. Nonetheless, by the end of March many of this species have already reached the Northern Pacific regions where they breed, and they are reported at over a quarter of feeders there. Records along the Mexican border and Gulf Coast are in sites where over-wintering can occur, and a few feeders do report this species all winter long.

Frequent feeder foods: *Sugar water.*

Infrequent choices: Plain water.

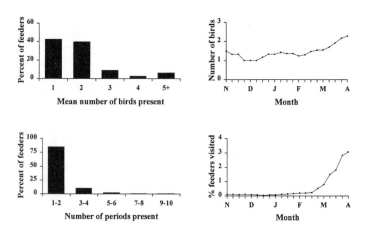

Rufous Hummingbird: percent of feeders visited

Abundance at feeders

Red-bellied Woodpecker

Melanerpes carolinus

The Red-bellied Woodpecker seems rather inappropriately named, given that it has bright-red plumage only on the head (male) and nape (both sexes). The "red" belly has only a pale rosy wash, at best. The bird is nonetheless comparatively noisy and conspicuous, making it a familiar woodpecker species at feeders in the eastern United States. Red-bellies from northern parts of the breeding range routinely undertake a fall migration, and some southern birds may move short distances, as well. There has been northward expansion of the winter range over the last one hundred years (that is, reduction in migration), in which bird feeding may have played a role.

The densest winter populations of the Red-bellied Woodpecker are in warm, productive lowlands where food is particularly abundant. Unlike most other woodpeckers, Red-bellies sample nearly every food available and will readily eat corn and other seeds. When acorns are abundant, these nuts constitute up to 70% of the natural diet.

The enterprising Red-belly also eats fruits, insects, an occasional frog or lizard, and has even been recorded eating hens' eggs.

As might be expected of birds with generalized diets, Red-bellies use a wide variety of foraging techniques. They are as likely to search for food on the ground as to glean tree trunks and branches, especially in second-growth deciduous woods with dense understory, where the foraging birds have some protective cover. Unlike the more specialized Hairy and Downy Woodpeckers, Red-bellies do little hammering and probing of tree bark with their bills. Instead, they winkle out insects hiding in bark crevices with their long, maneuverable tongues, which can be extended well beyond the end of the beak.

These woodpeckers carefully hide food in the fall, presumably to create a supply for the winter, although nothing is known about how important such caches may be to survival. Sometimes they hide food in other seasons, too. Acorns, poison ivy berries, insects, or seeds from feeders are all candidates for storage. Food is sometimes carried long distances before being pressed deep into natural crevices, the agile tongue used like a finger to manipulate items within the chosen cavity. The only other bird that is capable of routinely pilfering Red-bellied Woodpecker stores is the larger Pileated Woodpecker, which may learn to search for food at sites recently worked over by Red-bellies. Perhaps to reduce such theft, Red-bellies sometimes conceal their caches with bits of nonedible vegetation.

Red-bellied Woodpeckers usually visit feeders alone because individuals set up solitary housekeeping for the winter after family units break up in early fall. As spring approaches, males become more tolerant of females and they start visiting feeders in pairs. While birds that defend winter territories are often aggressive, Red-bellies feed peacefully among smaller birds. They are by no means pushovers, however, and will hold their ground against such feeder bullies as Northern Mockingbirds.

Key references: Bock and Lepthien 1975a, Connor 1980, Dennis 1981, 1986, Kilham 1963, Martin et al. 1951, Morse 1972, Rodgers 1990, Root 1988, Wallace 1974, Williams 1975.

FeederWatch Findings

This woodpecker visits over 80% of feeders in its core wintering range. About two-thirds of sites that report Red-bellies do so regularly throughout the winter, while others are most likely to have visits in midwinter only. These woodpeckers are slightly more faithful and more numerous at rural and suburban than at urban sites, but the differences are too small to be noticeable to casual observers.

Frequent feeder foods: *Suet, bird puddings,* striped sunflower, peanut butter mixes.

Infrequent choices: Black-oil and hulled sunflower, mixed seed, safflower, whole and cracked corn, milo, peanuts (any form), fresh and dried fruit, meat scraps, baked goods, water.

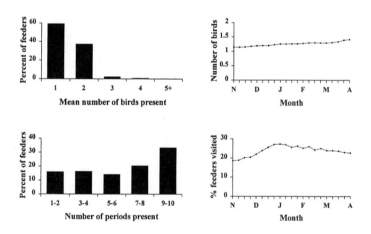

Red-bellied Woodpecker: percent of feeders visited

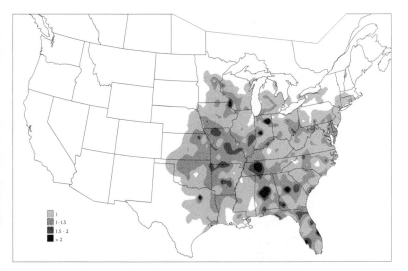

	0
	<30
	30–60
	61–90
	>90

Abundance at feeders

	1
	1 - 1.5
	1.5 - 2
	> 2

Yellow-bellied Sapsucker

Sphyrapicus varius

The Yellow-bellied Sapsucker is the only North American wood-pecker with essentially no overlap of the summer and winter ranges. Females (which have white chins) winter farther south than the red-chinned males, and at the southern edge of the wintering range there are more than three females for every male.

These woodpeckers are relatively uncommon at feeders. They are more likely to sample bird "puddings" than suet and are known to enjoy sugar water and even jelly. Such taste preferences are understandable in light of the sapsucker's natural diet. Conspicuously absent are the beetle larvae sought by many woodpecker species, while important summer foods include fruit, insects (especially ants), tree sap, and "bast"—the soft inner layers of tree bark that transport and store sap and sugars.

Less is known about the sapsucker's natural diet in winter. Yellow-bellies store nuts and seeds occasionally in this season, and insects are probably a staple food. While we tend to think of sap flow as a summer event, even leafless deciduous trees may produce a little dilute sap when temperatures rise above freezing, and evergreen trees in the southern United States possibly produce enough sap in winter to serve as a regular food source. However, no one has studied the relative importance of sap, seed stores, or other foods to the birds' winter energy budget.

Sapsuckers begin to drill for sap in earnest on spring migration, at first favoring hickory trees. These produce a slow-flowing sap with 10 to 11% sugar content. Once deciduous trees begin to photosynthesize, sap flow becomes more copious, and sugar content rises to 20% or more. The birds then collect sap and bast from a vast array of tree species, both deciduous and coniferous. Introduced and cultivated trees are patronized in particular—as some rueful homeowners can attest. Sapsuckers feeding on bast in early spring may drill as many as fifty holes an hour, so tree damage can be high.

To test whether sap is flowing, the birds often start by drilling a horizontal row of several holes. Shaped like inverted cones, these holes hold sap inside and reduce seepage. Once flow is established the sapsucker returns repeatedly to feed—one bird was recorded sipping over five hundred times an hour for eight and a half straight hours. When one hole runs dry, another is drilled directly above it, and eventually a band consisting of many vertical columns of sap wells is formed around the tree.

Sapsuckers switch to eating insects during the breeding season, but once the young fledge, sap feeding again becomes paramount. Newly fledged families move to favored groves of trees—in northern regions these are often birches—and defend them from other sapsuckers. Over three thousand holes can be drilled annually within the summer territory, so each year a few trees may die from the sapsuckers' attentions. However, the victims often have prior wounds or damage and are apparently chosen because sap flow at wound sites is especially heavy.

Many other bird species, insects, and small mammals are attracted to sapsucker wells to take advantage of this otherwise unavailable food source. North America's most northerly nesting hummingbird species may even be dependent on sapsuckers to provide food in early spring, before nectar-bearing flowers come into bloom.

Key references: Connor and Kroll 1979, Dennis 1981, Foster and Tate 1966, Howell 1953, Kilham 1956, 1964, Lawrence 1967, Miller and Nero 1983, Sutherland et al. 1982, Tate 1973, Williams 1980.

FeederWatch Findings

The Yellow-bellied Sapsucker is rather an uncommon feeder visitor, even though it visits over a quarter of sites in some states. Only 10% of sites report it present for more than half the winter. Peak visitations occur in midwinter and during spring migration. Most visits are by a single bird.

Frequent feeder foods: *Bird puddings,* suet. No FeederWatch data were available for fruit or sugar water, but these foods are also known to be eaten by sapsuckers.

Infrequent choices: Small samples suggest peanut butter mixes may be acceptable.

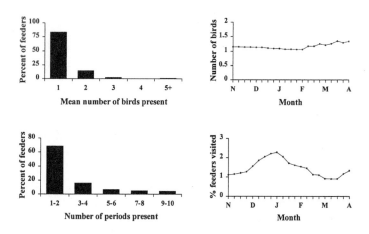

Yellow-bellied Sapsucker: percent of feeders visited

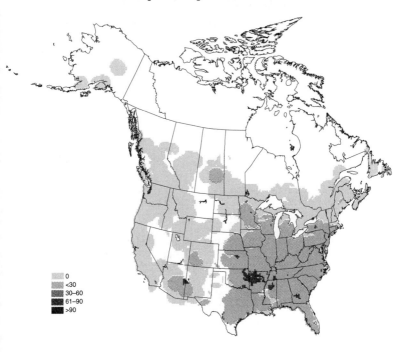

0
<30
30–60
61–90
>90

Abundance at feeders

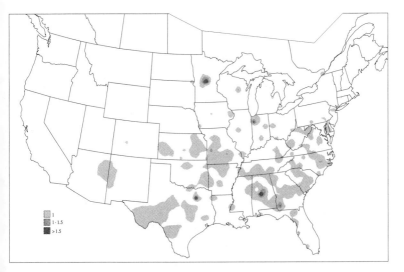

1
1-1.5
>1.5

Downy Woodpecker

Picoides pubescens

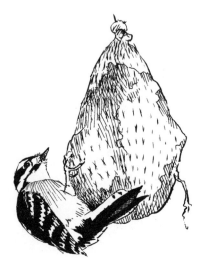

Downy Woodpeckers are among the most widespread species at North American feeders—at least where suet or fat is offered. Suet is similar to this woodpecker's favorite natural food of fat-rich beetle larvae. Downies also eat a wide variety of other animal and vegetable foods, however, and they sometimes surprise feeder owners by carrying off a sunflower seed or a morsel of cracked corn.

Pictures of Downy Woodpeckers often show them perched on the large woody galls commonly found on goldenrod stems. These galls are favored because they each house an overwintering fly larva that the birds consider a delicacy. By midwinter Downy Woodpeckers may have attacked nearly every gall within a few yards of woody cover. (Galls distant from cover are more likely to be worked over by chickadees.) Some galls are rejected by the woodpeckers, and research has shown that the larvae in these galls have been parasitized by another insect, lessening the food value. A bird distinguishes the quality of the gall by giving it a light tap with its bill.

Evidently the resonance reflects the size of the larva inside.

While larvae are favored treats, they apparently are not abundant enough to fulfill all needs. This can be deduced from the fact that a male Downy Woodpecker (dominant to its mate, with whom he may be loosely associated throughout the winter) hogs the habitat where larvae are most accessible and drives the female off if she ventures too close. Even when foraging in the same tree, the female is likely to probe for surface insects on the lower trunk, while the male excavates deeper holes in the upper reaches of the tree where bark is thinner and wood-boring larvae are easier to dig out. In midwinter when weather is most severe, members of a pair often separate entirely and forage out of one another's sight. This allows a female to use the habitat that the male normally commands, perhaps making it easier for her to get sufficient food.

The male's domination of the "best" habitat may seem unchivalrous, but he does display some regard for his mate. If a predator is detected while the female is absent, he remains silent; but if his mate is within earshot, he will give an alarm call even though that might attract the predator to him. Perhaps this kind of protection helps explain why the female usually remains with her mate through most of the winter even though she may be excluded from certain foraging areas.

In the depths of winter, tension between the sexes can often be observed at feeders. If a male arrives while the female is present, you may see her retreat and hide behind a branch until he is gone. Indeed, one sure sign of spring on the horizon is an increased tendency for Downy Woodpeckers to visit feeders in pairs.

Although Downy Woodpeckers defend their winter territories against neighboring pairs, they are very tolerant of other species. The woodpeckers respond to alarm calls of other birds, freezing motionless for minutes on end. They only resume feeding when the other birds begin their normal calling—a sort of "all-clear" signal. If you alarm a woodpecker and then play a tape recording of chickadee chatter, you can trick it into relaxing just as it would if other birds were actually present.

Key references: Confer and Paicos 1985, Connor 1980, Dennis 1981, Kilham 1970, 1974, Matthysen et al. 1991, Peters and Grubb 1983, Sullivan 1984, 1985.

FeederWatch Findings

Downy Woodpeckers are very widespread at North American feeders, visiting over 90% of them in some regions. Over half of feeders host this species all winter long. Most sightings are of lone individuals or pairs.

Frequent feeder foods: *Suet, bird puddings,* peanut butter mixes.

Infrequent choices: Mixed seed, canary seed, sunflower (any type), safflower, corn (any form), peanuts (any form), milo, oats, canola, pet food, fresh and dried fruit, meat scraps, baked goods, popped corn, water.

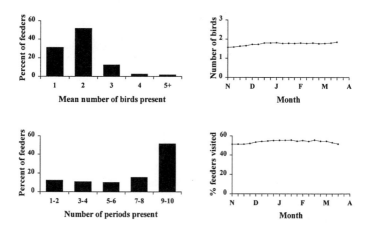

Downy Woodpecker: percent of feeders visited

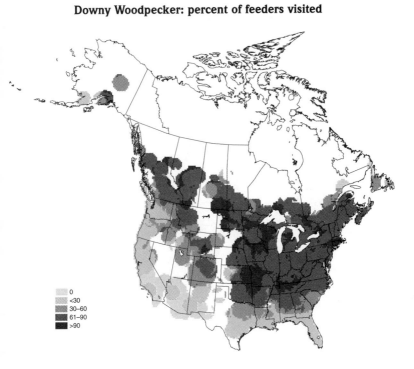

0
<30
30–60
61–90
>90

Abundance at feeders

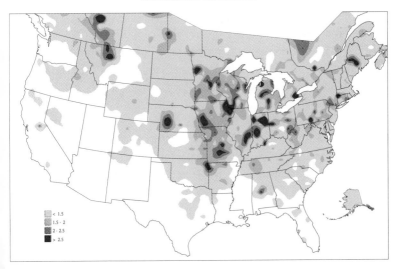

< 1.5
1.5 - 2
2 - 2.5
> 2.5

Hairy Woodpecker

Picoides villosus

Hairy Woodpeckers can be distinguished from the more common Downies by their larger size. If you do not have both species for comparison, check the length of the bill relative to the size of the head. The Hairy's beak is nearly as long as the distance from the base of the beak to the back of the head, whereas Downies have relatively short and dainty bills. The male Hairy uses his hefty beak to dig deeply into tree trunks in a quest for beetle larvae, while the female spends more time scaling off bark and probing for insects near the surface. Sometimes the beak is whacked against a tree in a series of side-to-side blows, a behavior hypothesized to produce echos that indicate the degree of insect infestation.

Beetle larvae make up only about one-third of the Hairy Woodpecker's natural diet, and most people are surprised to learn that ants are the next most important food item. Hairies also eat a wide variety of other insects and a few fruits (including poison ivy berries). Sometimes Hairies spend a great deal of time digging seeds out of pine cones. They evidently have a sweet tooth, too, as they are known to visit sapsucker wells and hummingbird feeders, and they have even been reported piercing sugar cane stems to enjoy a sweet drink. The main food taken at feeders is fat or suet, but seeds are occasionally carried off to a spot where they can be wedged for pounding open.

One might wonder how woodpeckers manage all of their pounding for insects without ever losing their grip and falling off a tree—not to mention never getting a headache from all their hammering— but they are well built for the job: Two toes point backward (instead of one, as in most small birds), allowing the birds to cling tightly to vertical tree trunks; special stiff tail feathers are pressed against the substrate to join the short legs in forming a firm tripod that supports the bird as it lifts its upper body and throws itself into a vigorous blow; and air bubbles incorporated into the skull act as shock absorbers to protect the brain. Woodpeckers do not need to dig all the way down to an insect's hiding place, but just have to break into the tunnel system. Then the woodpecker's long, sticky tongue takes over. The roots of the Hairy's retractable tongue reach entirely around the back of the skull, over the top, and into a coil around the right eyeball.

The Hairy Woodpecker is something of a loner and less likely than a Downy Woodpecker to join in mixed-species flocks. Despite this lack of sociability with other species, Hairy Woodpeckers are often found in twos, as pairs may remain together year-round. The differences in foraging technique between the sexes (males excavate more while females probe the surface) may prevent competition and allow mates to remain together through periods of low food abundance.

Quite a bit of Hairy Woodpecker behavior can be observed at feeders. Although Hairies can easily displace smaller birds if they wish, they usually feed with others quite peacefully—until another Hairy Woodpecker appears. Then you may witness a threat display in which the calling bird waves its bill and tail from side to side. A similar display in spring, but with the tail fanned, is a friendlier gesture that is directed at a female. (She is slightly smaller than her mate and is easily distinguished by the lack of any red on the back of her head.)

Key references: Bull et al. 1986, Kilham 1965, Morrison and With 1987, Spring

FeederWatch Findings

Although the Hairy Woodpecker visits fewer feeders than the Downy, it is still reported at over 75% of feeders in some regions. It is marked-ly more likely to be seen at rural than at urban feeders and is a more regular visitor in rural areas, too. Finally, rural feeder owners have a slightly greater chance of seeing two Hairy Woodpeckers at a time (instead of just one).

Favorite feeder foods: *Suet,* bird puddings, peanut butter mixes, meat scraps.

Infrequent choices: Mixed seed, sunflower (any form), safflower, whole corn, peanuts (any form), baked goods, water, and (based on small samples) popped corn.

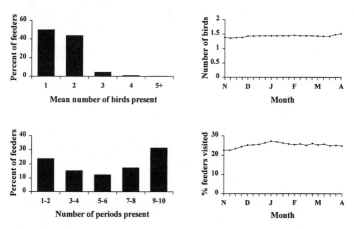

Hairy Woodpecker: percent of feeders visited

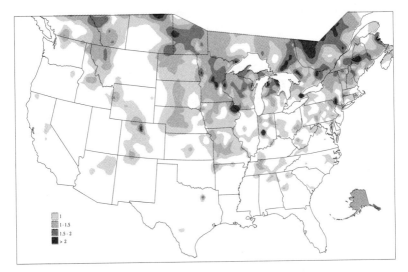

- 0
- <30
- 30–60
- 61–90
- >90

Abundance at feeders

- 1
- 1 - 1.5
- 1.5 - 2
- > 2

Northern Flicker

Colaptes auratus

People sometimes forget that the Northern Flicker is even a woodpecker because it spends nearly three-quarters of its time on the ground foraging for ants. Instead of "pecking wood" in a search for tree-boring larvae, a flicker will rip open ant colonies found in the ground or old tree stumps, or it may merely probe tunnels of undisturbed colonies with its long, barbed tongue. That handy appendage can be extended two inches beyond the tip of the beak and is coated with enough stickum from the flicker's enormous salivary glands to entrap any ant encountered. The winter diet consists far less of ants, shifting strongly toward fruits of trees and vines. Poison ivy and poison sumac berries are particular favorites, and flickers may be important in distributing their seeds. These birds must have iron stomachs indeed to stand up to the twin insults of poison ivy and the formic acid exuded by angry ants!

Wintering flickers utilize a wide variety of open areas and lightly treed parkland, but they especially favor cut-over or burned forest and pine barrens. Ants are probably abundant in such areas, as are scrubby berry bushes. Reforestation throughout eastern North America has reduced the availability of these favored habitats, perhaps contributing to the thirty-year decline that has been documented in Northern Flicker populations. Another possible contributing factor may include chemical control of fire ants in the southern United States, where most eastern flickers spend the winter.

Given the flicker's dietary tastes, we should not be surprised that these woodpeckers are relatively uncommon at feeders. Foods of interest may be present—suet and fats, a few nuts or seeds, plain or sugar water, or bits of fruit—but rarely are these offered on the ground in wide-open areas. Flickers will sometimes overcome their wariness of backyards, however, and seem fairly comfortable on suet logs and tree-mounted feeders.

The flicker is among the earliest of spring migrants, and its appearance in the north is welcomed as a sign of spring by people who recognize the loud call, white rump, and flash of color under the wings that make the flying bird so conspicuous. (On the ground, the bright colors are concealed and the bird is well camouflaged.) There are several races of flickers—formerly considered separate species—that differ in the colors of both the underwing (yellow or red) and the male's "mustache," or cheek stripe (red or black).

One of the few studies of flicker winter ecology, on roosting behavior, was perhaps undertaken only because the flicker is large enough to carry a radio transmitter. The study involved attaching transmitters to the feathers, which would have added too much weight for a smaller species. Results showed that males tend to roost at different places each night. They do not move far—less than 1 mile from the previous night's roost—but over several weeks the flicker sleeps at sites scattered throughout an area of about ½ square mile. The birds tend to sleep out in the open, often on tree trunks, building walls (generally up under eaves), or under bridges, but sometimes they tuck themselves into chimneys or natural holes.

Key references: Connor 1980, Cruz and Johnston 1979, Dennis 1988, Royall and Bray 1980.

FeederWatch Findings

Northern Flickers visit quite a large proportion of feeders over the course of the winter—more than half in many states—but usually not week after week. Fewer than 10% of feeders report flickers present all season, and usually only one or two birds visit at a time. Suet is not as clear a favorite as for other woodpeckers that visit feeders.

Favorite feeder foods: Suet, bird puddings.

Infrequent choices: Mixed seed, millet, sunflower (any type), corn (cracked or whole), peanuts (any form), niger, peanut butter mixes, baked goods, water. Small samples suggest oats and dried fruit are also acceptable.

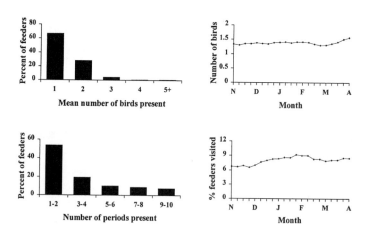

Northern Flicker: percent of feeders visited

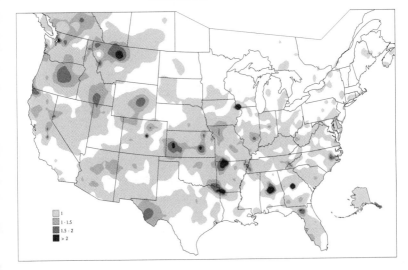

Abundance at feeders

Pileated Woodpecker

Dryocopus pileatus

The first view of a Pileated Woodpecker at your feeder can really set your heart pounding. This striking black-and-white crow-sized bird topped with a spectacular red crest simply cannot be mistaken for anything else. (The *pileatus* in the bird's Latin name means "crested").

Pileated Woodpeckers suffered declines during the mass felling of North American forests in the late 1800s. Although quite tolerant of second-growth forest, these birds disappear when woodlots become small and isolated. However, the species has recovered well: According to the Breeding Bird Survey, it is among the few woodpeckers whose continent-wide breeding populations increased significantly in the period 1966–89.

It is reported that Pileateds started visiting bird feeders in the 1950s, but this was probably not a factor in the population recovery. Pileateds visit relatively few feeder sites, although some individuals do become fairly tame and regular visitors after an initial period of wariness.

Male and female Pileated Woodpeckers use similar foraging

techniques and normally feed together quietly and in relative peace. Although the male may often displace his mate, particularly from upright tree trunks, he will occasionally defer to her. The pair stays together throughout the winter (unlike many other woodpecker species in which mated pairs may separate for part of the winter before reuniting in spring).

Pileated Woodpeckers eat a lot of fruit in winter, but about half their diet consists of termites, larvae of wood-boring beetles, and other insects common to decaying wood, especially carpenter ants. These ants prefer large trees (since small-diameter trunks break up quickly after infestation); therefore, any bird that particularly relishes these ants has to be large-bodied enough to deal with substantial tree trunks. Pileated Woodpeckers will forage on live deciduous or coniferous trees if the heartwood is infested with ants, but more often—and more than any other woodpecker species—they rely on dead trees and especially on fallen logs. Each bird spends about two-thirds of its feeding time excavating distinctive, fist-width holes of a vertical, round-cornered rectangular shape—a sure sign of Pileated activity. As soon as the bird stops for a break (sometimes even before), Hairy Woodpeckers and other bird species may come to feed on small larvae that the larger bird has exposed.

A single pair of Pileated Woodpeckers needs a lot of space, presumably to ensure an adequate food supply. The core of the territory is defended by the male, who announces his ownership (and attracts females) with loud drumming—and a piercing call that has been described as something out of a Tarzan movie. Especially persistent drumming signals the presence of a male still on the lookout for a mate.

Key references: Bock and Lepthien 1975a, Bull et al. 1986, Connor 1980, Dennis 1986, Kilham 1959, 1976, Maxson and Maxson 1981, Schardien and Jackson 1978.

FeederWatch Findings

The Pileated Woodpecker visits fewer than a quarter of feeders in any region, usually alone, and normally only occasionally during the winter. Nonetheless, about 15% of visited feeders host this woodpecker throughout the winter.

Favorite feeder foods: *Suet*, bird puddings.

Infrequent choices: Mixed seed, striped sunflower. Small samples indicate that other acceptable foods include millet, safflower, peanut hearts, peanut butter mixes, and meat scraps.

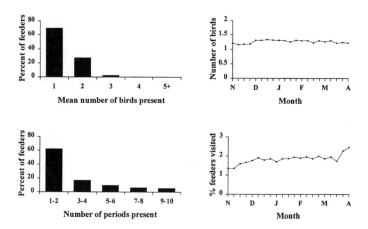

Pileated Woodpecker: percent of feeders visited

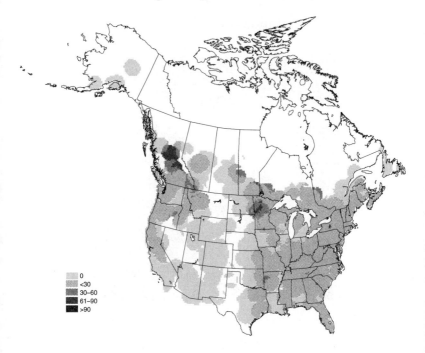

- 0
- <30
- 30–60
- 61–90
- >90

Abundance at feeders

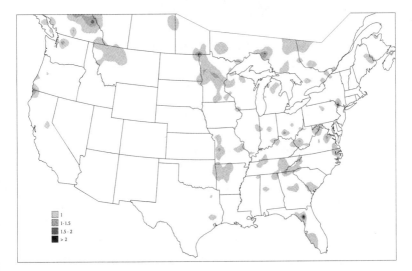

- 1
- 1 - 1.5
- 1.5 - 2
- > 2

Gray Jay

Perisoreus canadensis

The Gray Jay, or "Whisky Jack," is also known as "Camp Robber" because of its boldness and opportunism in finding food. These omnivorous birds are well-known to trappers, prospectors, and campers in northern spruce forests for trying to carry off everything from leather moccasins to soap and matches. Carrion can be an important winter food source, and Gray Jays learn to scavenge roadkill and to follow wolf packs and human hunters, waiting for a kill in which they can share. Sometimes they chase live prey, such as wounded ducks or small birds (usually without success), and jays will land on the backs of moose to feast on engorged ticks.

Much of the Gray Jay's life is focused on food storage. Small pellets of food are covered with copious, sticky saliva and glued to needle clusters, twigs, or tree trunks. Other North American corvids store food in the ground, but Gray Jays have to find cache sites above the deep snows that are normal within their range. Caching is most prominent through the summer, and on long Alaskan days these birds may cache over a thousand items. Some food stores may be recovered for eating within a few hours, but others are left for a month or more. Experiments have shown that the jays use memory to recover hidden items (as opposed to simply revisiting favored sites). The caching behavior doubtless contributes to Gray Jay survival through harsh northern winters. Indeed, where winter days afford only four to six hours of daylight, ready access to previously stored food is probably crucial.

Other adaptations to surviving winter are physiological. The Gray Jay's thick plumage has a special structure that is thought to let solar radiation penetrate deeply while remaining insulative, and Gray Jays often sunbathe in subfreezing temperatures. Body temperature is reduced several degrees at night as an energy-saving measure. A roosting bird fluffs its plumage so extensively that all you can see—literally—are the tips of the wings and tail protruding from a fluffy gray ball.

Astonishingly, Gray Jays begin nesting in late winter, long before snowmelt and when temperatures are as low as -22°F. The nest is well insulated, but the incubating female often has to protect eggs from late snowstorms. Why nest so early? Perhaps food caches used to help raise young could spoil if the jays waited until warm weather, or maybe carrion is especially plentiful in the late winter. Possibly the main reason, though, is that the entire warm part of the year must be used to store food if enough is to be saved to get the birds through the next winter.

Gray Jays are essentially resident, with mated pairs occupying an area of 100 to 200 acres for most of their lives. By midsummer the dominant juvenile has driven other siblings out of the territory. The majority of the excluded die, but some are able to attach themselves to unrelated pairs that did not raise young. The juveniles help the resident pair make caches and may inherit the territory when one of the adults dies, since the average life span after reaching adulthood is only about four to six years.

Presence of a bird feeder in a local pair's territory may attract regular intruders, such as a neighboring pair or a group of nonbreeders. As the mortality of nonbreeders is high, access to a feeder might prove crucial for survival. Preferred foods include fat, bread, and such miscellaneous items as meat scraps, cheese, baked beans, and oatmeal. Gray Jay beaks are relatively weak and some authors report that these jays never hammer open seeds; but they occasionally take sunflower seeds from feeders. Sometimes larger items, such as bread slices, are transferred to the feet for carrying in flight—a very unusual behavior for birds other than hawks and owls.

Key references: Addison et al. 1989, Bunch and Tomback 1986, Dow 1965, Gill 1974, Ha and Lehner 1990, Maccarone and Montevecchi 1986, Ostry et al. 1983, Ouellet 1970, Rutter 1969, Strickland 1991, Strickland and Ouellet 1993.

FeederWatch Findings

Although unfamiliar to most feeder owners, the northern-nesting Gray Jay visits nearly a third of feeders in Alaska and quite often visits them all winter long. This jay is most likely to be seen at rural sites and is more abundant and a more frequent visitor there than at urban feeders. The percent of feeders visited declines gradually throughout the winter.

Favorite feeder foods: *Baked goods,* suet, peanut butter mixes, water. Small samples suggest that pet food, bird puddings, and meat scraps are also favored foods.

Infrequent choices: Mixed seed, sunflower (all types), and (according to the few feeder owners who offer this) popped corn. The FeederWatch sample did not include feeders offering dried fruit, but Gray Jays are known to be fond of raisins.

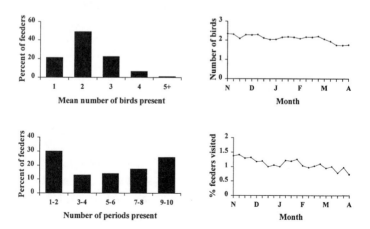

Gray Jay: percent of feeders visited

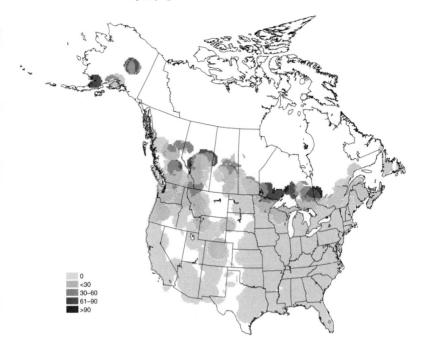

0
<30
30–60
61–90
>90

Abundance at feeders

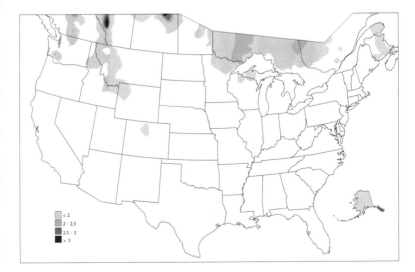

< 2
2 - 2.5
2.5 - 3
> 3

Steller's Jay

Cyanocitta stelleri

This crested jay of the West is quite closely associated with coniferous forest, and several species of western pines are thought to depend partly on Steller's Jays as a means of dispersing their seeds. These birds are not as specialized for carrying and caching seeds as are Pinyon Jays, but they can nonetheless carry several seeds at once in their extensible throat cavities. Seeds may be transported more than 3 miles prior to being hidden in shallow caches in the ground.

Conifers only produce cone crops every few years, and when pine seeds are in short supply, the Steller's Jay relies more on acorns. Their diet is extremely varied, however, and these omnivorous jays—which readily invade towns and cities in search of other foods—will eat fruits, grains, insects, and small vertebrates (including bird eggs and nestlings).

Steller's Jays are intelligent, as indicated by a number of published observations of them taking advantage of unusual food sources.

One feeder owner reported a jay killing and eating a Dark-eyed Junco during severe winter weather—a behavior likely to be repeated once a predation attempt has proven successful. In another example of intelligence, a few Steller's Jays in Seattle learned to tear off milk bottle tops to get at the milk inside. Small gangs of Steller's Jays may pursue and harass a Gray Jay that has just hidden food, distracting the victim while one gang member pilfers the cache. (Gray Jays are smart, too, though, and often will not make any caches when Steller's Jays are in the vicinity.)

Large flocks of Steller's Jays are likely to consist of dispersing juveniles, because paired birds prefer to remain year-round in their breeding territories. Nonetheless, local pairs may temporarily join together in flocks of up to a dozen birds. When one of these flocks visits an established territory, the pair that normally lives there dominates the other jays; when the flock moves on to another territory, dominance shifts to the owners of the new site. You may be able to detect the dominant individuals by looking for a twosome that will not tolerate other jays coming within about a bird's length, as subordinates are less fussy about maintaining individual distance. At feeders, Steller's Jays are relatively unassertive and will step aside for both Mexican Jays and Western Scrub-Jays.

In severe weather the normally homebody Steller's Jays will move to lower elevations. They also undertake periodic irruptions— undirected wanderings apparently caused by failure in the local food supply—although irruptions are more common in species heavily dependent on a single food type for winter survival, such as the Clark's Nutcracker and Pinyon Jay. While Steller's Jays do rely on a wider variety of foods than those species, they nonetheless irrupt on occasion and travel up to several hundred miles from their usual haunts. At such times they are especially likely to be seen at feeders.

Key references: Brown 1963, Burnell and Tomback 1985, Carothers et al. 1972, Dennis 1981, Goodwin 1976, Oliphant 1991, Morrison and Yoder-Williams 1984, Stewart and Shepard 1994, Vander Wall 1990, Westcott 1969.

FeederWatch Findings

Steller's Jays visit rural feeders more frequently, and are more abundant there, than at urban feeders. About half of sites that report the species host two or three jays throughout the winter. Our data suggest that feeders are visited most consistently (week after week) in regions where relatively few sites report the species—perhaps indicating that feeders are important to jays when they wander far from their normal range. The gap in distribution shown on the maps for Nevada is not simply a function of no FeederWatch coverage there—this species avoids the arid Great Basin region.

Favorite feeder foods: *Striped sunflower, peanuts (in shell or not)*, mixed seed, black-oil sunflower, cracked corn, suet, peanut butter mixes, water. Small samples indicate *baked goods*, whole corn, and pet food are also favored.

Infrequent choices: Millet, hulled sunflower, and bird puddings. (Acceptable as well, based on small samples, are milo, peanut hearts, oats, fresh fruit, and meat scraps.)

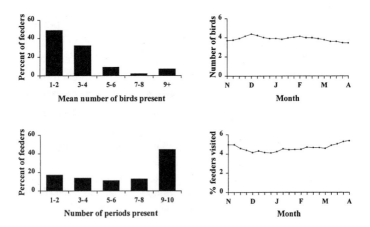

Steller's Jay: percent of feeders visited

0
<30
30–60
61–90
>90

Abundance at feeders

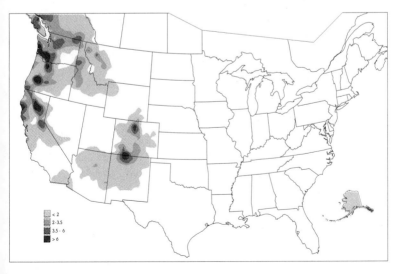

< 2
2 - 3.5
3.5 - 6
> 6

Blue Jay

Cyanocitta cristata

The bold and handsome Blue Jay is usually a welcome visitor at feeders, although its pushy behavior is sometimes less than endearing. Smaller birds scatter when jays sail in, and the jays' habit of carrying off several food items per visit makes them look like pigs. (One jay was observed gorging its gullet with over one hundred sunflower seeds in one visit to a feeder.) Jays are also notorious nest robbers, and they will even kill other birds as the opportunity arises, including at feeders. Nonetheless, the birds are so gorgeous that we usually end up tolerating their assertive nature.

The seed-gobbling behavior of the jay is actually one of the keys to its winter survival. Acorns, beech mast, hickory, and other nuts are often not swallowed immediately but transported several at a time to be buried in the birds' breeding territories, as far as 2½ miles from the original source. One researcher studying jays that were collecting beechnuts estimated that each bird cached two thousand seeds in a single month. Individual jays made over a thousand trips per day in the peak storage period. When storing acorns, Blue Jays may strip over half the crop from trees even before it is fully ripe.

At least eleven species of oaks and several other trees with heavy nuts may in fact depend on Blue Jays for distant dispersal of their seeds. Although there would seem to be plenty of dispersal agents, since about 150 vertebrate species are reported to eat acorns, only Blue Jays routinely carry nuts more than several hundred yards from the parent tree and bury them in sites where germination is quite probable. Moreover, jays select only undamaged nuts for burial, avoiding the 90% that would likely not germinate due to insect or other damage.

Acorns are full of tannin, a compound that is difficult for animals to digest and therefore helps the tree protect its seeds. Indeed, Blue Jays eating acorns alone quickly start to lose weight—unless those nuts are full of weevils. It seems that the protein content of the weevils makes it easier for the jays to digest the acorns' tannin. Acorns eaten in fall instead of being buried are nearly always infested with these insects. Perhaps the sound nuts that are buried are edible in spring because there are so many more insects available in that season to be eaten as a side dish.

Blue Jays are only partially migratory in that some move while others stay behind. Occasional larger-scale movements may result from food shortages. Following migration, groups of fifteen to fifty jays spend the winter together within a relatively small area. A winter flock will often concentrate at one feeder, for example, ignoring others nearby. Many flock members—or their offspring—return to the same wintering area the next year. Flock turnover is quite rapid because about half of adult jays die each year.

Blue Jay flocks are exceptionally alert and quickly give alarm calls at the first signs of danger. Many other animal species react to their alarms, too, much to the disgust of hunters trying to ambush game. Blue Jays are even reported to use other species' reactions to their own advantage; for example, by sounding alarms or imitating hawk calls as they swoop into feeders—causing other birds to dash for cover. There is a dominance hierarchy within each flock, so when several jays come to a feeder together, only one eats at a time while the others wait their turn at a distance.

Key references: Darley-Hill and Johnson 1981, Dennis 1981, Ehrlich and McLaughlin 1988, Hickey and Brittingham 1991, Johnson and Adkisson 1985, Johnson and Webb 1989, Johnson et al. 1993, Racine and Thompson 1983, Scarlett and Smith 1991, Smith 1979a, 1986.

FeederWatch Findings

Blue Jays are extremely widespread, visiting virtually all feeders in much of their winter range, regardless of habitat. However, numbers seen at one time are more than twice as high in rural as in urban areas, and rural feeders are more likely to report Blue Jays all winter long. Numbers are also higher at northern feeders than at southern ones (even though wintering populations are no larger in the North), which suggests greater feeder attendance in harsh weather. Note that some of the mapped records of Blue Jay in California may be errors, as the species is only a casual winter visitor there. Blue Jays appear to prefer feeder foods with shells, which may delay spoilage of food items that are cached.

Favorite feeder foods: *Striped sunflower, peanuts in shell,* mixed seed, black-oil sunflower, cracked or whole corn, hulled peanuts, pet food, meat scraps, baked goods, water.

Infrequent choices: Millet, canary seed, hulled sunflower, safflower, milo, wheat, peanut hearts, suet, peanut butter mixes, bird puddings, fresh or dried fruit, sugar water, popped corn.

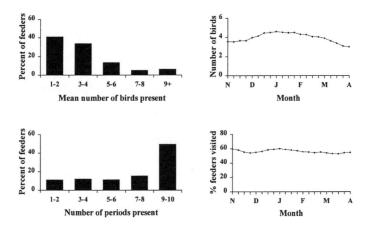

Blue Jay: percent of feeders visited

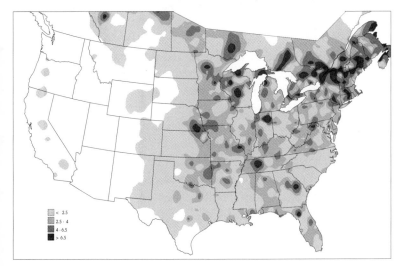

Abundance at feeders

Western Scrub-Jay
Aphelocoma californica

Scrub-Jays are split geographically into several populations that were recognized in 1995 as separate species. The Western Scrub-Jay is a widely distributed feeder visitor, living in oak scrub and pinyon-juniper woodland. The Florida Scrub-Jay also lives in oak scrub and visits feeders, but it has markedly different social behavior than its western counterpart. Unfortunately, it is also an endangered species and too rare to merit a full account here.

Western Scrub-Jay youngsters disperse in fall and hang out in loose winter bands before settling down to breed. The noisy winter flocks of five to fifteen teenagers may wander out of their normal breeding habitat into oak-grassland foothills. There they often mix with Steller's or Mexican Jays, although Scrub-Jays stick closer to trees and shrubs than these other species.

Resident Scrub-Jays habitually store acorns (a behavior that is less common in roving bands of first-year birds). This propensity for food storage is evident at feeders, where one individual was seen removing over one hundred sunflower seeds in a half-hour period. However, stored acorns and pine seeds make up only 50 to 60% of the winter diet, and adults will venture quite far from their territories in search of a wide variety of other foods. The only oak tree widely available to Scrub-Jays is Gambel's Oak, whose acorns are fairly low in tannin (which is hard for jays to digest), but also relatively low in fat and protein. Scrub-Jays eating acorns alone will lose weight.

In contrast to other jay species, Scrub-Jays are comparatively quiet when visiting feeders. Even families that are aggressive with each other along territorial boundaries may mingle peacefully at feeders located on neutral ground. If you have a flock foraging in your yard, look for the presence of sentinels: birds taking turns sitting high in the vegetation to watch for predators. If guards spot something, the whole group may join in mobbing behavior.

You may also witness other signs of the intelligence that Scrub-Jays share with fellow corvids. These birds have been reported harassing house cats (a potential predator) by sneaking up to peck at the hapless beasts from behind. Additionally, Scrub-Jays learn to recognize freebie food sources, and with patience you can teach them to take food from the hand. One unfortunate domestic hen that gave a distinctive cackle before laying each of her eggs unwittingly trained Scrub-Jays to come pilfer her nest whenever they heard the tell-tale call.

Key references: Balda and Kamil 1989, Dennis 1981, Ehrlich and McLaughlin 1988, Fleck and Tomback 1996, Goodwin 1976, Koenig and Heck 1988, Wiltschko and Balda 1989.

FeederWatch Findings

Scrub-Jays are a regular, season-long visitor at the majority of feeders where they are seen at all. For example, in California they visit over 85% of feeders at least once a winter. They usually visit in twos or threes but are somewhat less abundant at urban sites. Like Blue Jays, Scrub-Jays seem to prefer nuts with shells, which may play a factor in storage quality when cached. On the maps, a gap in Feeder-Watch coverage masks an area of abundance in West Texas.

Favorite feeder foods: *Sunflower (striped or black-oil), peanuts in shell, peanut butter mixes,* mixed seed, corn (whole or cracked), suet, bird puddings, water. Small samples indicate the jays also like *hulled peanuts,* fresh fruit, and baked goods.

Infrequent choices: Millet, hulled sunflower, milo. (Small samples indicate acceptability also of wheat, peanut hearts, pet food, and meat scraps.)

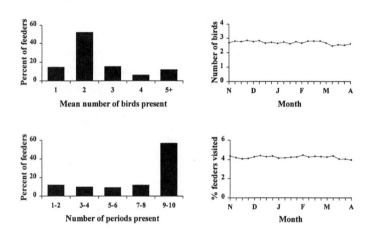

Western Scrub-Jay: percent of feeders visited

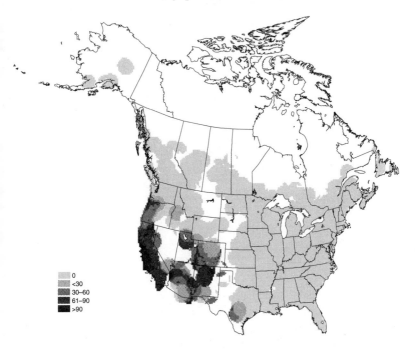

Abundance at feeders

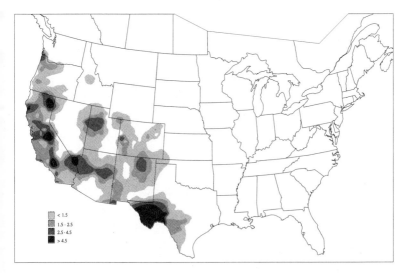

Pinyon Jay

Gymnorhinus cyanocephalus

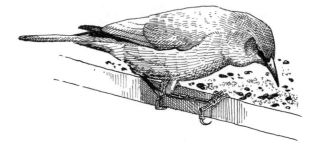

Large flocks of this remarkable jay may descend on your feeders, up to a hundred strong. They eat all the things that other jays like, from suet to peanuts and sunflower seeds, but if you can afford to offer pinyon seeds (the same "pine nuts" that people enjoy), this will be the food of choice.

The relationship between Pinyon Jays and pinyon pines is exceptionally close. Jays are the primary dispersers of the seeds, carrying them off to cache, usually in the ground. Unrecovered seeds later germinate, to the benefit of the trees. The jays in turn depend heavily on the nutritious pinyon seeds for their own successful reproduction.

Pinyon Jays check the quality of the pine nuts by "chewing" on them with the bill. The clicking noise that is produced lets the bird know if the seed is sound. Carrying as many as forty-five at once in the extensible throat, the jay transports nuts up to about two-thirds of a mile to cache sites that will be snow free in winter. Numerous jays in the flock may cache in communal areas; each bird can store up to twenty thousand seeds annually, building a food resource that can provide as much as 70 to 90% of the jays' winter food.

A big seed crop stimulates Pinyon Jays to breed during the winter, and a second nesting may follow in late summer if there are still good supplies of cached nuts. Conifers do not produce good cone crops every year, however, so Pinyon Jays sometimes nest in springtime along with most other birds, depending on insects as their main source of food. In these years nest success can be very low.

When nesting starts, flocks break into several subgroups and nest in loose colonies near the food storage sites. Females incubate while the males forage in flocks and return together to nest sites to feed their mates. Nonbreeding birds maintain separate flocks and may spend a lot of time at feeders.

When the nesting season is over, Pinyon Jays join into cohesive, noisy flocks of forty to five hundred birds. When these flocks visit feeders, they usually do so only briefly, in contrast to the flocks of nonbreeders that loaf at feeders during the nesting season. Instead, the postbreeding flocks forage throughout the large, apparently undefended home range, covering up to 8 miles daily. In years when conifer crops are especially small, neighboring flocks may join together and emigrate in search of better food supplies, visiting feeders far from the breeding range. Eventually wandering birds return to their home territories.

Pinyon Jays employ a variety of foraging techniques, from gleaning insects on leaves to prying flakes of bark off trees, hammering open cones, or probing the ground. Each busily foraging flock is guarded by up to a dozen sentinels that sit high in trees and give alarm calls if danger threatens. The guards are usually adult birds, but about a quarter of them are one-year-olds. Other bird species that forage with jay flocks will respond to the guards' alarms and benefit from the jays' vigorous mobbing of any predators.

Feeder owners can observe caching behavior of Pinyon Jays because the birds will carry off sunflower seeds, peanuts, and even millet for the purpose of storage. This behavior is much more prevalent in fall and winter than in other seasons. Most seeds are hidden in a clump of sites that are very close together, but many of the cached items are later rehidden elsewhere. Because Pinyon Jays are so social, food storage is accompanied by a good deal of interference and aggressive interaction, and recaching may be a necessary means of reducing pilferage.

Key references: Balda and Bateman 1971, Balda and Foster 1972, Bock 1982, Ligon 1978, Ligon and Martin 1974, Marzluff and Balda 1988 and 1989, Stotz and Balda 1995.

FeederWatch Findings

The Pinyon Jay is a far less regular visitor to feeders than other jay species. It often visits only sporadically and visits few sites, although in irruption years feeder visitation may increase. Urban feeders may only get a couple of birds per visit, but flocks at rural areas are often made up of twenty-five to fifty individuals. The abundance map is strongly influenced by large flocks showing up in isolated locations.

Frequent feeder foods: Few data from the FeederWatch study, but probably mixed seed, black-oil sunflower, and peanuts.

Infrequent choices: Small samples suggest hulled sunflower, cracked corn, wheat, suet, and bird puddings are occasionally eaten, and water is an attractant.

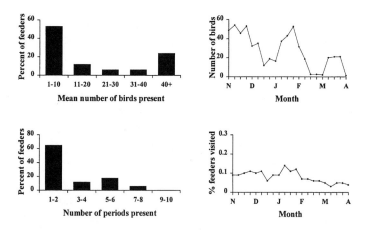

Pinyon Jay: percent of feeders visited

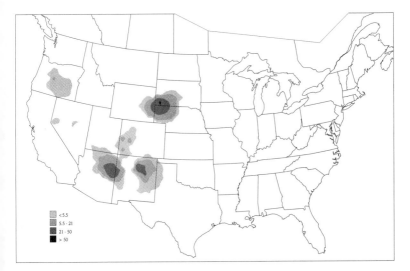

0
<30
30–60
61–90
>90

Abundance at feeders

<5.5
5.5 - 21
21 - 50
> 50

Black-billed Magpie

Pica pica

Black-billed Magpies are birds of arid, cool regions in the West; in fact, their distribution may be limited by a low tolerance for heat. They like open country but adapt easily to cities as long as there are patches of dense thicket or trees in which to nest.

Meat is a favorite magpie food, both in the wild and at feeders. Magpies are sometimes predators, robbing bird nests and even killing small mammals, but more often they try to steal prey that has already been killed by larger predators. A magpie attempting to get a share of a carcass alongside a fox or wolf demonstrates an impressive agility both on foot and on the wing. Despite their liking for fresh meat, the ground-foraging magpies will eat just about anything they run across—from grains and berries to garbage and carrion.

As soon as a Black-billed Magpie discovers a good food source, it quickly starts making temporary storage caches nearby (mostly within 100 yards. This hides the food from other scavengers, ensuring that the magpie can monopolize the largest possible share in a short time. Within a few hours, though, these caches are dug up, and the food is transferred to new sites within the bird's territory. Cached meat probably rots within a week unless temperatures are below freezing, so new sources of food must be found regularly.

If a feeder is well stocked with meat or suet, a dominant juvenile may decide to set up its breeding territory there. But if the feeder owner stops supplying food with the disappearance of snow, the magpie may find that it has chosen an area that is otherwise inferior and end up raising fewer young than magpies whose territories were chosen without regard to feeders. Most feeders, however, are not attractive enough to Black-billed Magpies to influence their choice of territory.

Once territories are established, they are defended year-round. Nonetheless, adult magpies in winter may leave during the day to join flocks of up to thirty others of their kind. This sociability probably reduces predation rates during foraging. Magpies in flocks still take frequent breaks from their meals to scan for danger, but the rate of vigilance declines as flock size gets larger. Specialized calls warn of danger: a long-syllabled alarm call causes other magpies to come investigate what the trouble is, and shorter, staccato alarm calls cause all listeners to flee immediately.

In particularly cold weather the birds of a foraging flock will spend the night together as well as the day, with up to several hundred gathering at a roost site. The magpies perch in dense conifers to reduce their exposure to wind and cold night air—and to protect themselves from predation by Great Horned Owls.

Contrary to the dominance relationships that are typically found in other bird species, magpie teenagers can dominate adult males at roosts and foraging sites. However, when it comes to establishing a territory or attracting a mate, experience and savoir faire carry the day for adults.

Key references: Bock and Lepthien 1975b, Boxall 1982, Buitron and Neuchterlein 1985, Dìaz and Asensio 1991, Goodwin 1976, Hayworth and Weathers 1984, Komers 1989, Komers and Komers 1992, Reebs 1987, Reebs and Boag 1987, Reese and Kadlec 1984, Sarno 1989, Stone and Trost 1991, Vines 1981, Verbeek 1972.

FeederWatch Findings

While the Black-billed Magpie is a season-long visitor at some sites, it is seen only sporadically at others—a variation that seems unrelated to habitat. Numbers seen at one time are fairly constant through the winter at one to three birds, but the number of sites visited drops off steadily as winter progresses.

Favorite feeder foods: Peanuts in shell, suet, peanut butter mixes, baked goods. Small samples suggest *pet food* and *meat scraps* are actually preferred choices.

Infrequent choices: Millet, striped or black-oil sunflower, cracked corn, bird puddings, water. Small samples show magpies will also eat whole corn, milo, hulled peanuts, oats, and fresh fruit.

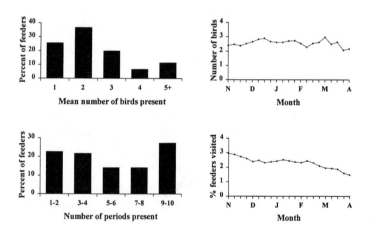

Black-billed Magpie: percent of feeders visited

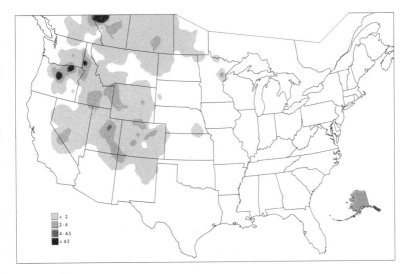

Abundance at feeders

American Crow

Corvus brachyrhynchos

The American Crow is recognized by almost everyone, no matter how ornithologically impaired. Despite this, crows have not been much studied, probably because their extreme alertness makes them difficult to observe. Only recently have we learned much about the day-to-day lives of these common birds.

Most crows nesting in the United States are permanent residents. Each family maintains a large territory, shared by the adult pair with several of their offspring from the past few years. Young crows may remain with their parents even during subsequent breeding seasons, helping to raise additional broods by participating in nest building, incubation, and feeding of nestlings.

During the winter, crows usually leave their territory in the late afternoon and join others from miles around in a large roost. In the morning, the family members return independently to their territory, often stopping along the way at a garbage dump or other communal foraging site. Family members do not squabble over food when in their own territory, but they may forego such niceties when feeding together elsewhere.

Most Canadian-nesting crows migrate to the United States for the winter. These birds apparently do not hold winter territories, and their winter behavior is rather poorly known. Migratory individuals probably make up the bulk of flocks that hang about such concentrated food sources as landfills. These flocks appear to contain different individuals on different days, and there are frequent scuffles among them.

Crows maintain good security systems and can be counted on to raise alarms when predators are near. If they discover an owl, they will harass it vigorously (a behavior that will also attract knowledgable bird-watchers interested in finding owls). When a crow flock is feeding on the ground, several birds may act as sentinels, perching high up to watch for danger. Although the whole flock can take advantage of this watchfulness, sentinels are probably not acting out of public spirit. Instead, they are guarding their own offspring within the foraging flock.

Crows are omnivores, consuming grains, berries, insects, crustaceans, or any other available food, including garbage. They are notorious predators of small vertebrates (especially nestling birds and eggs), and will eat carrion, too—rapidly cleaning up roadkill while somehow managing to avoid becoming victims themselves. At feeders, crows are especially likely to eat meat or suet, preferably from the ground. Nonetheless, only about one-quarter of the overall diet is made up of animal food, and waste grain is a very important food source in winter.

Food caching by crows is not often witnessed in the wild, but it may occur more often than realized. In one reported instance, two crows cached pecans in a lawn, working alone and appearing to shield their cache sites from observation by the other crow. Up to ten minutes was spent on each cache to select a site, hammer in nuts, and cover them with tufts of cut grass. So well hidden were the nuts that the human observers could not locate the sites afterward, even though they had watched the caching with binoculars from only about 10 yards away. One of the other known instances of food caching by crows was reported by some photographers who released one hundred mice in hopes of attracting raptors for a film. Instead, three crows arrived on the scene, and within a half hour they killed and cached seventy-nine of the mice.

Key references: Chamberlain-Auger et al. 1990, Connor and Williamson 1987, D'Agostino et al. 1981, George and Kimmel 1973, Knopf and Knopf 1983, Stouffer and Caccamise 1991.

FeederWatch Findings

American Crows visit over half of feeders in some regions, and at about half of those sites they are quite regular visitors. Typically they visit in small groups of two to four birds.

Favorite feeder foods: *Meat scraps*, corn (cracked or whole), peanuts in shell, pet food, baked goods, and (small samples suggest) popped corn.

Infrequent choices: Mixed seed, millet, canary seed, sunflower (any type), milo, hulled peanuts or hearts, suet, bird puddings, fruit (fresh or dried), water. Oats may also be sampled, according to sparse data.

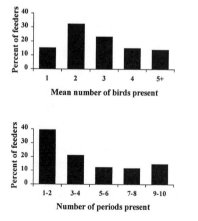

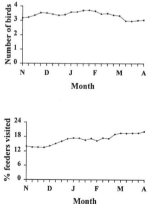

American Crow: percent of feeders visited

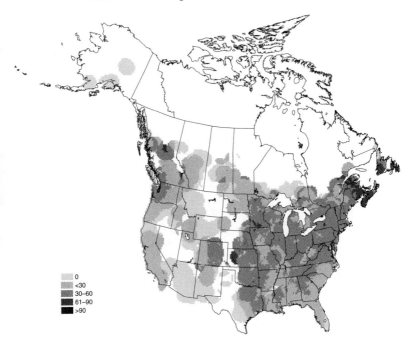

Abundance at feeders

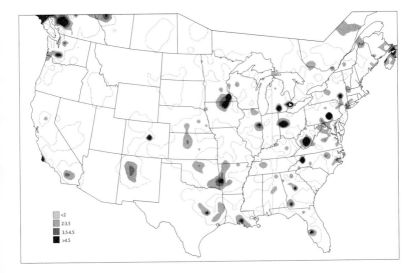

Common Raven

Corvus corax

Ravens are familiar birds whose wide range of unusual vocalizations and free-wheeling aerial acrobatics have earned them a prominent place in human folklore. However, like crows, these conspicuous birds are so wary that their life history was little known until quite recently.

Ravens are extreme generalists and opportunists when it comes to food, taking whatever is available: insects, fruits, seeds, crustaceans, garbage, small vertebrates, or eggs and nestlings of other birds. In areas where snow cover is persistent during the winter, ravens concentrate on scavenging carcasses. They locate these by following large predators (polar bears, wolves, humans), hanging around highways scouting for roadkill, or touring dumps and livestock ranges. Huge areas may be searched daily. The raven's long, relatively narrow wings are suited to long-distance flight, and an individual sometimes commutes up to 55 miles daily to a good food source. Ravens quickly adjust their behavior to focus on whatever food is most abundant, such as concentrating on grains in agricultural areas or on small birds during the migration season.

Outside the breeding season, ravens gather each evening into communal roosts of several dozen to several hundred birds. Mated pairs maintain their territories year-round, however, and return there daily from the roost to forage in familiar surroundings. The remaining ravens spread out to search for new food sources, and in one day birds from a single roost may cover more than 700 square miles. This maximizes the chance that at least some birds will discover food patches that are scattered few and far between. However, this is of no use as a cooperative strategy unless a find is communicated to the other birds. The resident ravens in whose territory a food source lies will try to defend it and will certainly not advertise its presence, but unmated vagrants have special calls they use to attract roost mates. Why would they do this if it reduces the size of their own share in the food? Apparently because a large number of nonbreeders must join together to overwhelm the defenses of the resident pair. As a result, all birds get to share in rare bonanzas, enabling ravens to survive in harsh regions where food sources are scarce and widely scattered. You may see evidence of this behavior at feeders: Usually only the local territorial pair will visit, but if you put out a suitably large food source (such as a dead farm animal), you may attract a flock of unpaired vagrants.

Captive ravens are known to cache food, particularly fat, especially if the bird is hungry. However, if a human inspects a raven's cache, that raven will refuse to hide food again while under observation. This wariness may explain why caching has only rarely been reported in wild ravens, and food storage may be a more common behavior than we realize.

Ravens are one of the few bird species that can overwinter in the high arctic. Thick, horny soles protect their feet from cold, and raven plumage is so thick that metabolism need not be raised to fight off cold until temperatures drop below -4°F. In the southwestern United States ravens face extremes of heat, so presumably there is geographic variation in physiology and plumage to accommodate different climates.

Key references: Connor and Adkisson 1976, Engel and Young 1989, Engel et al. 1992, Goodwin 1976, Heinrich 1988, Kilham 1988, Marzluff and Heinrich 1991, Schwan and Williams 1978.

FeederWatch Findings

Common Ravens are seen at more feeders in Alaska than elsewhere, but southwestern and northeastern parts of North America also host them fairly frequently. Only a very few sites report ravens all winter, however, perhaps because few feeder owners provide the foods they like best. Ravens are especially unusual at urban sites. In fall, three to four ravens may visit together, but by January most sites are hosting only two.

Favorite feeder foods: Baked goods, although small samples indicate *meat scraps* are preferred.

Infrequent choices: Mixed seed, sunflower (striped or black-oil), cracked corn, suet, peanut butter mixes. Limited data suggest whole corn, pet food, and popped corn may also be accepted.

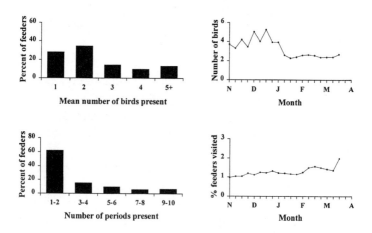

Common Raven: percent of feeders visited

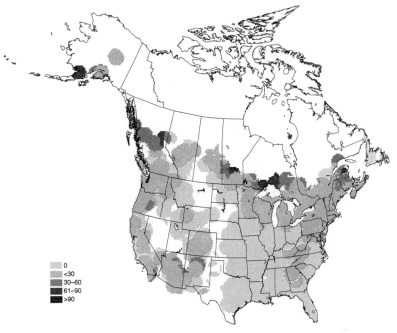

0
<30
30–60
61–90
>90

Abundance at feeders

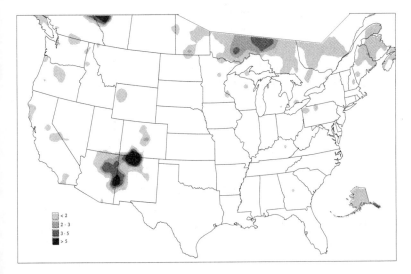

< 2
2 - 3
3 - 5
> 5

Carolina Chickadee

Poecile carolinensis

This is the most common chickadee species in the Southeast United States, the counterpart of the Black-capped Chickadee of the Northeast. In summer there is only a narrow zone of contact between the two species—but in winter young Black-caps may disperse into Carolina territory for the winter, and the similarity of the two species makes them very difficult to separate at feeders. Surprisingly, genetic and behavioral studies suggest that the Black-capped Chickadee is actually more closely related to the distinctive Mountain Chickadee than it is to the look-alike Carolina.

Carolina Chickadees usually mate for life, but due to high mortality only about two-thirds of pairs remain intact more than two seasons in a row. While young of the year sometimes find mates before cold weather sets in, winter flocks often have unequal sex ratios—which suggests that some birds remain unpaired until spring (unlike the usual practice of Black-capped Chickadees). In addition, Carolinas are less likely than Black-caps to have a stable, linear dominance hierarchy. The rank of a female Carolina Chickadee depends on whether or not her mate is nearby, whereas in Black-caps these ranks are quite rigidly observed, regardless of who else is present.

Carolina Chickadees also differ somewhat from Black-caps in visual displays. However, body language takes a backseat to conversation in chickadee communications, and the two species have many similar vocalizations. Humans may not find much musicality in chickadee calls, but research has shown that the songs carry a lot of meaning to the birds. The *chick-a-dee-dee* call, for example, has been shown in Black-caps to serve as a general alert. It attracts other birds, coordinates group movements, calls attention to a new food source, and announces the "all-clear" after a predator alarm. In the Carolina Chickadee, the length of the *dee* portions of the call signals what kind of action the caller is about to take. The familiar high-pitched *tseets* of foraging flocks are used to keep flock members in touch as they roam through the woods. Aggression is signaled with a "gargle" call that is often heard near feeders.

Carolina Chickadees are not well adapted physiologically to cold temperatures, relying instead on behavioral means to reduce energy costs during winter. In cold and windy weather they spend more time in sheltered habitat, feeding at lower heights than usual and spending more time sitting motionless than in foraging. At night they roost in a cavity or very dense vegetation. This can reduce energy use by 60 to 100% over what would be expended if the bird sat out in the open. Roosting cavities are usually very small, and following cold nights you may see birds at your feeder whose tail feathers are bent from having been crammed into small spaces. Carolina Chickadees can further save energy by letting body temperature decline at night, although the metabolic level is maintained high enough for the bird to take flight at a moment's notice.

While Black-capped Chickadees at the southern end of their range store food infrequently, Carolinas cache readily in winter, especially when their reserves of body fat are low—perhaps yet another indication that their physiology is not tuned for withstanding cold weather. A Carolina Chickadee needs only about fifteen seconds to cache a seed, usually hiding it on the underside of a medium-sized branch.

Key references: Brackbill 1987, Dixon 1963, Grubb 1977, 1978, Lucas and Walter 1991, Mayer et al. 1982, Petit et al. 1989, Pitts 1976, Smith 1972, Smith 1991.

FeederWatch Findings

Carolina Chickadees are similar to Black-caps in being faithful, winter-long visitors and visiting the vast majority of feeders within their winter range. Flock size is a little smaller than for Black-caps, however—two to three vs. four to six—and only slightly smaller at urban feeders than elsewhere. Note that feeders reporting a mix of Carolina and Black-capped Chickadees are excluded from the maps shown here, so there are relatively few data on Carolinas from the overlap zone (approximately from Kansas to Ohio to Virginia).

Favorite feeder foods: Sunflower (any type but especially *black-oil*), safflower, hulled peanuts, suet, peanut butter mixes, bird puddings, water.

Infrequent choices: Mixed seed, millet, cracked corn, milo, niger, peanuts in shell or hearts, baked goods.

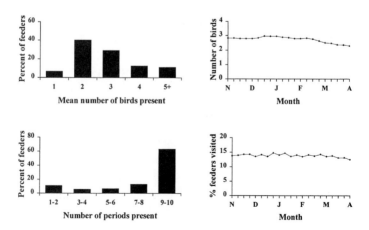

Carolina Chickadee: percent of feeders visited

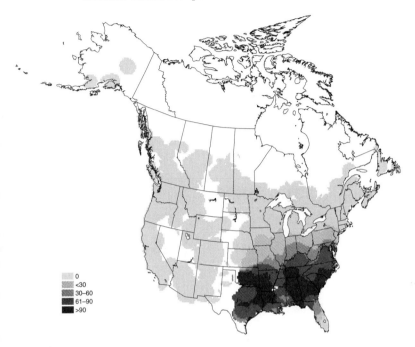

Abundance at feeders

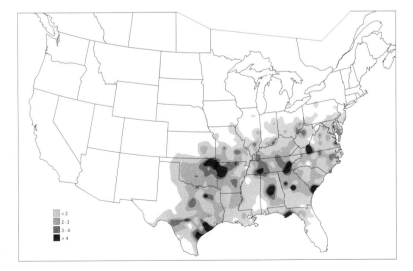

Black-capped Chickadee

Poecile atricapillus

Chickadees are among the most welcome visitors to feeders, cheering us on dull winter days with their busy to-and-fro traffic and bold manner. Carrying off only one seed at a time, they seem more polite than the gobbling jays and starlings, even though a chickadee may return time and again for additional handouts. (Individuals have been recorded taking as many as seventy sunflower seeds in a day.) However, a study of chickadees in Wisconsin estimated that only about 20% of the birds' daily energy intake came from feeders, and about half of the overall winter diet was made up of such animal matter as spiders, dormant insects, and even carrion.

Black-capped Chickadees have been a popular subject for studies on the effects of bird feeding. Ready access to feeders proved to have no effect on their overwinter survival under mild winter conditions, but if temperatures dropped below zero for more than five days in a row, chickadees that were able to visit feeders did slightly better than birds without a food supplement.

Much of the food gathered by chickadees is stored for later use, especially in colder northern regions. Under natural circumstances a chickadee might discover a rich food source only once in a while, so it pays to salt some away. Seeds, insects, and fat are tucked into bark cracks, needle clusters, or under leaves. A single bird may hide hundreds of items in a day. Feeder owners can easily observe this behavior, as most items are stashed within 100 feet of the food source.

Ingenious studies of chickadees hiding and recovering seeds in laboratory settings have shown that twenty-four hours after caching, the birds not only remember where they hid things but also which sites they have already emptied. They also remember which cache sites hold the highest quality seeds and will visit those first. The act of caching itself appears important in establishing the memory, as chickadees are poor at recovering seeds that they have watched other birds hide. Most hidden items are probably recovered within a day or two, but occasionally they are not picked up for as long as twenty-eight days. Some of the shorter-term recoveries may simply be steps in moving seeds to more permanent storage sites.

Chickadees spend the winter in flocks that vary widely in size but average six to ten individuals. Each flock is composed of a resident pair and a number of unrelated juveniles that dispersed from their nesting areas during late summer. Usually the young birds move less than 1½ miles from their birthplace, but if natural food supplies are low, they sometimes disperse much farther. The resident pair dominates all other flock members, gaining preferential access to food and thereby the highest chances of surviving the winter. In spring the dominants drive most lower-ranking birds away. Subordinate chickadees nonetheless benefit from joining a winter flock, often finding a mate there or inheriting a portion of the winter territory as a place to breed.

Chickadees pairs that have nested successfully usually stay together for future breeding seasons, but as the average chickadee only lives a few years, there is a fair bit of turnover in mates. Occasionally there are even "divorces," usually initiated by a bird that can rise to the top of the flock by pairing with a dominant chickadee that lost its previous mate. Social climbing of this sort has a clear evolutionary advantage because dominant pairs survive better than other chickadees in the flock.

Since Black-capped Chickadees are among the best studied of feeder birds, only a few topics of wintering ecology can be mentioned here, but some additional information is included in the accounts for other chickadee species.

Key references: Baker et al. 1988, Brittingham and Temple 1988, 1992a,b, Ficken et al. 1987, Hampton and Sherry 1994, Hitchcock and Sherry 1990, Kilham 1975, Lima 1985, Myton and Ficken 1967, Petit et al. 1989, Sherry 1984, 1989, Smith 1986, 1991, 1992, 1993.

FeederWatch Findings

Black-capped Chickadees visit feeders faithfully all year long. They are also very widespread and visit virtually all feeders in northern parts of their range. Urban and rural feeders are visited at equal rates, but flock sizes in the country are close to twice as large. Flock size is also slightly higher at northern than at southern feeders (even though wintering populations are no larger there), suggesting that chickadees come to feeders more readily in cold weather. Feeders reporting a mix of Black-capped and Carolina Chickadees are excluded from the maps shown here, so there are few records for Black-caps from the overlap zone (approximately from Kansas to Ohio to Virginia).

Favorite feeder foods: *Sunflower* (any type, but especially *striped* and *black-oil*), safflower, hulled peanuts, suet, peanut butter mixes, bird puddings, water.

Infrequent choices: Mixed seed, millet, canary seed, cracked corn, milo, niger, peanuts in shell or hearts, oats, canola, pet food, fruit (fresh or dried), meat scraps, baked goods, popped corn.

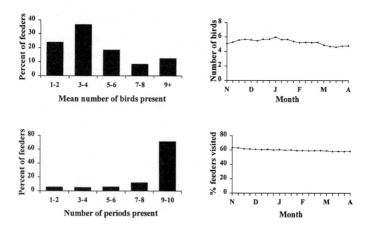

Black-capped Chickadee: percent of feeders visited

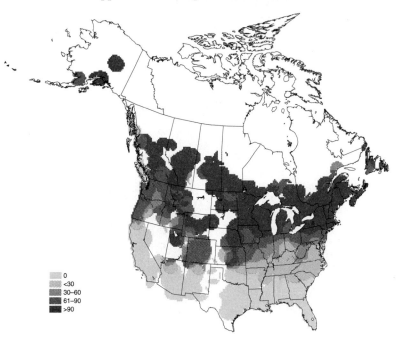

0
<30
30–60
61–90
>90

Abundance at feeders

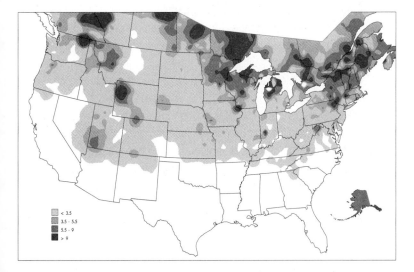

< 3.5
3.5 - 5.5
5.5 - 9
> 9

Mountain Chickadee

Poecile gambeli

The Mountain Chickadee is well named, as it inhabits montane slopes right up to timberline. It prefers coniferous woodlands, especially those of ponderosa pine, but also lives at lower densities in areas vegetated with pinyon and juniper. Where Mountain and Black-capped Chickadees both occur in the same region, the Black-caps' preference for more deciduous woodlands tends to keep the species apart. During the winter, however, many first-year Mountain Chickadees visit less coniferous habitats at lower altitudes, where they may meet Black-caps at feeders. In such encounters Mountain Chickadees are usually the subordinate species.

The winter social system of Mountain Chickadees appears similar to that of the better-studied Black-cap—its closest relative, according to genetic evidence. Youngsters disperse in the autumn, then join winter flocks made up largely of pairs mated "for life."

These stable winter flocks are often smaller than in other chickadee species, consisting of only two to six individuals. There is a fairly linear pecking order in which males tend to dominate females, and older birds take precedence over younger ones. The dominant males suffer less winter mortality in years with poor cone crops, suggesting that they get first crack at food resources. However, dominant Mountain Chickadee males undertake most of the aggressive interactions with neighboring flocks, so there may be an energetic cost to dominance, as well.

Experiments with Black-capped Chickadees that probably apply to other species as well show that lower-ranking individuals can sometimes obtain more food if they forage alone, and those living in flocks survive less well than dominants. Why, then, would a subordinate bird join a winter flock? It turns out that low-ranking birds fare better in a flock than alone when food is distributed in rich but widely scattered batches, probably because the flock is better able to find such bonanzas. Flocks may also be less vulnerable to predation. Finally, subordinate birds in a flock have the opportunity to mate with a higher-ranking individual if the latter's previous mate dies.

Like other chickadees, Mountain Chickadees are often seen with other species in mixed foraging flocks. Young Mountain Chickadees wintering at low altitudes may be followers rather than leaders and often join resident flocks of Bushtits. Joining a mixed-species flock probably offers many of the same benefits as joining a winter flock of a single species: enhanced abilities to find scattered food resources and less chance of predation. (See the account of the Chestnut-backed Chickadee for more on this topic.)

Mountain Chickadees are mainly foliage gleaners, searching for spiders and larvae at the tips of branches. A significant portion of their food consists of conifer seeds, which are stored whenever there is a surplus. One individual was observed taking seeds from fallen cones, removing the seed wings, then storing the seeds on tree trunks or large branches—repeating this twenty-one times in less than ten minutes. Seeds stored in autumn may not be eaten until the following June, in contrast to the short-term hoarding of the Black-capped and Carolina Chickadees of deciduous woodlands.

The tendency for longer-term hoarding by the Mountain Chickadee may be related to its harsher montane winter climate or to the relative unreliability of conifer seed abundance.

Key references: Dixon 1965, 1986, Ficken et al. 1990, Glase 1973, Haftorn 1959, Hill and Lein 1989, Manolis 1977, McCallum 1990, Minock 1971, 1972, Smith 1991, With and Morrison 1990.

FeederWatch Findings

Mountain Chickadees are less common as feeder visitors than Black-capped or Carolina Chickadees, but they do visit over half of sites in much of their range. The majority of these are visited all season long. As with other chickadees, this species is reported at urban feeders less frequently than elsewhere and in lower numbers. The Nevada-Utah gap in the maps results from lack of FeederWatch coverage there.

Frequent feeder foods: *Black-oil sunflower, peanut butter mixes,* striped sunflower, suet, bird puddings, water, and (based on small samples) baked goods.

Infrequent choices: Mixed seed, millet, cracked corn, peanuts in shell. Small samples suggest acceptability also of hulled peanuts, hulled sunflower, oats, fresh fruit, safflower, canola, and popped corn.

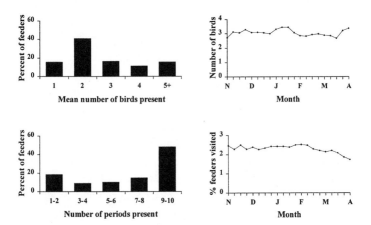

Mountain Chickadee: percent of feeders visited

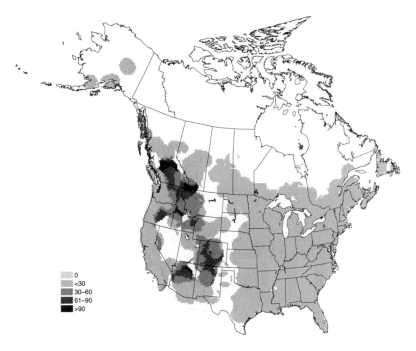

- 0
- <30
- 30–60
- 61–90
- >90

Abundance at feeders

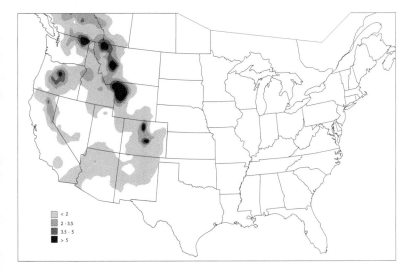

- < 2
- 2 - 3.5
- 3.5 - 5
- > 5

Chestnut-backed Chickadee

Poecile rufescens

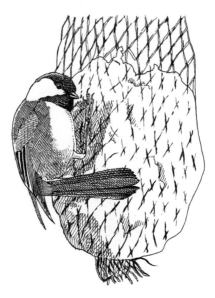

Chestnut-backed Chickadees have a relatively restricted range in western North America. Originally confined to mature coniferous forests, they have demonstrated a tolerance for second growth, as well. Chestnut-backs recolonized the Sierra Nevada after the forest regeneration that followed clear-cutting, and the species is still expanding its range in the San Francisco area. In a few places it has even invaded oak woodlands. Nonetheless, Chestnut-backed Chickadees still prefer to spend their time high in tall conifers, particularly Douglas fir.

Any easterner familiar with the Black-capped Chickadee would immediately recognize the Chestnut-back as a close counterpart. These birds demonstrate all the characteristics that endear chickadees to feeder owners: bold, active birds calling frequently to fellow flock members, curiously investigating novelties in their environment, and performing amazing acrobatics on all kinds of feeders. Chickadees' legs are particularly long and strong for birds their size, allowing them to forage while hanging upside down. In contrast to Black-caps, however, Chestnut-backs are more likely to be found foraging higher up in trees, closer to the outer tips of branches, and on upper surfaces (spending less than half their time hanging upside-down).

Like other North American chickadees and titmice, the Chestnut-back is frequently joined in its foraging by other birds, such as nuthatches, woodpeckers, kinglets, and even warblers. Research on Black-capped Chickadees has demonstrated the advantages of such behavior. As permanent residents, chickadees may be better at finding food than migratory birds. Indeed, mixed-species flocks form more frequently when food is in short supply and in cold weather when food demands are greatest. In addition to being good guides to local food sources, chickadees often "advertise" a good find with a *chick-a-dee-dee* call. This advertising is probably meant only to alert the mate—as chickadees usually pair for life and stay together through the winter—but other birds take advantage of the information, too.

Foraging in mixed-species flocks may reduce risk of predation as well as help in finding food. Alarm calls are more likely to be given by chickadees than by other species—once again, probably for the benefit of mates. Other species respond as well to the chickadee's "all-clear" signal, usually given by the dominant male in the flock.

Part of the chickadee's ability to find food depends on its exceptional learning abilities. Laboratory studies have shown that Chestnut-backed and Black-capped Chickadees keep an eye on the food-finding success of other individuals. If one bird is doing especially well, the foraging behavior of others converges toward the food-finding strategy of the successful one, whereas unproductive tactics are not copied.

Key references: Berner and Grubb 1985, Brennen and Morrison 1991, Ficken 1981, Ficken and Witkin 1977, Hertz et al. 1976, Klein 1988, Krebs 1973, Root 1964, Smith 1991, Sturman 1968.

FeederWatch Findings

About one-third of feeders that record Chestnut-backed Chickadees are visited on a weekly basis. Urban and suburban sites are more likely to host this species than are rural feeders. The number of feeders visited rises in midwinter, but the flock size decreases steadily all season.

Favorite feeder foods: *Black-oil sunflower, suet, bird puddings.* Small samples indicate that other favorite feeder foods include *striped and hulled sunflower, peanut butter mixes,* and hulled peanuts.

Infrequent choices: Mixed seed, millet, niger, sugar water, plain water, and (based on small samples) peanut hearts, safflower, and barley.

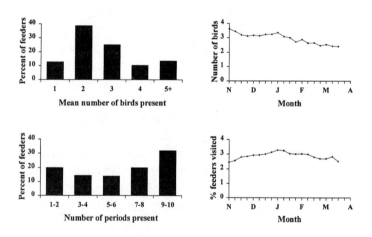

Chestnut-backed Chickadee: percent of feeders visited

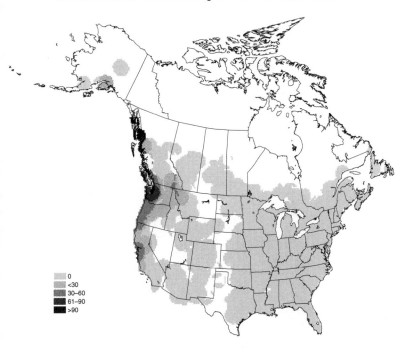

0
<30
30–60
61–90
>90

Abundance at feeders

< 2
2 · 3
3 · 5
> 5

Boreal Chickadee

Poecile hudsonicus

The Boreal Chickadee is rarely seen at feeders except in Alaska and Canada, where its range extends right to the arctic tree line. Within the boreal forest, however, this species is a very common visitor. It may not be as bold and inquisitive as many other chickadee species, but Boreals were visiting trappers' cabins for food handouts long before formal bird feeding became a common practice. This tame bird has been given such affectionate nicknames as Tom-tit and Chick Chick.

Little is known about Boreal Chickadee winter ecology, probably because few humans care to brave harsh winter conditions to study it. Available data suggest that Boreal Chickadees form flocks of four to ten birds as soon as young have fledged, although some birds overwinter alone, and these flocks persist until spring. They sometimes join in mixed foraging parties with other birds, including Golden-crowned Kinglets or other chickadee species. Birds in these flocks respond to each others' *chick-a-dee-dee* calls. Boreals in mixed flocks glean upper branches along with kinglets, while Black-capped Chickadees concentrate on lower portions of the trees. Boreal Chickadees have also been recorded in association with Three-toed Woodpeckers, taking advantage of food exposed by that larger bird's excavations.

This chickadee is basically resident (although northernmost breeders may have a regular short-distance migration), but at intervals of about six to eight years they stage large-scale irruptions toward the south. These irregular flights are thought to occur when winter food supplies are poor. Such movements by Boreal Chickadees always take place in the same years as Black-capped Chickadee irruptions but only about half as often. The emigrants are wanderers, usually visiting southern feeders for only a few days before moving on. While on the move, they continue to prefer coniferous woods but will utilize a broader range of habitat than the dense boreal forests of their summer home.

Boreal Chickadees are able to survive cold snaps with temperatures as low as -49°F, a level at which Black-capped Chickadees would probably freeze. This is an extraordinary achievement considering that a Boreal weighs about a third of an ounce or about as much as two quarters. While little is known about Boreal Chickadee physiology, cold tolerance must be even better than that of the Black-capped Chickadee. The latter birds, at least in the southern parts of their range, reduce their body temperature at night to save as much as 25% in overnight energy expenditure. In northern regions they are better acclimated and instead rely on warmer "clothes." Plumage of the Black-capped Chickadee is denser than on other species of similar size, with awesome insulative properties—almost no heat escapes through the feathers, even when the temperature gradient from skin to ambient air spans more than 70°F.

Boreal Chickadees store food extensively in fall, which may provide a significant source of energy in midwinter when temperatures are lowest and there are only a few hours of daylight in which to forage. It is not known how large a proportion of the winter diet is derived from fall caches, but in northern Europe some related species store fifty to eighty thousand seeds each autumn. Boreals have been recorded caching about forty-five items an hour in August, even before the fall period in which storage is most common.

They store not only spruce seeds but also insects, spiders, and larvae—even tiny aphids. Cache sites are commonly chosen on the underside of branches, perhaps because upper surfaces get covered by snow. Some items are camouflaged, concealed by a wide variety of materials from lichen and bark to spider webs or saliva.

Key references: Chaplin 1974 and 1982, Ficken et al. 1996, Grossman and West 1977, Haftorn 1959, 1974, Hill et al. 1980, Hooper 1988, Kessel 1976, McLaren 1975, Yunick 1984.

FeederWatch Findings

The Boreal Chickadee visits half of feeders in Alaska and also makes respectable showings in the Maritime provinces of Canada and other northern jurisdictions. Many sites host the species all winter, but the majority report Boreals only a few times. Urban sites are visited rarely; rural sites, the most. At one to three individuals, flock sizes are usually smaller than for the Black-capped Chickadee.

Favorite feeder foods: *Suet,* black-oil sunflower. Small samples suggest *hulled sunflower, peanut butter mixes,* and *bird puddings* may be preferred choices.

Infrequent choices: Small samples show that striped sunflower and baked goods are accepted on occasion.

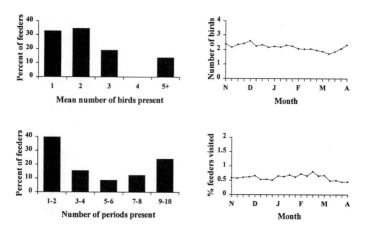

Boreal Chickadee: percent of feeders visited

	0
	<30
	30–60
	61–90
	>90

Abundance at feeders

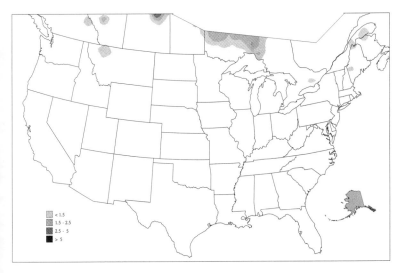

	< 1.5
	1.5 - 2.5
	2.5 - 5
	> 5

Oak Titmouse and Juniper Titmouse

Baeolophus inornatus and *B. griseus*

The coastal and inland forms of western titmice have recently been recognized as separate species: Oak and Juniper Titmouse, respectively. Here we refer to the two together under their old name of "Plain Titmouse," which was still in use when our data were gathered. The grayer titmice of the interior use pinyon-juniper areas more than birds of the coastal race and are more likely to form local flocks in winter.

Titmice in California are homebodies, spending nearly their entire lives within a territory of about 6 acres (2½ hectares). While youngsters disperse in early summer, they rarely move more than a few territories away, so adjacent pairs are quite likely to be related. This territorial habit ensures that only a few titmice are likely to visit your feeder at one time, and the same individuals may visit regularly throughout their lifespan (typically about three years once adulthood is reached).

Titmice have much stouter bills than their chickadee relatives, and they put these beaks to good use hammering open nuts. Over 80% of their winter diet consists of seeds and nuts—mostly acorns or pine seeds. Titmice live in dry scrub and brushland habitat, where there are plenty of the live oak, pinyon, and juniper that produce their favorite feeder foods. This same taste for seeds is also indulged at feeders, where these titmice prefer safflower and sunflower seed—especially if shelled.

In years with abundant nut crops, titmice spend a lot of time, alone or in pairs, searching the ground for fallen acorns and cones. Seed crops vary annually, however, and when production is low, the birds change their foraging strategy. In such years they are more likely to be found in trees, seeking food among leaves or small branches high in the canopy, and the titmice also become more sociable, mixing more freely with other species.

The Bushtit is one of the species that titmice will join in group foraging, and they respond to the Bushtit's distinctive "confusion" call when predators are spotted. The titmouse's own alarm call is also remarkable: a loud scold that fades off as if the bird is moving into the distance—perhaps fooling predators into chasing a phantom while the titmouse stays safely hidden.

Key references: Dixon 1949, 1954, 1956, Hertz et al. 1976, Root 1964, Wagner 1981, With and Morrison 1990.

FeederWatch Findings

Within their core winter range, Oak and Juniper Titmice visit over a third of feeder sites, usually in twos. Rural and suburban feeder owners are more likely to report these birds than urbanites, and to see them more regularly and in larger numbers. The majority of visited feeders host titmice throughout the winter season. Both the number of sites visited and the number of birds seen per visit decline slightly but steadily from fall to spring. The absence of Plain

Titmice from Nevada and Utah (see maps) is an artifact of low FeederWatch coverage there.

Favorite feeder foods: *Black-oil sunflower,* peanut butter mixes, bird puddings and probably (based on small samples), *hulled sunflower, safflower* and striped sunflower.

Infrequent choices: Mixed seed, millet, suet, water. Small samples indicate peanuts in shells and milo are also eaten on occasion.

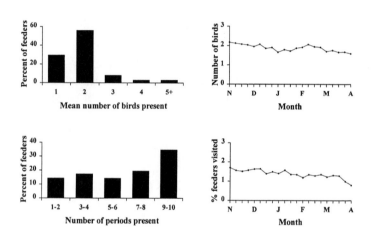

Oak and Juniper Titmouse: percent of feeders visited

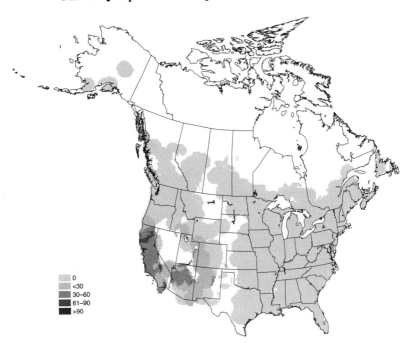

0
<30
30–60
61–90
>90

Abundance at feeders

< 1.5
1.5 - 2
2 - 2.5
> 2.5

Tufted Titmouse

Baeolophus bicolor

With its jaunty tuft and bold manner, the acrobatic Tufted Titmouse is a favorite at eastern bird feeders. It can be induced to investigate a whistled version of its song and may become tame enough to take seeds from the hand. Part of its attraction is its look of wide-eyed innocence, but in fact the Tufted Titmouse is quite assertive and can displace most other species from feeders.

The Tufted Titmouse's preferred milieu is mature, mixed-oak woodland—the more extensive the better. There it seeks insects and cocoons among dead leaves, whether still attached to a tree, fallen to the ground—or even built into squirrels' nests. The bulk of the titmouse's winter diet, though, consists of acorns and beech mast. Perhaps this liking for large seeds explains why Tufted Titmice at feeders enjoy peanuts and large striped sunflower seeds, whereas most other feeder species that eat sunflower prefer the smaller black-oil variety.

A Tufted Titmouse will make a fast trip to a feeder for a single seed, then fly off to a perch where it can hold the seed underfoot while pecking it open. Up to half the seeds may be cached for later consumption, usually after husking. These are hidden under loose bark, pushed into cracks on the tops of branches, or pressed into the ground. Given how common this bird is, it is surprising how little is known about cache recovery or the importance of food-hoarding behavior to its winter survival.

Tufted Titmice are permanent residents and defend territories year round, although they are often joined in winter by youngsters of their own or from nearby areas. Their territorial behavior explains why only a few of them visit feeders at any one time. If you seem to have more than a single family visiting, you may be in a zone of overlap between winter ranges of neighboring pairs.

Other social interactions that you can observe at feeders involve dominance relationships. If you notice one Tufted Titmouse displacing another, you are probably watching an older bird or a young male demonstrating its superior rank. Dominant individuals gain first access to feeders and eat more quickly, while subordinates spend more time watching out for danger.

Despite being permanent residents, Tufted Titmice do not live in one place forever. Juveniles often disperse about ½ to 1¼ miles and sometimes stage slightly longer fall or winter "mini" irruptions. Also in winter, local titmouse populations may gravitate to areas with large acorn or beech crops or to dense river-bottom habitat that provides protection from severe weather.

While the propensity for leaving home is small, it is nonetheless sufficient to allow Tufted Titmouse populations to expand when conditions are suitable—and indeed, this species has gradually expanded to the north over the past thirty years. Climate change is probably part of the cause, but bird feeding is thought to have played a role, as well. In one of the few experiments carried out on the effects of supplemental feeding, winter density of Tufted Titmice as much as doubled once feeders were provided. These birds are much more likely to visit feeders in northern areas, suggesting that feeders are a more important food source in colder climates.

Key references: Brawn and Samson 1983, Cimprich and Grubb 1994, Dunn 1995, Grubb and Pravosudov 1994, Kricher 1981, Petit et al. 1989, Samson and Lewis 1979, Waite 1987a.

FeederWatch Findings

The Tufted Titmouse is a very regular visitor, reported from over 90% of feeders in much of its range. Three-quarters of these host the species all winter long, although there are slight declines in flock size from January on. Tufted Titmice are slightly less regular and abundant in urban than in rural areas, but the habitat differences are small. That territorial pairs are often joined by a few juveniles for the winter is reflected in the numbers present at feeders (typically two to three but up to five or more).

Favorite feeder foods: *Sunflower (striped or black-oil), hulled peanuts,* hulled sunflower, safflower, peanut butter mixes, bird puddings.

Infrequent choices: Millet, mixed seed, canary seed, cracked corn, milo, niger, peanuts in shell or hearts, pet food, suet, meat scraps, baked goods, water.

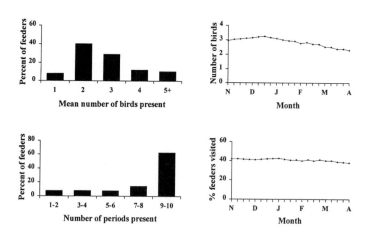

Tufted Titmouse: percent of feeders visited

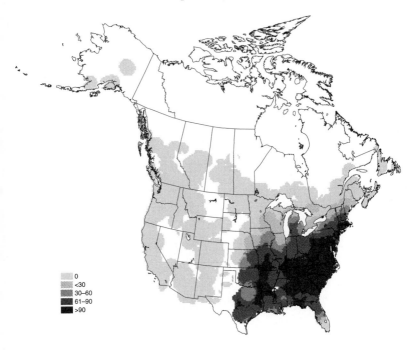

0
<30
30–60
61–90
>90

Abundance at feeders

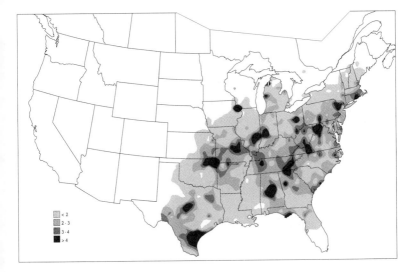

< 2
2 - 3
3 - 4
> 4

Bushtit

Psaltriparus minimus

A Bushtit is almost never alone. This tiny bird spends almost the entire year in a flock with fifteen or twenty other individuals. During the nesting season mated pairs remove themselves temporarily to a breeding territory within the flock range, but as soon as possible they rejoin the group, bringing their young along with them. The flocks are very cohesive, and a Bushtit finding itself left behind when the flock has moved on hurries after the others, loudly uttering a special "where-are-you" call.

This species is well known for its "confusion chorus": When a predator is detected—usually a hawk or other avian predator sighted when still a long way off—a Bushtit gives an alarm note similar to that of most flocking species to alert the rest of the flock. Once warned, however, Bushtits do something special. All the birds in the flock immediately take up a cicadalike monotonous trilling that makes it very difficult to pinpoint the location of any individual bird. Other species respond to their chorus by taking their own defensive measures and heading for cover. Indeed, the Bushtits' effective defense may be the reason why many other species will join them temporarily when a flock passes nearby.

Most of a Bushtit's foraging time is spent in low foliage, where the bird hangs upside down and acrobatically picks small insects off the bottoms of leaves—although it also feeds readily on the ground. These birds are not too fussy about microhabitat and will utilize a wide variety of coniferous and deciduous plants within the oak or juniper woodland areas where they are most common. They are willing to visit towns but are rather difficult to attract to feeders. When they do appear, the busy flocks stay only a short while, nibbling suet or fat and perhaps taking some water before moving off.

At about a fifth of an ounce, a single Bushtit weighs only as much as a quarter, ranking them among the world's smallest songbirds. Small size generally leads to high energy costs, and Bushtits are no exception. They eat up to 80% of their body weight daily during cold weather. At roost, flock members usually maintain a personal distance of a few inches, but when temperatures drop to freezing, they pack tightly together. Huddling at low temperatures can reduce overnight energy expenditure by about 20%, so there is sufficient reward for overcoming the usual aversion to body contact.

Key references: Austin and Smith 1972, Chaplin 1982, Dixon 1949, Ervin 1977, Grinnell 1903, Hertz et al. 1976, Smith 1972, Wagner 1981.

FeederWatch Findings

Bushtits visit only about a fifth of feeders in their winter range, and most of those sites report just occasional visits. However, these birds are winter-long visitors at some feeders. While the number of feeders visited remains steady throughout the season, flock size drops precipitously—from about fifteen to about five—between mid-January and the end of March. Lack of Bushtits in Nevada (see maps) is an artifact of poor Feeder-Watch coverage there.

Favorite feeder foods: *Suet,* bird puddings, and probably (although samples are small) peanut butter mixes.

Infrequent choices: Black-oil sunflower, water. Small samples show sugar water may also be taken.

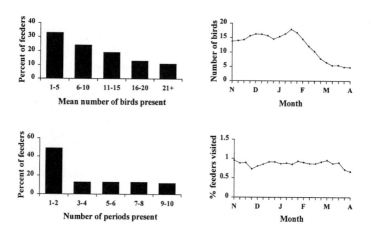

Bushtit: percent of feeders visited

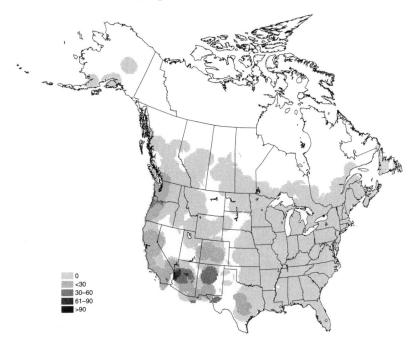

0
<30
30–60
61–90
>90

Abundance at feeders

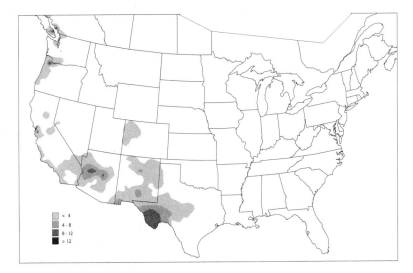

< 4
4 - 8
8 - 12
> 12

Red-breasted Nuthatch

Sitta canadensis

The Red-breasted Nuthatch is unexpectedly feisty for such a small bird. Approaching a feeder boldly, it easily displaces many larger species. It rarely lingers, though, and other birds quickly come back once the nuthatch has darted off with a seed. Most feeder owners observe only one or two nuthatches at a time because these birds maintain individual home ranges during the winter of about 10 acres. The ranges may overlap, bringing two or three birds into loose association, but Red-breasted Nuthatches do not form winter flocks per se.

This nuthatch is quite dependent on conifer seeds as a food source, and because cones are not produced in equal abundance each year, Red-breasts periodically have to search for food farther afield. In such years large numbers of nuthatches irrupt southward, emigrating deeper into the United States. Typically an "invasion" occurs every two to three years but sometimes twice in a row or with a three-year gap. Other species that depend heavily on tree seeds, such as Common Redpoll and Pine Siskin, frequently irrupt in the same years as nuthatches.

Many feeder owners within the permanent wintering range of Red-breasted Nuthatches are unaware of these large-scale movements, because their feeders attract only one or two nuthatches at best, and they scarcely notice when there are no birds at all. Moreover, the few nuthatches staying behind in northern areas during low-food years may visit feeders more frequently than usual, thereby masking their decline in numbers in the wild. South of the breeding range, however, irruptions are more obvious. While some emigrants set up home ranges, many apparently do not, and as many as ten Red-breasts can sometimes visit a feeder at one time.

Red-breasted Nuthatches cache seeds and other foods, poking them into crevices on tree trunks or rough-barked branches. One bird that was offered a supply of mealworms carried them off and hid them at the rate of nearly three a minute. Cache sites are usually chosen quite close to the food source and occasionally are covered with bits of nearby lichen or bark.

A few caching species, such as Clark's Nutcracker and Pinyon Jays, hide thousands of seeds within their territories and recover them months later, perhaps tiding them over seasonal shortages. When an especially lengthy food shortage causes these species to emigrate to unfamiliar areas, they often will not make any caches there. In contrast, Red-breasted Nuthatches have been recorded storing food in winter while far from their breeding range. This behavior would not be expected in a species using its stores months later, so nuthatches, like chickadees, are evidently short-term cachers—mainly stashing convenience food for a same-evening "top-up" and a quick breakfast the next day.

Key references: Davis and Morrison 1988, Dennis 1986, Grubb and Waite 1987, Larson and Bock 1986, Kilham 1974, 1975, Widrlechner and Dragula 1984, Yunick 1982, 1988.

FeederWatch Findings

The feeder visitation rates of Red-breasted Nuthatches varies between irruption and nonirruption years. Because the maps show average distribution and density for a three-year period, they illustrate the extent of irruptions while also showing that abundance of feeders is highest in the northern and western regions, where these birds are present every winter. The gap in Nevada is an artifact of poor FeederWatch coverage there. The Red-breasted Nuthatch is slightly more regular and abundant at rural than at urban feeders, although the differences are smaller than most people would notice. Feeders in northern areas are more likely than those in the south to host two nuthatches at once, as opposed to only one. Percent of feeders visited declines steadily throughout the winter.

Frequent feeder foods: *Suet,* sunflower (any type), hulled peanuts and hearts, peanut butter mixes, bird puddings.

Infrequent choices: Mixed seed, safflower, corn (any type), niger, peanuts in shell, meat scraps, baked goods, water, and (according to small samples) oats.

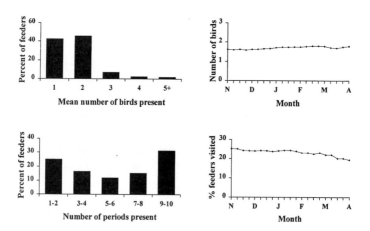

Red-breasted Nuthatch: percent of feeders visited

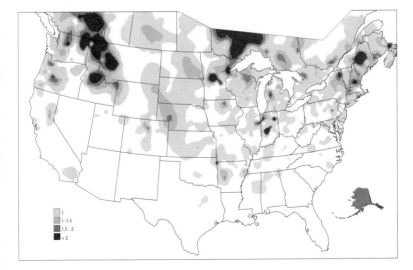

0
<30
30–60
61–90
>90

Abundance at feeders

1
1-1.5
1.5 · 2
> 2

167

White-breasted Nuthatch

Sitta carolinensis

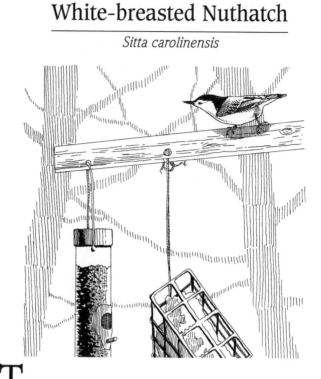

The White-breasted Nuthatch is a frequent choice for favorite feeder visitor. While a stubby plumpness gives this species an air of being a couch potato among birds, that appearance is belied by the White-breast's bold behavior. Both males and females are dominant over most other species at feeders and give way only to woodpeckers. Indeed, aggression appears to play a large role in the lives of White-breasted Nuthatches. Pairs defend quite large territories year-round: some 25 to 30 acres in woodland and up to twice that in more fragmented habitat. As a result, each feeder site is normally visited by only one or two individuals, although a feeder near a territorial border may sometimes attract three or four.

The female stays close to her mate throughout the winter, keeping in constant vocal communication when the pair is separated by more than a few yards. However, the male can be rather testy and may demonstrate his dominance by displacing his mate at food sources or stealing food she has just cached. As a result, she is likely to go on caching trips in the opposite direction from the male and hide her food farther away from the food source than he does.

Indeed, White-breasted Nuthatches spend quite a bit of their time caching food, carrying seeds a short distance (usually under thirty yards) and carefully concealing them in bark furrows high up on large tree trunks or on the undersides of thick branches. A White-breast that is storing food may visit your feeder frequently for a period of an hour or more—especially early in the day when it is building a stock of food to be eaten just before going to roost—while a noncaching bird makes two or three quick visits and then disappears for an hour or two before returning for more.

You are especially likely to observe caching near your feeder if you offer "convenience foods," such as shelled sunflower seeds or mealworms. Seeds that require wedging into a crack and hammering with vigorous blows of the beak are quite likely to be eaten on the spot. Why the difference? For a final preroost meal, the bird will want items that do not take a lot of preparation prior to consumption.

The local pair of White-breasted Nuthatches will frequently join flocks of other species as the latter move through a territory, keeping a close eye on visiting chickadees and Tufted Titmice, checking out their feeding sites—and often robbing their food caches. When foraging with other species, White-breasts relax their own level of predator vigilance and rely instead on the increased numbers of eyes to do some of the work. This system works because the nuthatches recognize and react appropriately to other species' alarm calls.

The White-breasted Nuthatch has a broader winter diet than the conifer-loving Red-breasted and lives in deciduous forest where it eats acorns, beech mast, and many other foods. Evidently this ensures that wholesale shortage of food is rare because irregular winter irruptions southward occur far less often than in Red-breasted Nuthatches.

Key references: Butts 1931, Grubb 1982, Petit et al. 1989, Pravosudov and Grubb 1993, Waite 1987b, Waite and Grubb 1988a, 1988b, Woodrey 1990, 1991, Yunick 1988.

FeederWatch Findings

The majority of feeders host White-breasted Nuthatches week after week, but the total number of feeders visited declines steadily throughout the season. A gap in the mapped distribution for Nevada is an artifact of poor FeederWatch coverage there, but the gap in West Texas (also missing coverage) is real.

Favorite feeder foods: *Suet*, sunflower (any type), hulled peanuts or hearts, peanut butter mixes, bird puddings.

Infrequent choices: Mixed seed, safflower, corn (whole or cracked), niger, peanuts in shell, meat scraps, baked goods, water, and (based on small samples) oats.

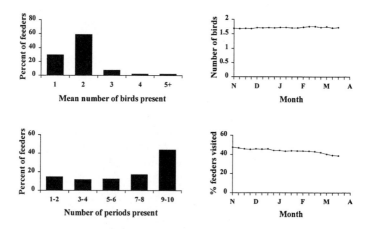

White-breasted Nuthatch: percent of feeders visited

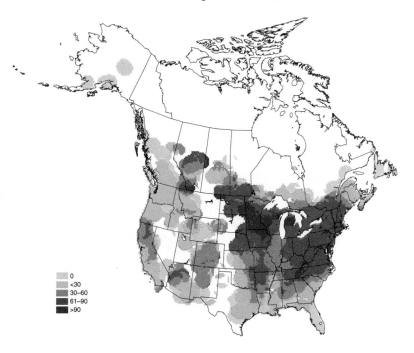

0
<30
30–60
61–90
>90

Abundance at feeders

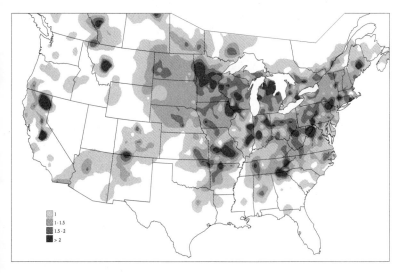

1
1 - 1.5
1.5 - 2
> 2

Pygmy Nuthatch

Sitta pygmaea

The tiny Pygmy Nuthatch is aptly named—but it's tough for its size. Though weighing in at only about a third of an ounce, about the same as a Black-capped Chickadee, it makes its home in western ponderosa forests where winter climate can be severe.

One of the key adaptations to winter survival in these nuthatches is their habit of communal roosting, in which birds fly as much as 1¼ miles to join a sleepover in a tree cavity. Typically a roost contains two to forty-five birds snuggled together, but more birds join in when temperatures drop especially low. One observer counted bird after bird entering a roost hole—reaching an astonishing total of 167! Inside the cavity, the nuthatches cling to the walls or stand on the floor, sometimes in several layers, with their heads all pointing in the same direction.

The energetic benefits of this roosting behavior are threefold. First, each nuthatch body is in close contact with others, which reduces heat loss. Next, the cavity itself keeps out the wind and holds in the birds' body heat, warming as much as 18°F over outside temperature. Finally, Pygmy Nuthatches let their body temperature decline, probably reducing metabolic expenditure by at least a third. As a by-product of metabolic decline, the roosting birds sleep very soundly—so much so that they must sometimes be prodded considerably before showing signs of life. The energy savings gained by this roosting behavior make it possible for Pygmy Nuthatches to stay in the roost cavity as long as forty hours without feeding, which gets them through short periods of severe cold or heavy snowfall.

The communal roosting habit is perhaps an outgrowth of the Pygmy Nuthatch's propensity for year-round group living. Each bird belongs to a highly social flock that only breaks up for the breeding season. Even then many nesting pairs are not alone, being accompanied by one or a few helpers (typically yearling males that are related to one of the nesting birds). These extra birds help the pair rear nestlings and protect nests from predation; in return, they apparently earn a place in the winter social group and perhaps increase their chances of breeding on their own the following year.

Once reproduction is out of the way, Pygmy Nuthatches join together for the rest of the year. Flocks may subdivide temporarily during foraging or coalesce with neighboring groups to form noisy assemblages of up to one hundred birds, but the usual flock size ranges from five to fifteen. About half the time that you see a Pygmy Nuthatch flock, it will have an admixture of other kinds of birds traveling along with it, from other species of nuthatch to chickadees or Brown Creepers. The Pygmy Nuthatches concentrate on gleaning insects from tree trunks, branches, and needle clusters of ponderosa and yellow pine. When cone crops are abundant, pine seeds take over as the primary winter food, and the nuthatches switch from insect hunters to seed pickers, searching cones both on the tree and on the ground.

Pygmy Nuthatch flocks are noisy but relatively peaceful when it comes to interactions among flock members. They often visit feeders in small groups (unlike the territorial White-breasted Nuthatch). Each bird carries off a seed to a spot where it can be wedged into a crack for hammering open with the bill, since Pygmy Nuthatches are unable to hold seeds under the foot as chickadees do. There are a few records of Pygmy Nuthatches caching seeds, but no one knows how important this may be to their winter survival.

Key references: Bock 1969, Güntert et al. 1988, Manolis 1977, Norris 1958, Pravosudov and Grubb 1993, Sealy 1984, Stallcup 1968, Sydeman et al. 1988, Sydeman and Güntert 1983.

FeederWatch Findings

The Pygmy Nuthatch is an uncommon feeder visitor even in its core winter range, visiting under a quarter of sites there. However, where it does occur, it is present week after week. It is a less frequent visitor in urban areas, and probably also less abundant there. Unlike more territorial nuthatches, Pygmies visit in small groups. Numbers drop off in spring while the number of feeders visited rises, suggesting that the birds spread out more at winter's end.

Favorite feeder foods: *Suet, bird puddings,* black-oil sunflower, water.

Infrequent choices: According to small samples, mixed seed, millet, and peanut butter mixes are occasionally eaten.

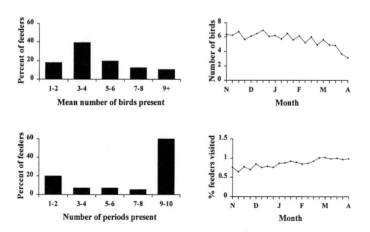

Pygmy Nuthatch: percent of feeders visited

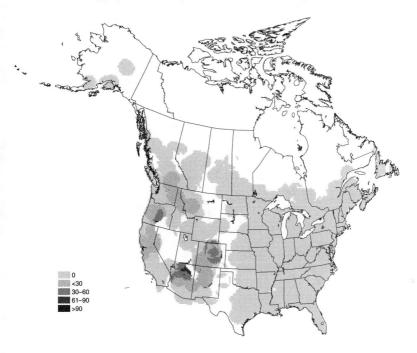

0
<30
30–60
61–90
>90

Abundance at feeders

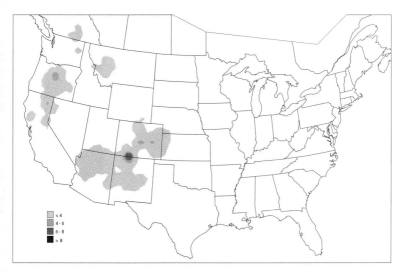

< 4
4 - 6
6 - 8
> 8

Brown-headed Nuthatch

Sitta pusilla

Brown-headed Nuthatches are restricted to mature pine forests of the Southeast and are especially common in loblolly-longleaf pine stands more than forty-five years old. They generally shun the pine plantations that are rapidly replacing natural stands in some parts of the South.

When pine seeds are abundant, Brown-headed Nuthatches concentrate on them for winter food. They store at least a few of the seeds, caching them one at a time on branches or in the furrowed bark of tree trunks. However, every five to seven years conifers fail to produce sufficient seeds for a good food source, and in these years the normally sedentary Brown-headed Nuthatches may venture out of their usual haunts. Alternate foods include insects, which are sought primarily in pine needle clusters but occasionally also on tree trunks, stumps, fence posts, or even buildings. Sometimes these nuthatches will use a loose scale of bark to pry up other bits of bark, placing Brown-headed Nuthatches in the record books as one of the few bird species known to use tools.

Nuthatches can be divided neatly into two groups based on social behavior. Red-breasted and White-breasted Nuthatches are territorial and usually are found alone or in pairs. In contrast, Brown-headed Nuthatches and western Pygmy Nuthatches are very gregarious. This sociability extends right into the breeding season, when up to 20% of Brown-headed Nuthatch pairs may be assisted in raising nestlings by an extra male. Unlike Pygmy Nuthatches, however, this species does not roost communally in cavities. Instead, each Brown-headed Nuthatch sleeps alone, typically perched on a pine branch.

Outside of the breeding season Brown-headed Nuthatches live in flocks of five to twenty-five birds. The superficial lack of social structure actually has an underlying order. Each flock has its own home range, which may be as large as 5 acres, although it may overlap territories of neighboring groups. Within the flock, each pair continues to defend a small area around its nest site. And within the pair, the male is likely to be the leader as pairs move from tree to tree. There appears to be some habitat division between the sexes, with males foraging lower on tree trunks than their mates.

Flocks of Brown-headed Nuthatches are quite noisy, which helps attract other species: Downy Woodpeckers, Carolina Chickadees, creepers, kinglets, and various warblers all associate temporarily with these nuthatch flocks. They have to hurry to keep up, though, as the restless nuthatches may spend less than a minute in one tree before moving on. Progress is a little slower when the Brown-headed Nuthatches are eating pine seeds, as these take longer to handle.

Key references: Haney 1981, Norris 1958, O'Halloran and Connor 1987, Morse 1967a,b, Pravosudov and Grubb 1993, White et al. 1996.

FeederWatch Findings

Despite the large flock sizes found in the wild, Brown-headed Nuthatches typically visit feeders in ones and twos. They are recorded at about a third of feeders in the Southeastern United States as a whole and at over half of feeders in Georgia and the Carolinas. Appearing sporadically at some feeders, especially in midwinter, they are faithful weekly visitors at others. No habitat differences could be detected.

Favorite feeder foods: Black-oil sunflower, bird puddings. Small samples indicate striped and hulled sunflower are also eaten regularly.

Infrequent choices: Suet, water, and (based on small samples) safflower, hulled peanuts, and peanut butter mixes.

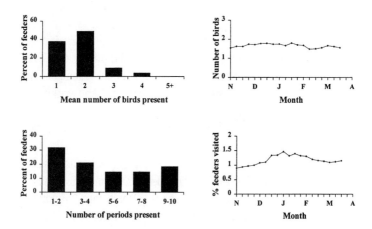

Brown-headed Nuthatch: percent of feeders visited

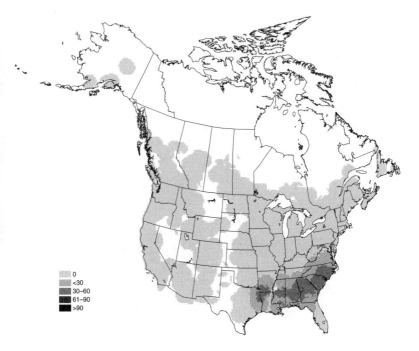

Abundance at feeders

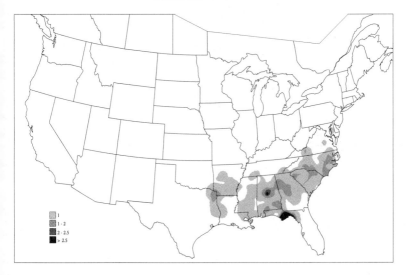

Brown Creeper

Certhia americana

Asmall brown bird with mothlike flight lands at the base of a tall old tree. It moves upward, detouring around branches, sometimes spiraling around the trunk. Occasionally the bird heads out along the underside of a branch, then returns along the top to the tree trunk. When the bird reaches denser branches, it leaves that tree and drops to the base of another tree to start all over again. If alarmed, the beautifully camouflaged bird spreads its wings and flattens almost invisibly against the tree trunk. What better name for this bird than "Brown Creeper"?

The creeper is specially suited for foraging on tree trunks. Short legs end in big toes with large claws, and the long pointed tail feathers help the creeper keep its balance while it probes bark crevices for insects with its slender, decurved bill. Besides eating insects, creepers also consume seeds, such as corn, acorns, and sunflower—but only if these have already been broken into very small pieces. Brown Creepers have been observed stuffing bits of sunflower into bark crevices, but caching of food is apparently uncommon.

Most of the food taken at feeders consists of tiny crumbs of seed or suet that other birds have left behind, and even when feeders contain plenty of suitable food, creepers are reluctant visitors. They may forage in the vicinity, but only venture out to a feeder after a long inspection to check that the coast is clear of other birds—then stay only long enough to swallow a morsel or two before leaving again. Some authors suggest that creepers are more likely to accept suet and fat mixtures that have been spread directly on tree bark. If you try this, choose the tallest and oldest conifer available. To avoid causing birds to inadvertently smear their feet or feathers, be sure to make each patch of food thick enough to be clearly visible, and limit it to a small area (perhaps an inch or two in diameter).

When creepers first arrive on the wintering grounds following fall migration, they may be quite gregarious, joining readily in foraging flocks of other species. Later in the winter, though, the creepers tend to become more solitary and perhaps even territorial. One feeder owner reported two creepers fighting over a suet basket. In response to an alarm call, they froze for a full fourteen minutes— and then resumed their altercation where they had left off.

Brown Creepers in the northern parts of the breeding range migrate south for the winter, while others move to lower altitudes, but evidently they remain sensitive to cold because severe winters are correlated with population decline. Nonetheless, creepers are among the earliest of spring migrants and often run into poor weather in that season, so they must at least be tolerant of moderately low temperatures. Normally creepers sleep solitarily, clinging closely to a tree trunk several yards above the ground, but cold nights break down this asocial tendency and up to a dozen may roost together in a small cavity.

Key references: Dennis 1981, Franzeb 1985, Graber and Graber 1979, Lima and Lee 1993, Morse 1970, Williams and Batzli 1979.

FeederWatch Findings

Most people do not think of Brown Creepers as typical feeder birds, but they do visit up to a fifth of feeders in some regions (especially in midwinter), slightly more often visiting rural feeders than those in other habitats. Generally they are reported only a few times a winter, and usually as single birds.

Favorite feeder foods: Suet, bird puddings, and probably (according to small samples) peanut butter mixes.

Infrequent choices: Sunflower (all types—probably taking broken bits), water. Small samples suggest peanut hearts and baked goods may also be taken on occasion.

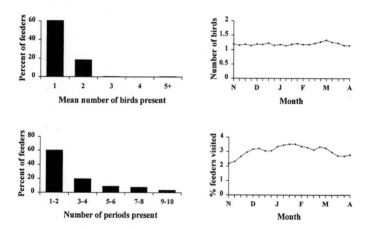

Brown Creeper: percent of feeders visited

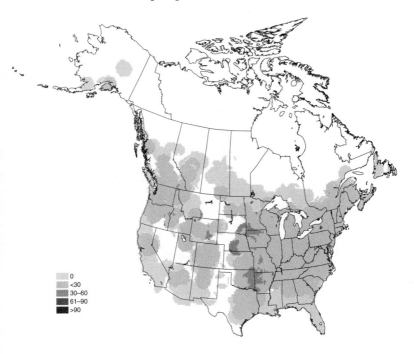

0
<30
30–60
61–90
>90

Abundance at feeders

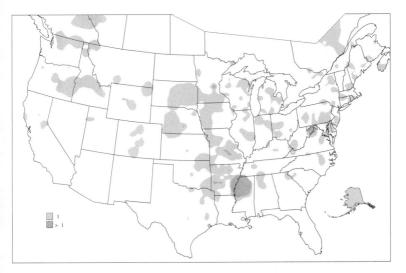

1
> 1

Cactus Wren

Campylorhynchus brunneicapillus

In the arid Southwest dwells a giant among wrens: the Cactus Wren. The name is appropriate because this bird is closely associated with the native vegetation common within its low-altitude habitat, including cacti, creosote bush, and mesquite. Cactus Wrens tolerate human activity well as long as there is plenty of appropriate plant life in the neighborhood.

Members of the wren family generally live their lives in the fast lane, always busy and bustling about, and this bird is no exception. One of the Cactus Wren's main activities is nest building. Not only is an elaborate, gourd-shaped home built for nesting, but additional abodes are constructed as winter roost sites. Each nest takes about ten days to build, and the owner may fuss with improvements for another several weeks. The domed structure has an entrance in the form of a downward curving "spout," and the interior cavity is lined with fur, feathers, or fine plant material—a cozy castle, indeed. Frequent repair or rebuilding is required when Curve-billed Thrashers are part of the local bird fauna, as these competitors for prime cactus real estate will destroy wren nests when they can.

Roost nests are conspicuous affairs, protected by the cactus spines among which they are built rather than by camouflage. A wren may start to roost there only two or three days into construction by perching on the open platform, suggesting that the roost nest provides protection from predation as well as shelter from cold night temperatures.

Roost nests are often found in loose clusters within a pair's year-round territory. The male and female each build their own roosting structure, usually within 130 feet of one another. Several other wrens, usually the pair's young-of-the-year, may hang about until mid-February and add their own roost nests to the landscape. These extra birds disperse a little farther when the breeding season begins in February, stimulated by the flush of new plant growth and insect abundance that follows winter rains. In dry winters the onset of breeding is delayed, but it still takes place before the snowy season has ended in colder climates.

Cactus Wrens may abandon their territories temporarily in winter to move into denser cover. If they wander at all, however, they return frequently to check over their home turf. It turns out that males are the real territory "owners," and females who lose their mates are unable to defend a territory alone. Even though the Cactus Wren's survival rate is relatively good for a small songbird, with about 70% coming through each winter, most individuals will have more than one mate during their lifetime due to loss of a former partner.

Cactus Wrens spend much of their food-searching time on the ground foraging in surface litter for a wide variety of insects. This behavior, combined with a relative tameness, makes them frequent victims of cat predation. They are safer when foraging above ground, usually in cacti and mesquite. Fruit and seeds supplement the insect diet to a total of about 10 to 20%, perhaps a little more than in other wren species, and Cactus Wrens will eat these at feeders, as well as in the wild.

Key references: Anderson and Anderson 1973, Bent 1948.

FeederWatch Findings

Cactus Wrens are abundant in West Texas and the apparent gap there (see maps) results from poor FeederWatch coverage. These wrens are reported from up to half of all sites in some areas, and are quite likely to visit week after week. They are especially likely to visit suburban feeders, even though numbers seen at one time are larger at rural sites.

Favorite feeder foods: The few data available suggest *suet* and mixed seed are favored, while striped and black-oil sunflower, milo, peanuts in shell, peanut butter mixes, bird puddings, fresh fruit, baked goods, water may be sampled occasionally.

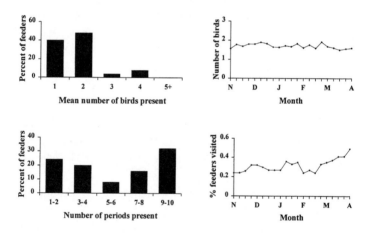

Cactus Wren: percent of feeders visited

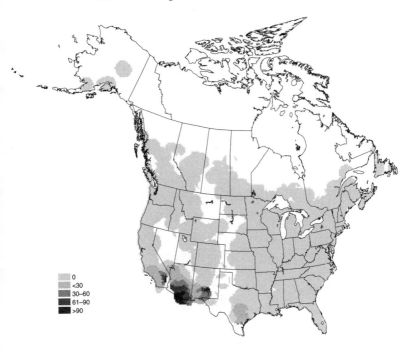

Abundance at feeders

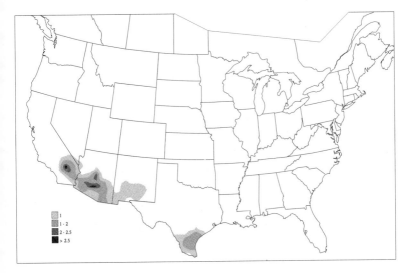

Carolina Wren

Thryothorus ludovicianus

Of all the wren species, the Carolina Wren is the one most commonly seen at feeders. You can improve your chances of enticing these welcome visitors by building a brush pile in your feeding area because these birds like a bit of cover to retreat to.

The energetic Carolina Wren investigates every nook and cranny while searching for insects. Sometimes it climbs tree trunks like a creeper; more often it rummages through leaf litter, interspersing short flights to new foraging locations. Although primarily insectivorous, this wren also eats some fruits and seeds. These tastes are reflected in the food choices at feeders, where suet and peanut butter mixes stand in for insects, while seeds and fruit are sampled less frequently.

Pairs of Carolina Wrens (and unmated males) work hard at defending their territories year-round, using song as one signal of ownership. You will certainly hear singing if wrens are present in your neighborhood, as these birds are unexpectedly loud for their size. A single male can have over forty song types, and sometimes the male and female perform duets. The unusually high degree of winter territoriality, compared to other bird species, suggests that protection of familiar food sources is important to overwinter survival in Carolina Wrens.

Members of established pairs stick very close together, usually foraging within a half yard or so. A female wren is unable to defend the territory alone if her mate dies, so it pays for her to watch out for his safety. She spends more time than the male does in watching out for predators and gives alarm calls to warn him of danger. Perhaps this species has to be especially vigilant for predators because the leaf-litter foraging habit is relatively noisy and conspicuous.

Partly due to their territorial tenacity, Carolina Wrens do not join foraging flocks made up of other species. However, they are fairly tolerant of other birds—as long as those others are not Carolina Wrens—and will spend long periods near feeders neither disturbing others nor being disturbed by them.

Over a series of mild winters the northern edge of the winter range will expand slowly—until a severe winter or disastrous late-spring storm knocks the population down again. One northward range expansion of Carolina Wrens took place at the turn of the century, and another occurred more recently. There are limits, however. Carolina Wrens are unlikely to maintain permanent populations where minimum January temperatures regularly fall below 19°F, and they suffer high mortality when snow covers the leaf litter where they forage. After one especially cold winter in the late 1970s, numbers of wrens at one Ohio site dropped from 537 to 1 in a single year.

Possibly bird feeding helps reduce mortality at the northern edge of the range, and availability of roost cavities for nighttime protection may also contribute to winter survival. Homeowners wanting to provide such cavities do not have to build fancy nest boxes—there are reports of Carolina Wrens sleeping in any suitable spot, including the pockets of old clothes.

Key references: Graber and Graber 1979, Haggerty and Morton 1995, Hess 1989, Morton and Shalter 1977, Tamar 1978.

FeederWatch Findings

This is the only wren that makes widespread use of feeders, visiting over three-quarters of sites in the southeastern United States. Nearly twice as many feeders are visited in midwinter as in fall and spring, although many locations report these birds all winter long. Carolina Wrens are slightly more regular visitors at rural feeders as compared to suburban or urban. They nearly always visit alone or in pairs.

Favorite feeder foods: *Bird puddings*, hulled peanuts and hearts, suet, peanut butter mixes.

Infrequent choices: Mixed seed, millet, sunflower (all types), safflower, cracked corn, milo, peanuts in shell, pet food, fruit (fresh or dried), baked goods, water, and (based on small samples), meat scraps and popped corn.

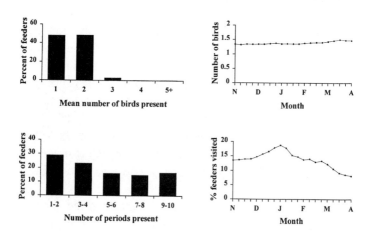

Carolina Wren: percent of feeders visited

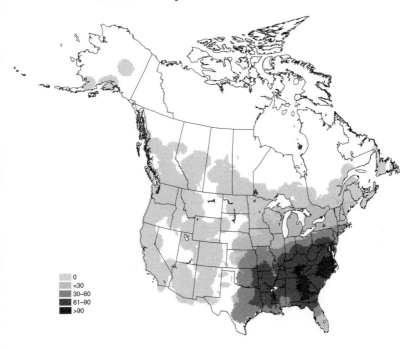

0
<30
30–60
61–90
>90

Abundance at feeders

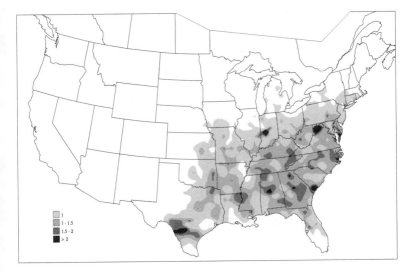

1
1 - 1.5
1.5 - 2
> 2

Bewick's Wren

Thryomanes bewickii

Though a year-round resident in most parts of its range, the Bewick's Wren will usually visit feeders only in winter. Its tastes in feeder foods parallel those of other insectivorous visitors such as kinglets and warblers: fat, peanut butter mixes, and suet.

Bewick's Wrens are constantly busy, foraging for insects with their tails cocked perkily above their backs. They investigate every hiding place in their search for insects and spiders. Sometimes they forage on the ground—flipping over leaves or digging with the bill—but most of their attention goes to low shrubbery within a few feet of the ground. The male tends to work areas above the female, if they are together at all. Between feeding bouts the wrens prefer to perch higher up, probably to make spotting of predators or territorial intruders easier.

Bewick's Wrens are described as gentle, but they are aggressive toward both House and Carolina Wrens when defending territory. House Wrens appear to have the upper hand in interactions and have been blamed for the historic near disappearance of Bewick's Wrens from the Appalachians and Midwest, where House Wrens have become more abundant. Where these two species coexist, Bewick's often forsake the habitats preferred by House Wrens and restrict themselves to swampy woodlands. In regions where Bewick's are the sole wren species present, they are more likely to live in the open woodland and fencerow habitats favored by House Wrens. As a further indication of competition between the species, Bewick's Wrens will move temporarily into areas occupied by House Wrens when the latter birds migrate northward for the breeding season.

Some Bewick's Wrens leave their territories in cold weather and move to lower altitudes or heavier cover for the duration of the season, and birds from the northern parts of the range may be short-distance migrants. They generally return to the same breeding area the following spring, but little is known about migrants' territorial behavior or site fidelity in winter.

The majority of Bewick's Wrens are year-round residents. Males continue to defend territories through the winter and may even expand their area of activity. Intruders inspire them to under-take vigorous choral battles along territory boundaries. Females usually separate from males in winter—although a few do remain mated—and occasionally young-of-the-year will also stay on parental territory through the winter.

Key references: Bent 1948, Kennedy and White 1997, Miller 1941, Root 1988, Root 1969, Wagner 1981.

FeederWatch Findings

In contrast to Carolina Wrens, the Bewick's Wren is a fairly casual feeder visitor, at relatively few sites (about 30% in Oklahoma and Arizona, for example). It is more common in West Texas than is shown on the maps, which suffer from lack of FeederWatch coverage there. Suburban feeders are most likely to be visited overall; rural sites are more likely to record Bewick's Wrens present throughout the winter. Most visits in fall are by lone birds, but the chances of seeing two at a time increase steadily through the winter.

Favorite feeder foods: The few data available indicate that *peanut butter mixes* and *bird puddings* are the main attractants, with suet close behind.

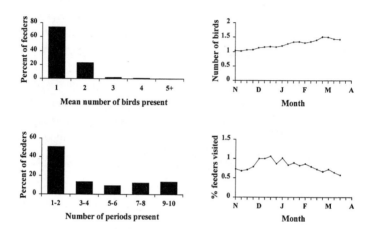

Bewick's Wren: percent of feeders visited

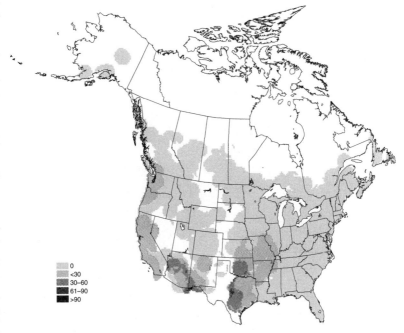

0
<30
30–60
61–90
>90

Abundance at feeders

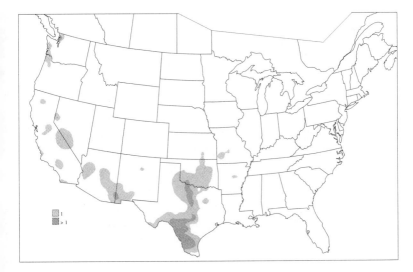

1
> 1

Ruby-crowned Kinglet

Regulus calendula

Ruby-crowned Kinglets are uncommon but regular visitors to feeders. You are most likely to see them during their migration, although feeder owners in the southern United States may attract these little woodland birds throughout the cold months.

Bird banders have noticed that kinglets will often return to the same wintering area year after year—and that nearly three-quarters of the kinglets caught in Florida during the winter are females. Most likely the males prefer to stay farther north. This partial separation of the sexes is known for several other migrant songbirds (Dark-eyed Junco and Evening Grosbeak, for example) and is probably quite common. One explanation proposed is that in a race to beat out competitors in claiming good real estate that will help attract a mate, those males that can reach the breeding grounds early in the spring can establish territories before the females arrive.

The tiny Ruby-crown is one of the last insectivorous birds to leave its northern breeding grounds on fall migration and one of the first to arrive back in spring. Despite this apparent hardiness, the kinglet confines its wintering range to warm regions, and mortality rises when midwinter temperatures are low, with extensive die-offs in severe winters. The kinglet is not known to have any specialized physiological adaptations to conserve energy at night, but it may take behavioral measures to retain warmth. Though the typical roost perch is simply a spot out of the wind, often near a tree trunk, some kinglets find snug beds in the abandoned nests of other birds.

Only male kinglets have the "ruby crown": a swatch of scarlet feathers frequently obscured by surrounding green plumage that can be erected conspicuously during aggressive interactions. Kinglets frequently flick their wings—perhaps another aggressive signal—although the true purpose is not known. Following a period of autumn gregariousness, kinglets chase and fight with each other, suggesting that they are territorial in winter. They are also aggressive on occasion toward Golden-crowned Kinglets and to Orange-crowned and Yellow-rumped Warblers. The feisty little Ruby-crowns are nonetheless capable of peaceful coexistence and frequently join other species in foraging flocks. They learn to react appropriately to Carolina Chickadee calls, ceasing all activity at the sound of alarm and resuming foraging at the chickadee's "all clear."

Ruby-crowns on the hunt for spiders or insects spend nearly all of their time foraging among the thin, outer twigs in the upper parts of deciduous or coniferous trees, especially those with dense foliage. Usually they stand on a perch and glean small prey from the foliage; sometimes they hover. For unknown reasons, the wings are frequently flicked as the birds hop about. The kinglets focus on flowers or newly emerging leaves, apparently because insects are concentrated on tender new growth. Within the kinglet's wintering range different tree species drop and regrow leaves on different schedules, while others are evergreen, so there is a steady supply of insects throughout the winter. The Ruby-crown also eats a few fruits and seeds, though the most common food choices at feeders are suet and bird puddings. Even if kinglets turn up their beaks at your food offerings, they may partake of water.

Key references: Fareley 1993, Franzeb 1984, Graber and Graber 1979, Homan 1982, Ingold and Wallace 1994, Laurenzi et al. 1982, Lepthien and Bock 1976, Robbins et al. 1986.

FeederWatch Findings

Ruby-crowned Kinglets are occasionally winter-long feeder visitors, but in most cases they are seen for only part of the year. Up to a quarter of sites may be visited at least once a season. Ruby-crowns do occur in West Texas (the gap on maps results from low FeederWatch coverage there). Suburban feeders are slightly more likely to host kinglets, but frequency of visit and abundance does not vary with residential density. Visits drop off as spring approaches. Although kinglets are nearly always seen one at a time, they do visit some feeders in small flocks.

Favorite feeder foods: *Bird puddings, suet,* and probably (based on small samples) *peanut butter mixes.*

Infrequent choices: Black-oil sunflower, water, hulled peanuts (although these birds probably eat only broken bits of the seeds).

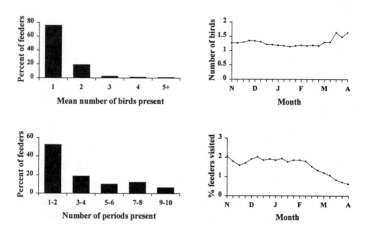

Ruby-crowned Kinglet: percent of feeders visited

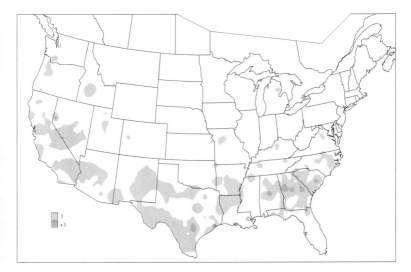

0
<30
30–60
61–90
>90

Abundance at feeders

1
>1

Eastern Bluebird

Sialia sialis

Feeder owners able to attract bluebirds are the objects of envy, as the gorgeous coloration and distinctive manners of these birds thrill observers wherever they appear. Although Eastern Bluebirds are less common than they once were—apparently because their preferred habitat of overgrown farmland is disappearing—the widespread provision of nesting boxes is helping to maintain healthy populations.

Bluebirds search open country for prey items on the ground, from perches about 2 yards high. Their eyesight must be remarkable: Camouflaged and immobile caterpillars can be spotted from 6 to 7 yards away—sometimes as much as 50 yards—even in rough pastures where grass is much longer than homeowners would tolerate on their lawns. The bluebirds then swoop down and pounce on their quarry, eating small items immediately; larger prey may first have to be beaten into submission on a hard surface. Often large foodstuffs are carried to a perch for leisurely consumption.

During a feeding session, a bluebird may make one feeding

attack per minute—or even more. Following a successful attack, the bird moves to a nearby perch from which it can look over part of the previously hunted area as well as some new ground. If no prey has been captured, the bluebird's next perch is far enough away so that an entirely new area can be surveyed.

We know little about the social behavior of Eastern Bluebirds in winter except that they are commonly seen in flocks of ten to twenty-five birds, frequently associating with groups of Yellow-rumped, Pine, or Palm Warblers. Resident birds that were marked with leg bands in summer have been reported traveling as intact families within larger winter flocks. But it is not known whether migrants from northern areas mix with local residents in winter or form separate flocks.

Most Eastern Bluebirds migrate south and spend the winter in warm, moist areas that have more than 180 frost-free days a year. A few remain in the North instead of migrating, most commonly in seacoast regions (where the climate is relatively mild) or areas with low snow accumulation and dense cedar growth. The cover is needed for shelter from poor weather conditions, but from there the birds can venture into open woodland and old pastures to forage.

Severe cold and snowfall can cause substantial mortality among bluebirds, not only in winter but also in the nesting period if there are late-spring storms. In very cold periods up to fourteen birds may roost together in a single tree cavity, with their heads all pointing toward the center, forming a dazzling blue pinwheel. The roosting birds are very sluggish, suggesting that they drop their body temperature to aid in energy conservation.

Fruit is an important source of food to bluebirds from late summer to early spring, making up nearly half the winter diet, and it is the main choice of foods at bird feeders. If you are especially eager to attract bluebirds, try offering mealworms in a dish on the ground near a suitable hunting perch. Other bird species also like these expensive treats, however, so you may want to offer them only when bluebirds are already in the vicinity.

Key references: Frazier and Nolan 1959, Goldman 1975, Graber and Graber 1979, Musselman 1941, Pinkowski 1977, 1979, Stiles 1984.

FeederWatch Findings

Eastern Bluebirds are reported at a quarter of feeders in some regions, but very rarely do they visit week after week. They are seen slightly less frequently at urban feeders than elsewhere. Flock size declines at feeders from January on, but as the number of feeders visited increases at the same time, this probably represents the beginning of northward migration.

Favorite feeder foods: Water, although small samples indicate that *dried fruit* is highly favored.

Infrequent choices: Mixed seed, striped sunflower, suet, bird puddings. Small samples indicate that bluebirds may also eat peanut hearts and peanut butter mixes as well as peanuts in their shells (possibly only taking broken bits of the latter).

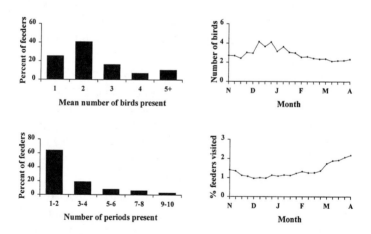

Eastern Bluebird: percent of feeders visited

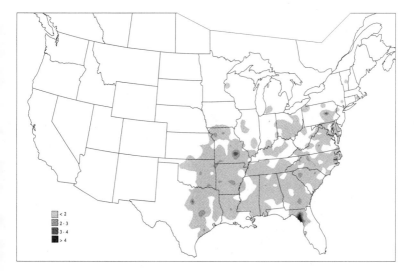

0
<30
30–60
61–90
>90

Abundance at feeders

< 2
2 · 3
3 · 4
> 4

203

Hermit Thrush

Catharus guttatus

All the closest relatives of the Hermit Thrush migrate to Central or South America for the winter. Why Hermits winter at least partially in North America is unknown, but perhaps diet is a contributing factor. While the majority of its winter food consists of berries, nearly half consists of insects and other invertebrates—a relatively high proportion compared to the foods eaten by Veerys, Swainson's Thrushes, and Gray-cheeked Thrushes. The Hermit Thrush may also be unusual in its preference for the fruits of evergreens. Evergreen berries are relatively low in nutrition and energy content, but they remain abundant in winter long after the berries of other fall-fruiting vegetation have been eaten.

Hermit Thrushes often feed on the ground, searching out insects from leaf litter, hopping and stopping in turn, peering at the ground in a manner reminiscent of robins. They punctuate these activities by cocking the tail upward, then slowly lowering it. Hermits also collect food from trees and shrubbery—more so than other thrush species—but nonetheless they suffer if snow covers food on the ground. Evidence from population surveys of breeding birds suggests that despite setbacks in cold winters, Hermit Thrushes increased in abundance in the thirty years up to 1996. This is also true for two other thrushes that winter in the United States, the American Robin and the Varied Thrush. In contrast, thrush species that winter south of the United States have declined or remained steady in population size.

There seem to be seasonal differences in Hermit Thrushes' favorite habitat. These birds breed in dry areas, such as oak and pine woodland, but are more likely to inhabit warm, moist forests in winter. In all seasons they avoid high elevations, concentrating around open areas within forests. This preference often brings them to well-vegetated residential areas that are surrounded by a wooded landscape.

Winter ecology of the Hermit Thrush has not been well studied, although recaptures of banded individuals show that they frequently return to the same wintering area each year. Some individuals establish small territories and maintain them for up to four months. Other, nonterritorial individuals wander locally, but do not form large nomadic flocks in the manner of American Robins. On the other hand, the Hermit Thrush is hardly the loner its name implies and will join foraging flocks of kinglets, chickadees, and other species.

Key references: Graber and Graber 1979, Jones and Donovan 1996, Morse 1971, Noon 1981, Skeate 1987.

FeederWatch Findings

The Hermit Thrush is most regular as a feeder species in California, where it is resident year-round and joined by migrants for the winter. It is nearly always a casual, solo visitor. Feeders are most likely to be visited in midwinter and on spring migration, although most visits are for water rather than sustenance. The gap in West Texas (see maps) results from poor FeederWatch coverage there.

Favorite feeder "food": Water.

Infrequent choices: Mixed seed and, according to small samples, niger, bird puddings, peanut butter mixes, and dried fruit. Other sources report that suet and bread crumbs are sometimes eaten.

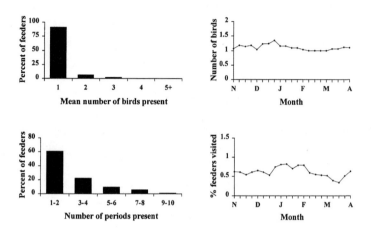

Hermit Thrush: percent of feeders visited

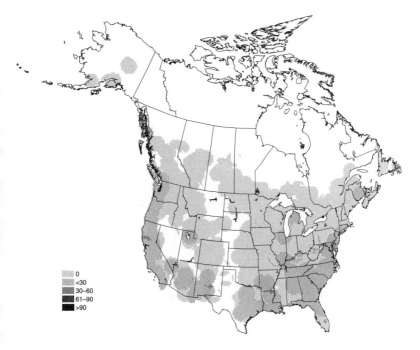

0
<30
30–60
61–90
>90

Abundance at feeders

1
>1

American Robin

Turdus migratorius

The American Robin is one of the most widely recognized birds of North America. Once hunted commonly for food, it now enjoys a more peaceful association with man.

Robins eat a broad variety of small invertebrates from insects to snails plus an astonishing array of fruits—representing more than fifty families of plants. Where grapes and cherries are commercially cultivated, it is sometimes necessary to take measures to keep robins out of fields.

In popular imagination the robin's favorite food is an earthworm, but in fact worms constitute only 15 to 20 percent of the summer diet. Nonetheless, earthworms are robins' food of choice on suburban lawns, especially after sprinklers or rain have forced worms to the surface. Experiments have shown that robins do not smell or hear earthworms, relying instead on vision to find their prey. The bird's familiar head cocking allows it to see straight ahead, overcoming the more peripheral view dictated by lateral eye placement. On lawns with longer grass, robins switch from pouncing on worms to gleaning insects from grass stalks or foliage. Mowing apparently causes invertebrates to be particularly vulnerable, and robins are especially likely to be seen foraging on lawns during the half hour after grass has been cut.

By wintertime, fruits make up to 80% of the diet, far above the 10% eaten in spring. The switch is made gradually in late summer while other foods are still available, and there are evidently physiological adjustments to digestive processes that must be made to accommodate the fruit. Many wild fruits contain compounds that are mildly toxic when accumulated in the body—perhaps an evolutionary tactic of plants to encourage birds to change food sources frequently and thereby distribute seeds widely. In one laboratory study, robins choosing among three wild fruits showed strong individual preferences, with the preferences changing from day to day.

Fruit sources (including feeders) may sometimes be defended by robins against other birds, especially if temperatures fall below freezing. A single robin was once reported keeping up to fifteen Cedar Waxwings away from a crab apple tree, although the robin gave up when additional waxwings joined the fray. Robins can also be on the other side of such contests, and flocks sometimes overwhelm the defenses of Northern Mockingbirds that are trying to protect fruit sources in their winter territories.

Bad weather can induce robins to change habitats or move into suburban areas, but as long as food is available, the birds are able to withstand quite severe cold. Nonetheless, late spring snowfalls can cause large die-offs if ground foraging is prevented because by that time all fruit sources have been exhausted. At such times large numbers of robins may descend on feeders and eat just about anything offered. To attract robins regularly, though, you should serve dried or fresh fruit and offer a source of water.

The migratory robin forms nomadic winter flocks. In the North these are usually well under fifty birds, but farther south flock sizes may grow to tens or even hundreds of thousands. The flocks break up somewhat during the day for foraging, spreading over as much as 450 square miles, then gather up again at night to roost in trees. An estimated one million robins have been reported sharing a giant blackbird roost in the southeast United States. Within a large roost, robins often segregate into smaller flocks, with each bird sitting a yard or two from its neighbors. There they sit for up to sixteen hours at a stretch during midwinter. Roosts offer little energetic savings to robins, and probably their main function is protection from predators.

Key references: Black 1932, Caldwell and Cuthbert 1987, Eiserer 1980, Graber and Graber 1979, Heppner 1965, Jung 1992, Levey and Karasov 1989, Meanley 1965, Moore 1977, Pietz and Pietz 1987, Sallabanks 1993, Skorupa and Hothem 1985, Walsberg and King 1980, Wheelwright 1986, 1988.

FeederWatch Findings

It is hard to judge how often American Robins actually take food from feeders—as opposed to simply being seen nearby—but it is clear from the food data that at least occasionally robins do sample a wide variety of feeder offerings. The percent of feeders visited rises dramatically once spring migration begins.

Favorite feeder foods: Fruit (fresh and dried), water.

Infrequent choices: Mixed seed, millet, sunflower (black-oil and striped), safflower, cracked corn, milo, hulled peanuts and hearts, suet, peanut butter mixes, bird puddings, baked goods. Small samples indicate that pet food, meat scraps, and popped corn are also taken on occasion.

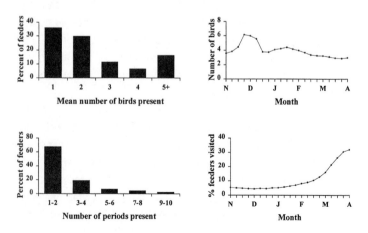

American Robin: percent of feeders visited

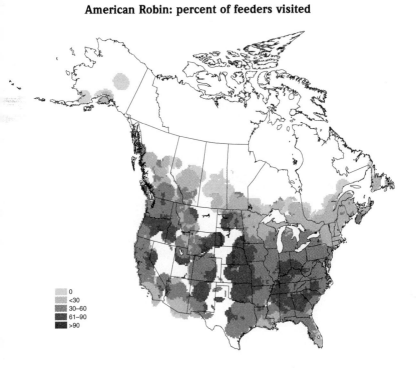

0
<30
30–60
61–90
>90

Abundance at feeders

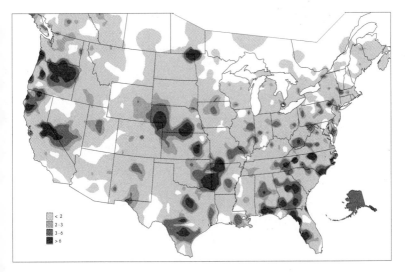

< 2
2 - 3
3 - 6
> 6

Varied Thrush

Ixoreus naevius

The handsomely marked Varied Thrush is one of the few thrush species that is seen quite often at feeders, at least in shady, wet, coniferous woodlands of the West. Seeming to relish constant rain and drizzle, the Varied Thrush prefers to winter in regions with over 63 inches of rainfall annually. About half of the summer range is vacated each fall by migrants withdrawing a short distance to the south.

This thrush sometimes pulls earthworms from lawns like an American Robin, but more often it forages in leaf litter. Hopping forward and grasping a beakful of vegetation, the bird then jumps backward, tossing aside whatever it has picked up. The forward and backward hops are almost continuous, with only occasional pauses to peer at the ground. Foods being sought include millipedes, sowbugs, beetles, snails, and quite a lot of plant matter. In fact, even in the breeding season when most bird species switch to insects, Varied Thrushes eat nearly 40% vegetable foods, and by winter the proportion reaches nearly 75%. Fruit and weed seeds are commonly consumed, and—perhaps surprisingly—so are acorns. Nuts on the ground are attacked with vigorous pecks, similar to those directed at acorns by Blue Jays.

Variation in food supplies probably influences the broad fluctuations in population size that characterize the Varied Thrush. Abundance of these birds in the normal wintering area peaks every two to three years (as does subsequent breeding population), then declines again—a cycle clearly visible in the number of Varied Thrushes visiting feeders. While some individuals wander widely and occasionally turn up at feeders as far east as the Atlantic Coast, these wanderings are not correlated with changes in the core population size. Could Varied Thrushes be like Blue Jays, Red-headed Woodpeckers, and certain other species that move greater distances in winters when acorn crops fail? So far no correlation has been found, and the cause of the approximately two-year cycle in Varied Thrush populations remains poorly understood.

One factor inducing Varied Thrushes to visit feeders requires no further study to understand: snow. Even a light snowfall can bring these birds to feeders, while severe storms may cause thousands to gather along newly plowed roadsides in last-ditch attempts to find food.

When foraging, each male Varied Thrush defends a small personal space—just large enough to keep other birds from feeding at a food patch or a feeder. Individual distance is maintained with a "tail-up" display that shows off conspicuous spots on the tail's underside. Subordinates beat a retreat when faced with a dominant bird extending his head forward in a close-up, face-to-face display, lifting his wings slightly to show off white wing stripes. Females will often forage elsewhere rather than contend with the fractious males.

Varied Thrushes differ from many birds in directing their threat displays to other species as well as to their own. At feeders they are aggressive toward many species and are dominant to most. Exceptions include Steller's Jays, with whom the thrushes prefer to strike an accommodation, and California Quail and Scrub-Jays, to whom Varied Thrushes lose regularly in scuffles. American Robins can also dominate Varied Thrushes but only in dry weather—evidently robins lose their assertiveness when wet.

Key references: Law 1921, Martin 1970, Ransome 1950, Wells et al. 1996.

FeederWatch Findings

Varied Thrushes visit feeders most often in the coldest part of the winter, though about a quarter of visited sites will host the species all winter long. Most feeders report only one thrush at a time. Larger flocks—up to ten or more—are more common in the years when most feeders are visited.

Favorite feeder foods: Mixed seed.

Infrequent choices: Black-oil sunflower, suet, water. Small samples indicate that millet, striped or hulled sunflower, cracked corn, bird puddings, fresh fruit, and popped corn may also be eaten occasionally.

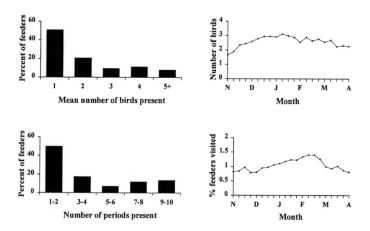

Varied Thrush: percent of feeders visited

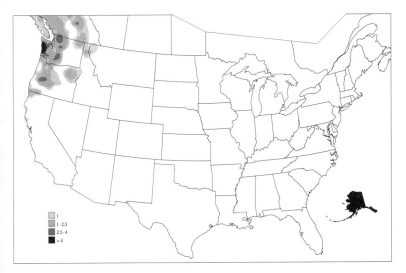

	0
	<30
	30–60
	61–90
	>90

Abundance at feeders

	1
	1 - 2.5
	2.5 - 4
	> 4

Northern Mockingbird

Mimus polyglottos

Mockingbirds, whose latin name means "many-tongued mimic," are justly famed for their vocalizations and at one time were commonly sold as caged songbirds. A single bird may sing up to two hundred different songs over the course of a year—over fifty in one day's concert alone—and the songs incorporate mimicked sounds of other bird species. The imitations are not perfect, but they are often good enough to lure bird-watchers into searching for a calling cardinal or jay—only to find themselves being mocked by a mockingbird. The greatest variety of songs comes from males seeking a mate, and unpaired birds sometimes make themselves unpopular to humans when there is a full moon by serenading the ladies all night long.

Song is just one of the means used in defense of year-round territories. Other techniques involve body language. You may witness two mockingbirds "dancing"—facing one another with bodies and tails erect, alternately hopping backward and forward—to define precise boundaries of mutual tolerance. "Wing-flashing" is a conspicuous display that has also been ascribed to territorial defense, consisting of raising the wings slightly to show off their prominent white stripes. However, this behavior has also been hypothesized to serve completely different functions, from startling insect prey to frightening potential predators, and a recent review concluded that the true function of wing-flashing remains unknown.

Many young mockingbirds set up territories in the fall, when most pair formation also occurs, while others delay through a foot-loose first winter; but once having staked some boundaries, mockingbirds stay within them for the rest of their lives. In winter the home turf may be split into separate male and female bailiwicks, especially in northern regions. This suggests that winter territory is important in the defense of food resources (food being scarcer in the colder North) and, indeed, territory size is smallest where there are dense, defensible sources of food.

Although mockingbirds are primarily insectivorous, running about on short grass searching for prey on the ground, fruit is an important and often guarded resource in winter. Mockingbirds can be quite fierce in defending a berry bush or fruit tree, both from other mockingbirds and from other species. They will harass Cedar Waxwings, American Robins, and European Starlings even when no fruit is in contention, showing that they can recognize potential as well as actual thievery. Although there is a report of a mockingbird killing a waxwing, most competitors are simply driven off. However, a mockingbird can only handle one or two invaders at a time, and a flock of fruit robbers can easily overwhelm its defenses. Occasionally such invading flocks consist of other mockingbirds—gangs of first-year birds that have not yet set up their own territories.

If an overly enthusiastic mockingbird is keeping other birds away from your feeders, try moving the feeder away from any fruit sources that may be the real focus of defense; or put out a separate feeder for the mockeringbird with raisins, fresh fruit, or other foods of the types it prefers.

Key references: Derrickson 1987,. 1988, Derrickson and Breitwisch 1992, Doughty 1988, Hailman 1960, Hedrick and Woody 1983, Logan 1987, Merritt 1980, Moore 1977, 1978, Roth 1979, Stewart 1980.

FeederWatch Findings

Northern Mockingbirds visit about half of feeders within their core winter range, nearly twice as many of them urban and suburban feeders as rural ones. Most feeders are visited in the coldest months, though about a quarter of sites have mockingbirds as winter-long visitors. Usually only one bird is reported at a time. Mockingbirds are common in west Texas; gaps on maps result from low FeederWatch coverage there.

Favorite feeder foods: *Peanut butter mixes, fresh and dried fruit,* bird puddings, water.

Infrequent choices: Mixed seed, sunflower (all types), hulled peanuts, pet food, suet, baked goods, sugar water.

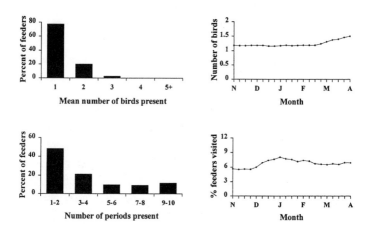

Northern Mockingbird: percent of feeders visited

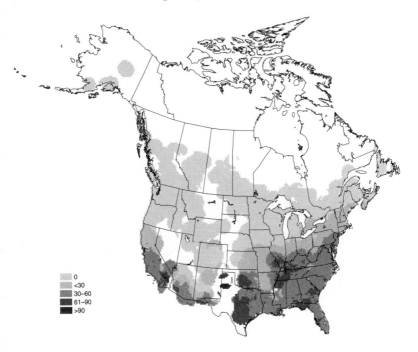

0
<30
30–60
61–90
>90

Abundance at feeders

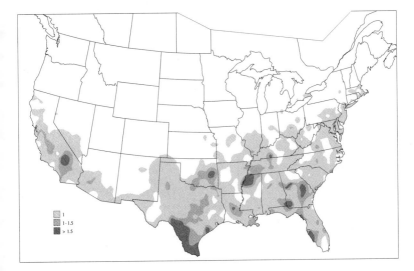

1
1 - 1.5
> 1.5

Brown Thrasher

Toxostoma rufum

The large Brown Thrasher is conspicuous when out in the open, with its bright rufous plumage and long tail. But as it does most of its foraging under cover of dense brush, it is frequently heard more readily than seen.

The territorial songs of Brown Thrashers are easy to recognize and are a delight to most listeners. Short phrases are often repeated a time or two before being dropped for another phrase, and the cadence is reminiscent of human conversation. The repertoire of this thrasher includes over 1,100 song types and is one of the largest of any North American songbird; in fact, other bird species' songs are sometimes mimicked (although not nearly as much as by the Northern Mockingbird). In spring a Brown Thrasher may sing for over an hour without repeating a particular phrase, while certain other phrases are repeated often. Sometimes neighboring males countersing; that is, one male sings, then pauses to listen as the other replies, and then the pattern repeats.

Brown Thrashers are largely vegetarian in winter, with fruits and acorns predominating in the diet. A thrasher on a foraging expedition spends 95% of its time on the ground, probing the soil or sweeping aside leaves and other litter with broad sideways swipes of the strong, decurved bill. Any thrasher perched in a tree is more likely to be resting or singing than it is to be looking for food. Like Blue Jays, thrashers may carry nuts away in their beaks for opening elsewhere. Unlike jays, they do not hold a nut down with a foot. Instead the thrashers direct vigorous blows at the loose nuts, which skitter away until pushed far enough into the ground to remain stationary for final opening.

Following fall migration, Brown Thrashers set up winter territories in dense scrub along rivers and old fields. Many squabbles occur among neighbors in early winter, with each ruckus stimulating a short chorus of singing by neighboring males. Later in the winter this subsides to ten or fifteen minutes of singing at dawn and dusk. Of thrashers marked with leg bands in winter in Texas, about one-third returned to the same territory the following winter, suggesting some site fidelity. Many of the nonreturnees probably died, but some may simply have moved. Brown Thrashers are relatively long-lived, with one bird known to have reached its twelfth birthday.

At the turn of the century, thrashers were considered rare visitors to feeders. A process of acclimation must have taken place since then, because thrashers are now regular visitors to feeders and birdbaths, especially in the South. The species is wary, however, and proximity to dense cover may be the most important feature for attracting thrashers to your feeders.

Thrashers that do visit feeders may display an aggressive nature, lunging at other birds to drive them off. However, thrashers feed mainly on the ground and in low numbers, so displaced species can usually find a spot nearby to feed in peace.

Key references: Boughey and Thompson 1981, Fischer 1981a,b, Kroodsma and Parker 1977.

FeederWatch Findings

Most feeders report one to two Brown Thrashers visiting at a time. Thrashers are fairly predictable visitors all season in the wintering areas, but many feeder owners elsewhere see them only on spring migration.

Favorite feeder foods: Mixed seed, bird puddings, and (according to small samples), millet.

Infrequent choices: Black-oil sunflower, cracked corn, water. Small samples suggest occasional selection of hulled sunflower, milo, wheat, suet, peanut butter mixes, baked goods, and whole corn.

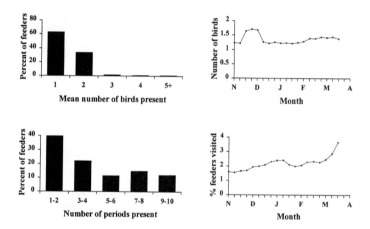

Brown Thrasher: percent of feeders visited

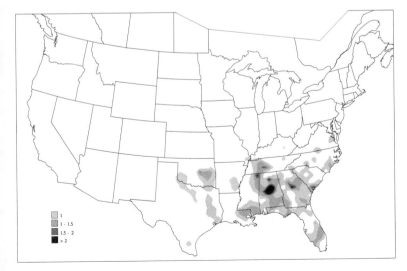

Abundance at feeders

Curve-billed Thrasher

Toxostoma curvirostre

The Curve-billed Thrasher has a much more limited winter range than its eastern cousin, the Brown Thrasher. It is found only in the Southwest, in low elevation open chaparral or in sparsely vegetated desert regions and especially in saguaro–polo verde habitat. Human development is tolerated as long as there is suitable native vegetation present, but habitat loss is thought to have contributed to population decline in this species.

A Curve-billed Thrasher looking for a meal strides or hops rapidly along the ground, stopping occasionally to peer downward or pick up a food item. It spends a lot of time digging—bracing woodpeckerlike on its tail and legs, pounding vigorously at the ground, and tossing aside soil and litter as it excavates holes up to several inches deep. This versatile forager will also climb about in trees and shrubbery in search of berries. If startled, it will fly directly to cover, skimming closely along the ground.

Beetles and other arthropods are among the favorite items a Curve-bill can dig up, with snails and isopods coming close behind.

The diet is rounded out with berries and cactus seeds, and vegetable matter probably makes up a larger proportion of the diet in the winter. Curve-bills will visit feeders for seeds and drinking water (whether in a dish or dripping from a tap) but have also been reported eating suet, bits of watermelon, and mealworms.

Curve-billed Thrashers spend most of their lives within a defended territory, following a youthful dispersal that may take them 20 miles from their natal site. They will leave their territories temporarily to visit nearby feeders, where they usually feed peacefully with other species of the region, such as Inca Doves and House Finches. If accompanied by their dependent young, however, thrashers may turn aggressive, running at foes and jabbing with their formidable beaks. It is possible to see youngsters at winter feeders because breeding (stimulated by rains) sometimes begins as early as February.

Curve-billed Thrashers have, in fact, less of a curl in their beaks than some other thrasher species. A more apt name might be Cactus Thrasher, as these birds often use the densely spined cholla cactus for nesting or winter roosting. Their nests are bulky and easily visible, but the surrounding cactus spines help protect them from predators. (Nests are nonetheless vulnerable to lizards, snakes, and ants—which we do not think of as predators, but can sometimes kill nestlings.) The downside of this close association with cholla cacti is that thrasher young are sometimes themselves impaled. Moreover, these cacti provide little of the shade that contributes to nest success in a hot climate.

In winter a thrasher (or pair) may sleep on a roost "nest," which is really just a broad platform. The roost platform may later be built into a proper nest for the breeding season, and a good site gets used over and over again.

Cactus Wrens also like to nest in cholla cactus, and during the breeding season both thrashers and wrens defend their nests vigorously against the other. Both species also maintain year-round territories, and Cactus Wrens, too, build winter roost nests. But whereas Cactus Wrens relax their defensive vigilance in winter, Curve-billed Thrashers do not and often destroy Cactus Wren roost nests during that season.

Key references: Anderson and Anderson 1973, Dennis 1991, Fischer 1980, 1981a,b, Tweit 1996.

FeederWatch Findings

In contrast to Brown Thrashers, Curve-billed Thrashers are winter-long feeder visitors at nearly three-quarters of the sites where they occur. They visit slightly more suburban than rural or urban feeders. Although these territorial residents visit feeders mainly alone or in pairs, it is not uncommon for an additional bird or two to join them.

Favorite feeder foods: Small samples suggest that the foods taken most regularly are *mixed seed,* cracked corn, suet, and bird puddings.

Infrequent choices: Small samples note acceptance of millet, striped sunflower, milo, and water.

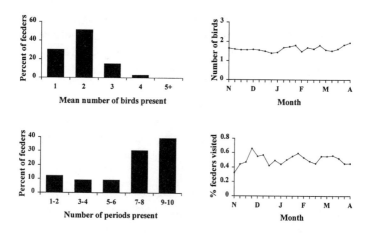

Curve-billed Thrasher: percent of feeders visited

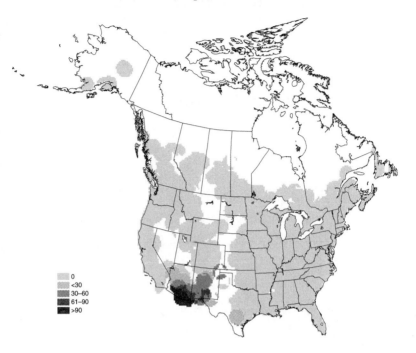

Abundance at feeders

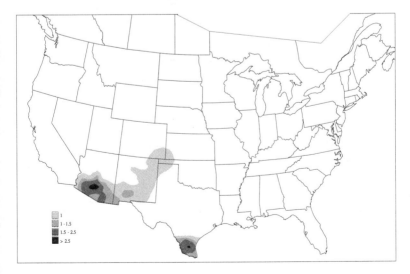

European Starling

Sturnus vulgaris

Euuropean Starlings arrived as immigrants to North America in 1890 and are now among our most abundant birds from coast to coast. They are the rowdies of bird feeders, often descending in screeching, bickering groups, jabbing at suet and gobbling food as fast as possible. This discordance with human views on table manners makes starlings almost universally unpopular at feeders. On the upside, starlings are only casual visitors as long as seeds are the main offering (as opposed to suet or kitchen scraps), and they are readily scared off by a minor disturbance. Fruit is also a strong attractant—not surprisingly, since fruit makes up nearly 70% of the natural winter diet—but few people offer it in their feeders. Given that starlings eat almost anything, it might be hard to believe that they have discriminating tastes, but experiments have shown that they can distinguish quite subtle differences in concentrations of some salts, sugars, citric acid, and tannin.

As well as eating fruit in winter, European Starlings glean insects and invertebrates from short vegetation in open areas—especially well-tended lawns. There you can watch them poking their beaks into the ground, opening wide to spread the soil and then picking out exposed larvae and earthworms.

Young starlings often migrate several hundred miles, as do a proportion of the adults, especially from cold regions. Whether resident or migrant, an individual may cover a fair bit of ground over the course of a winter because it has no specific territory. Starlings fly daily from roosts to foraging areas in fields or farms, usually in flocks of 70 to 150, often mixing with blackbirds, House Sparrows, or pigeons. They return to the same good feeding sites day after day and can cause considerable agricultural damage as a result. Starlings preferring to overwinter in residential areas and cities also key into centers of food abundance: The number of starlings present is a good indicator of the amount of food available.

Foraging ceases in late afternoon when starlings begin to gather into winter roosts of several thousands—or tens of thousands—of birds. Dominant males occupy the center of roosting flocks, where they are most protected from the weather and predators. Starlings show relatively little fidelity to roost site, as up to a third of the birds present each night can be different from the night before. Roosting behavior may differ in cities, where starlings use many man-made sites for roosting, often sleeping alone rather than in flocks and taking advantage of the warmth from chimneys or streetlamps.

Starlings sometimes roost with blackbirds and grackles in wood lots, and some of these mixed assemblages grow to over a million individuals. Because all these species can be agricultural pests in the breeding season, it can be tempting to practice population control while the birds are so conveniently concentrated. However, research has shown that each roost contains a few individuals from many different breeding populations, so control measures at a given winter roost would have relatively little impact on future bird numbers at any one breeding site.

Key references: Bailey 1966, Cabe 1993, Caccamise et al. 1983, Dolbeer 1982, Dolbeer et al. 1978, Francis 1976, Heisterberg et al. 1984, Johnsen and Van Druff 1987, Kessel 1953, Levey and Karasov 1989, Moore 1977, Peach and Fowler 1989, Summers et al. 1987, Williamson and Gray 1975.

FeederWatch Findings

The European Starling is a very widespread feeder species, and gaps in the distribution maps results from lack of FeederWatch data rather than lack of birds. The species is recorded at the highest proportion of feeders through midlatitudes of the United States, where it is also most abundant. Its visits to feeders may be sporadic or regular, probably depending on whether its favored foods are present. Number of feeders visited more than doubles from fall to midwinter, then remains high; but number of birds present at one time declines steadily.

Favorite feeder foods: *Suet, bird puddings,* mixed seed, cracked corn, hulled peanuts and hearts, pet food, peanut butter mixes, baked goods, water.

Infrequent choices: Millet, canary seed, sunflower (any type), whole corn, milo, wheat, peanuts in shell, fresh or dried fruit, meat scraps, sugar water, popped corn, and (according to small samples) oats.

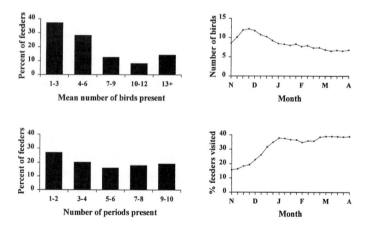

European Starling: percent of feeders visited

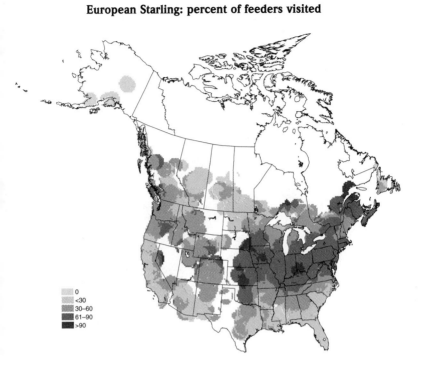

0
<30
30–60
61–90
>90

Abundance at feeders

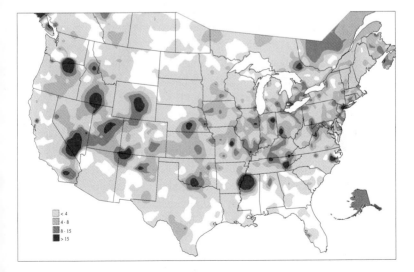

< 4
4 - 8
8 - 15
> 15

Bohemian Waxwing

Bombycilla garrulus

Bohemian Waxwings are unusually peaceful birds. Their large winter flocks seem free of the jostling for hierarchical status that occurs whenever chickadees or sparrows get together. Bohemian Waxwing flocks are relatively quiet, too. The soft notes are similar to the thin, high-pitched calls of Cedar Waxwings (often one of the first birdsongs that aging bird-watchers can no longer hear), although Bohemians call at a somewhat lower pitch. The characteristics of this species inspired one writer to call Bohemian Waxwings "gentlemen in feathers" because they are handsomely dressed, are not harsh or boisterous, and do not shout.

These waxwings nonetheless have some habits that humans might consider less than polite, including a notorious gluttony. Bohemians subsist mainly on fruit, and can eat two or three times their weight in berries every day. Between bouts of feeding, the birds sit almost comatose for twenty to thirty minutes, apparently working hard on digestion (and producing much physical evidence thereof). Regurgitated seeds are another by-product of waxwing digestion. In spring the Bohemians feed also on flowers, tree sap, and midges or mosquitoes. Tree bark is sometimes consumed, perhaps for roughage, as are mineral sources, such as dirt, chalk, and bits of white-washed walls. The latter choices are reminiscent of the mineral cravings of certain tree-seed-eating finches and may reflect a lack of some essential minerals in the regular diet. Like other fruit-eating birds, the Bohemian Waxwing takes in a lot of water, either as liquid or snow. Both Bohemian and Cedar Waxwings have been reported catching falling snowflakes.

Bohemian and Cedar Waxwings share many adaptations for their specialized diet, and the main physical difference between the two species is that Bohemians are larger. Both species have slightly hooked and notched bills, and the wing is pointed but also broad, aiding in hovering and sallying during foraging. Internally, the intestine is relatively short (typical of fruit eaters), and an especially large liver helps in converting sugar to energy, which is then stored as glycogen. These and other digestive adaptations allow waxwings to survive on a pure fruit diet if necessary, whereas most other songbirds will die unless they can supplement fruit with other foods.

Bohemian Waxwings occasionally make large-scale, irregular emigrations far beyond their normal winter range, most likely in response to widespread failure of berry crops. Wandering flocks may reach several hundred birds but generally are smaller than flocks of Cedar Waxwings. Although Bohemians commonly visit human-populated areas, they have not been well studied—which seems surprising given that they are such striking birds.

Most studies of winter flocking in birds have found that this behavior helps birds find patchily distributed food and protects them from predators. In waxwings there may be an additional benefit: Flocks have the potential to overwhelm territorial birds that are trying to defend fruit sources for themselves. A lone American Robin can hold off fifteen waxwings, and a Northern Mockingbird was seen to kill one in the vigor of its territorial defense; but in the face of large waxwing flocks, such territorial defense collapses.

Key references: Berthold 1976, Brewer and Drewiskie 1980, Cramp 1988, Goodwin 1905, Hedrick and Woody 1983, Pietz and Pietz 1987, Pulliainen 1985.

FeederWatch Findings

The erratically wandering Bohemian Waxwing is a species that rarely comes to feeders to take food, even when large numbers are present in a yard, because most people do not provide the fruit that these birds like to eat. The mapped distribution includes a year when Bohemians invaded the East; often they are limited to areas west of the Mississippi. Numbers of Bohemian Waxwings seen at one time at feeders are highly variable, from one or a few individuals to flocks of more than fifty.

Favorite feeder foods: Small samples indicate that fruits are the only real attractant. Some feeder owners collect fruit from the trees in which waxwings forage, freeze them, and then offer them in feeders later in the winter.

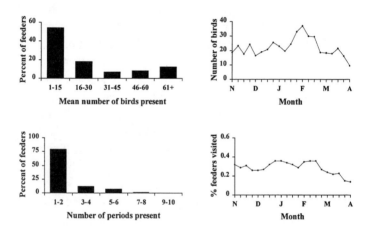

Bohemian Waxwing: percent of feeders visited

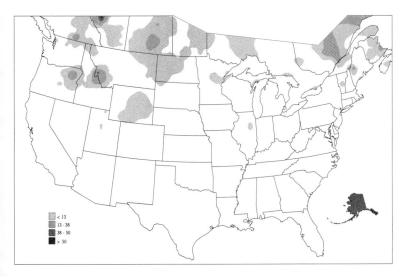

Abundance at feeders

235

Cedar Waxwing

Bombycilla cedrorum

Cedar Waxwings are among the most fruit-dependent of all North American birds. Even in the breeding season, when most species feed predominantly on insects, waxwings are still largely frugivorous, and the winter diet is 99% fruit (of which half is made up of juniper berries). Fruit abundance varies widely in time and space, however, perhaps explaining why Cedar Waxwings have low fidelity to breeding sites between years and why winter flocks are so nomadic. These flocks sometimes number in the thousands but are in fact extremely variable; one study in New York showed that half of them fell in the range of ten to seventy individuals.

The name "waxwing" refers to the shiny, droplet-shaped structures at the ends of the inner wing feathers, where red pigment is concentrated and covered with a clear cuticle. The waxy tips are normally grown only after birds are at least fourteen months old. Cedar Waxwings with red feather tips prefer to mate with others that are similarly endowed and perhaps use the red ornaments to identify more experienced birds—which nest earlier and more successfully than younger ones. Pairing takes place during the winter months when the waxwings are living in flocks, and courtship includes some unusual group displays—such as passing a berry from beak to beak along a row of perching birds.

Many North American fruiting plants depend on waxwings and other fruit-eating birds to disperse their seeds, and they have a variety of ingenious strategies to ensure that their berries get eaten. Some produce fruits that are relatively high in fat, which are avidly consumed by many frugivores during fall migration. However, waxwings have digestive specializations for high-sugar fruits and tend to avoid those that are high in fat. Low-fat fruits are not as attractive to other species but have better keeping qualities, thus providing a source of waxwing food all winter. Some of the lowest fat fruits of all (including apples) are ignored all winter but remain well preserved and finally get eaten by birds moving northward in spring.

Because seeds are generally destroyed when eaten by mammals, plants that are dependent on birds for seed dispersal try to repel seed predators. This seems to be the function of capsaicin, which puts the heat into hot peppers. Fruits loaded with this chemical compound are distasteful to mammals—but are consumed quite happily by Cedar Waxwings. The seeds pass unharmed through the avian digestive system and are often deposited far from the parent plant.

Once berries have been depleted in spring, waxwings eat the flowers of such trees as elm or maple, probably getting a shot of protein from the flower stamens. The waxwings also eat sap when a source can be found. Given their liking for sweets, it is perhaps surprising that waxwings are not regular visitors to hummingbirds' feeders. The reason may be that hummingbird syrups are made of sucrose (table sugar), which lab studies show to be poorly digested by waxwings. They prefer the glucose and fructose that are most commonly found in the fruits of those very plants that depend on birds to disperse their seeds. Interestingly, fruits cultivated for human consumption are often high in sucrose content, and this may help to reduce bird depredations.

Before there were extensive plantings of ornamental fruiting trees, waxwings relied heavily on cedar berries for their winter supplies (hence their name). Human alteration of the landscape has caused changes in the winter ranges of waxwings and probably has played a role in their increased abundance.

Most of the Cedar Waxwings that visit backyards are attracted primarily by fruiting shrubs and trees or by water for drinking or bathing, but sometimes they can be enticed to feeders if you put out native fruits that the waxwings are already eating. Once a flock starts visiting a feeder, watch out. Whole scoopfuls of raisins or apple slices may disappear within a few minutes.

Key references: Clark 1991, Martinez del Rio et al. 1989, Mountjoy and Robertson 1988, Muzny 1982, Norman et al. 1992, Stiles 1984, Stoner 1976, Witmer 1996, Witmer et al. 1997.

FeederWatch Findings

Cedar Waxwings, like Bohemians, only rarely come to feeders and are recorded on feeder counts primarily because they are attracted to yards by fruiting trees and shrubs. They are more widespread than Bohemians, however, and are reported at small numbers of feeders in a large number of states. Flock sizes vary widely, but the largest flocks are seen in urban areas, perhaps because more exotic fruiting trees are planted there.

Favorite feeder "food": water.

Infrequent choices: Small samples indicate that dried and fresh fruit will sometimes be accepted.

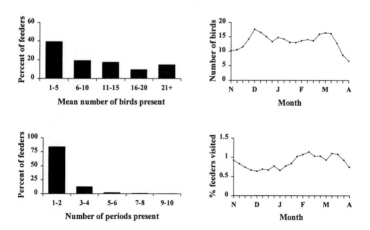

Cedar Waxwing: percent of feeders visited

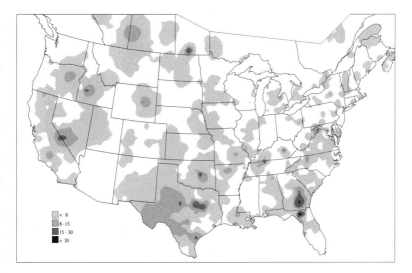

Abundance at feeders

239

Yellow-rumped Warbler

Dendroica coronata

Most North American wood warblers spend the winter in Central or South America, so the fact that many Yellow-rumped Warblers go no farther than the southeastern United States makes them unusual. They migrate quite late in the fall and are evidently flexible in where they decide to stop, moving farther south if weather deteriorates. Judicious choosing of protected roost sites probably helps them cope with cold. Occasionally a large flock will roost together, but more often individuals sleep alone. One enterprising Yellow-rump escaped a cold night in Arizona by fluttering against a glass door through which it could see a Christmas tree. When the homeowners opened the door, the bird flew in to roost in the tree until let out again the following morning. (It came back the next night, too!)

One of the key factors allowing the Yellow-rumped Warbler to winter in the United States is its ability to feed on the fruits of bayberry and wax myrtle (the origin of the old name, Myrtle Warbler). These berries have coatings that are rich in fat but also in waxes that few bird species can digest. Because Yellow-rumps have special digestive enzymes to cope with these waxes, they can utilize the food source relatively free from competition. An intake of about two hundred bayberries would be required to fill a Yellow-rump's energy needs for a typical winter's day if berries were the sole food eaten. However, other nutrients are also needed to maintain good health, and these are obtained primarily from insects and perhaps from other fruits that the warbler eats, such as cedar, poison ivy, and sumac.

Yellow-rumps use more generalized techniques for catching insects than do many other warblers, which may be another characteristic that contributes to their ability to winter so far north. They glean insects from the lower parts of trees, hawk occasionally for flying insects, work over decaying logs, and pick up foodstuffs from the ground. Often they forage in leaf litter underneath bayberry bushes. Feeding flocks of up to ten Yellow-rumps move through an area fairly rapidly, probing the vegetation only briefly before moving on to a new site.

Yellow-rumps often mix with other species in winter, a habit that is especially frequent in northern parts of the range. Sometimes chickadees are the leaders and warblers are the followers, but about half the time the reverse is true. There is little aggression among the species in a mixed flock, although squabbles begin to arise among the warblers themselves once spring approaches.

Occasionally a migrating or wintering Yellow-rump will try to defend a food supply, such as a berry bush or a source of insects, against all comers. Seeds are not likely to be defended, and a warbler can rarely defend a bird feeder, anyway, so it will usually give up and let others visit feeders in peace. In accordance with their generalized foraging styles and diet, Yellow-rumps will visit all designs of feeders and try out a variety of foods.

Key references: Anonymous 1978, Kilham 1961, MacArthur 1958, Morse 1970, Place and Stiles 1992, Terrill and Ohmart 1984, Wilz and Giampa 1978, Woolfenden 1962, Yarbrough and Johnston 1965.

FeederWatch Findings

Although the Yellow-rumped Warbler is an irregular visitor at most feeders where it occurs at all, close to 10% of sites host it all season long. It visits solo about as often as in small groups (with the latter more common in midwinter). Yellow-rumps are less likely to visit rural feeders, perhaps because rural sites offer more natural habitats in competition. The gap in West Texas (see maps) results from low FeederWatch coverage there. Records in the central United States, where Yellow-rumps neither breed nor overwinter, are of migrating birds.

Favorite feeder foods: Suet, bird puddings, water. Small samples indicate a preference also for peanut hearts, peanut butter mixes, and fresh fruit.

Infrequent choices: Black-oil sunflower, sugar water, and (according to small samples) baked goods.

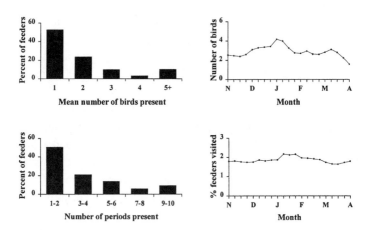

Yellow-rumped Warbler: percent of feeders visited

0
<30
30–60
61–90
>90

Abundance at feeders

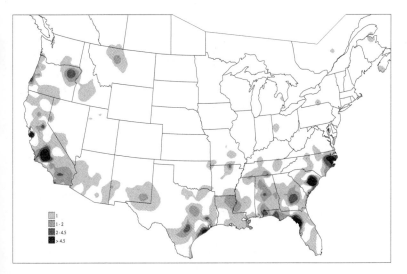

1
1 - 2
2 - 4.5
> 4.5

Pine Warbler

Dendroica pinus

Trues to its name, the Pine Warbler is nearly always found in conifers. Some people call it the Pine "Creeping" Warbler because of the way it inches along limbs and trunks as it forages, reminiscent of a nuthatch. This is one of the few warblers that winters throughout much of the southeastern United States, and the association with pine woodlands or plantations—and the food the pines provide—may be one of the features that makes its relatively northern distribution possible.

A wholly insectivorous warbler on migration eats well over its own weight in larvae every day, but such a cornucopia of caterpillars is simply not available to a Pine Warbler on its wintering range. One way of coping is to consume pine seeds, which Pine Warblers wedge into bark crevices before pecking them open (somewhat inefficiently) with their delicate bills. Given this component of the diet, it is not surprising that Pine Warblers visiting feeders will eat broken sunflower seeds and peanuts as well as the suet crumbs that are attractive to more insectivorous species. The Pine Warbler also feeds on a wide variety of fruits, including poison ivy, bayberry, sumac, dogwood, wild grape, and virginia creeper, although the quantities taken do not approach the intake of Yellow-rumped Warblers.

The behavior of Pine Warblers in winter appears to vary from fairly solitary to quite sociable. These birds do not defend specific territories, but they do sing all winter (a sign of assertive behavior) and do not wander far from a particular home district. They are occasionally quite aggressive toward their own species and other birds, such as Yellow-rumped Warblers and Brown-headed Nuthatches, and they normally appear at feeders only one or two at a time. Nevertheless, Pine-Warblers can frequently be found gathered in larger numbers, especially when mixed with other species in integrated foraging flocks. Common companions include Brown-headed Nuthatches, another species of the southern pine woods, as well as Carolina Chickadees, Tufted Titmice, Chipping Sparrows, bluebirds, creepers, other warblers, and kinglets. A half-dozen or so Pine Warblers may join such flocks and go about their business relatively quietly, flaking off bits of bark, hawking for insects, and poking about on the ground.

Beginning birders sometimes believe that they have large flocks of Pine Warblers as regular guests at their feeders. While it is true that as many as ten Pine Warblers may visit all at once, large flocks are much more likely to be American Goldfinches in their dull-green winter plumage. This mistake is encouraged by wide distribution of Christmas cards depicting bright yellow goldfinches on snow-covered trees—a combination that rarely occurs in nature because goldfinches do not acquire yellow plumage until spring.

Key references: Graber and Graber 1983b, Griscom and Sprunt 1979, Morse 1967a, 1989, Nesbitt and Hetrick 1976, Place and Stiles 1992, White et al. 1996.

FeederWatch Findings

Pine Warblers are much more likely to come to feeders in the coldest part of the winter than in the fall or spring. Accordingly, few sites report regular sightings throughout the winter. Pine Warblers usually visit in ones or twos but occasionally in larger groups.

Favorite feeder foods: *Bird puddings*, suet, and (based on small samples) peanut butter mixes.

Infrequent choices: Mixed seed, cracked corn and black-oil sunflower (both probably eaten only if in small bits), water. Small samples show the occasional choice also of striped and hulled sunflower and baked goods.

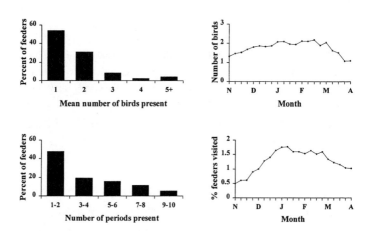

Pine Warbler: percent of feeders visited

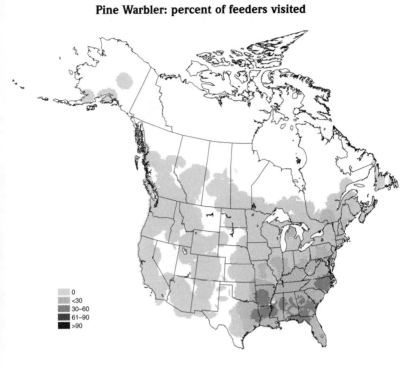

0
<30
30–60
61–90
>90

Abundance at feeders

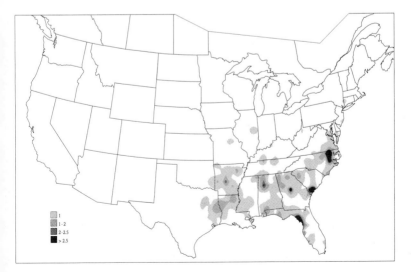

1
1-2
2-2.5
> 2.5

Eastern Towhee and Spotted Towhee

Pipilo erythrophthalmus and P. maculatus

Formerly known collectively as Rufous-sided Towhees, the Eastern and Spotted Towhees have recently been split into separate species. Breeding range of the two species is largely separate—Spotted Towhees in the West and Easterns, not surprisingly, in the East—but because winter ranges overlap in Texas and Oklahoma, we are unable to separate data collected prior to the split. We therefore treat both species together here.

Big birds are usually the bosses at feeders, forcing smaller species to give way; but "rufous-sided" towhees are an exception. These relatively large but shy skulkers rush for cover at the smallest disturbance. Once a towhee screws up enough courage to dash out to a feeder, it will often grab a single seed, then hurry back to a less exposed spot before dining. Some individuals are a little bolder, especially in autumn and when several towhees are present together—

but only if there is protective cover nearby. So accustomed are they to foraging under cover that towhees may be quite lacking in vigilance when in the open, as if they have forgotten where they are.

These towhees have a hop-and-scratch foraging style: Jumping forward, head and tail up, a towhee kicks its long legs backward, propelling leaf litter up to a yard behind. So vigorous is this movement that a second hop may be required to recover balance. After a few scratches the towhee stops to feed on any small invertebrates or seeds it has turned up, but research has shown that the amount of scratching before stopping to look for food increases if food-finding success is low. Towhees seldom pick up food without scratching first, even at feeders where seeds are clearly visible, and seeds may be sent flying in all directions before a bird pauses to eat. In fall and winter the foods eaten are mainly vegetable, including seeds of weeds and grasses, grains, fruits, and fallen acorns. Probably most of the acorns that towhees eat are damaged or broken, as these birds are not well constructed for breaking open whole nuts.

The Eastern Towhee has many common names, some of which refer to its foraging habits, such as "Ground Robin," or "Low-ground Stephen." Other names describe the bird's call notes: "Chewink" or "Jeroo," for example. In oak-hickory woodland or pine barrens where this species breeds, the call notes are as diagnostic as the distinctive *drink-your-tea* song. As the number of common names implies, these birds were once familiar to rural dwellers. In recent years, however, they have become much less well-known to the general public. Partly this reflects our more urbanized lifestyle, but towhees have also been declining steadily in abundance on a continent-wide basis, along with several other bird species that rely on scrub and thicket habitats.

Towhees from northern parts of the breeding range migrate to areas where there are year-round residents, either mixing with local towhees or joining separate winter flocks. A study in Kentucky showed that migrant Eastern Towhees formed stable winter flocks of eight to twenty-seven birds that roamed about within a certain home range, and these flocks consisted largely of males. This suggests that females migrate farther south than males, which is fairly common in migratory species. Towhees that do not migrate apparently also wander in winter and perhaps flock with other towhees, instead of maintaining winter territories. Towhees of both species mix readily in winter with other flocking species.

Key references: Bent 1968, Burtt and Hailman 1979, Davis 1957, Greenlaw 1996a,b.

FeederWatch Findings

Both Eastern and Spotted Towhees visit three-quarters of feeders in the core areas of their winter range. Towhees tend to visit feeders either very occasionally or week after week, with no middle ground. The likelihood of visitation is higher in the suburbs than elsewhere. Spotted Towhees appear at feeders in fairly stable numbers, but Eastern Towhees are twice as likely to visit during spring migration as in fall.

Frequent feeder foods: Mixed seed, millet.

Infrequent choices: Sunflower (any type), cracked corn, suet, peanut butter, bird puddings, water, and (based on small samples) canary seed, milo, and wheat.

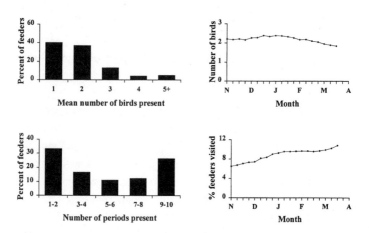

Eastern and Spotted Towhee: percent of feeders visited

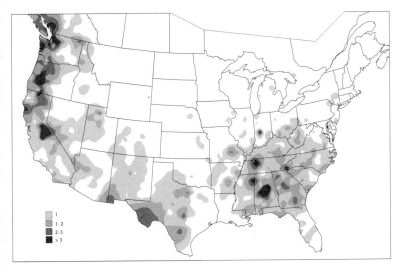

Abundance at feeders

Canyon Towhee

Pipilo fuscus

Canyon Towhees differ in several respects from the California Towhees with which they were formerly combined as a single species. One obvious distinguishing mark is a dark "stickpin" dot in the center of the chest, and there are clear differences in song. Canyon Towhees inhabit oak or pinyon woodland mixed with juniper, or sometimes cottonwood riparian lands within mesquite habitat, whereas Californias prefer chaparral. Finally, Canyon Towhees are more the "country cousin" when it comes to behavior, usually feeding under cover or within a few yards of shrubbery (although some individuals are much bolder).

Canyon Towhees stay at home year-round, maintaining territories centered about 1,000 feet apart. Some territory holders are paired, others are alone, and a few nonterritorial birds move about in small flocks that encroach from time to time on the territories of others. Few disputes result as long as it is winter, but territorial defense increases as spring approaches. Canyon Towhees then become so aggressive that they may attack their own reflections in windows. Singing also increases greatly in spring, whereas in winter most calling is done as the birds fly to roost.

Because Canyon Towhees pair for life, it is probable that single birds observed in winter are youngsters or adults whose mates have died. Paired birds are rarely separated, starting to call more frequently as the distance between them increases. During the mating season, this close association prevents any strange males from getting near the female during her fertile period.

Although Canyon Towhees live in treed habitat and like to be near cover, they spend most of their time foraging on the ground in fairly open areas: along roadsides, on bare ground, in plowed fields, or under bushes and weeds. With a thrushlike series of short runs and stops, the towhee searches for seeds, small invertebrates, and fallen fruit. Most food is simply picked off the ground surface, but about a third of the time the bird scratches to uncover foodstuffs in leaf litter. Only rarely will these towhees reach into overhead vegetation for seeds, buds, or insects.

Individual towhees may become fairly tame at feeders, although most are quite timid and retreat when other species arrive, or fly immediately to cover when startled. They will occasionally patronize platform feeders instead of feeding exclusively on the ground. The most preferred seeds are only slightly larger than those eaten by sparrows, even though the towhee is considerably larger bodied. Canyon Towhees are among the many feeder visitors that also appreciate water.

Given the fact that this species appears shy, it is surprising that Canyon Towhees regularly attack and supplant a wide variety of species encountered at feeders—from California Quail to doves, wrens, Pyrrhuloxia, and a variety of sparrows. Perhaps these "attacks" are really only a reflection of a food-finding strategy. When feeding with other birds, a Canyon Towhee tends to forage at the edge of flocks, then suddenly rushes to the center to spend a short time checking out the foods there—scattering other birds as it goes.

Key references: Bent 1968, Johnson and Haight 1996, Marshall 1960, Pulliam and Mills 1977.

FeederWatch Findings

Canyon Towhees visit feeders faithfully throughout the winter and normally come in pairs. Abundance is slightly higher at rural feeders, even though a higher proportion of feeders is visited in suburban areas.

Favorite feeder foods: *Mixed seed,* millet, striped sunflower, cracked corn, water, and probably (according to small samples) peanut butter mixes.

Infrequent choices: Black-oil sunflower, suet, bird puddings. Small samples also show an occasional choice of hulled sunflower, canary seed, peanut hearts, and fresh fruit.

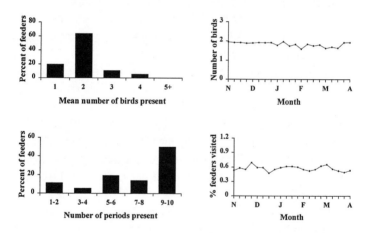

Canyon Towhee: percent of feeders visited

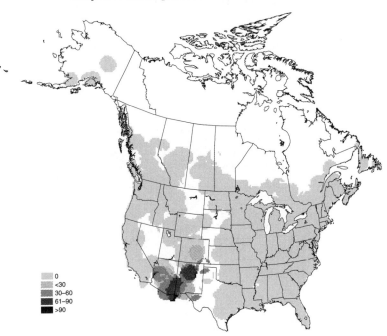

0
<30
30–60
61–90
>90

Abundance at feeders

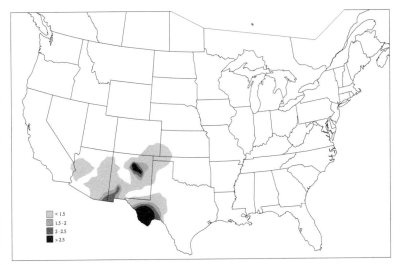

< 1.5
1.5 - 2
2 - 2.5
> 2.5

California Towhee

Pipilo crissalis

"Little brown job" is a birders' term that is apt enough for describing the California Towhee's looks—but this bird's nature is far from bland. It is quite a bold species that will venture onto suburban lawns, explore picnic areas, and chase smaller birds away from feeders. Indeed, a relatively bold nature is one of the features that distinguishes the California Towhee from the closely related Canyon Towhee, with which it was formerly combined as a single species ("Brown Towhee").

The California Towhee is also more adventurous than the rather retiring Spotted Towhee. The latter species hops about, scratching vigorously, and hastens to a sheltered spot with food items before eating them. The California Towhee would rather run than hop, usually picks up food only if it is already visible, and is happy to dine on the spot wherever food happens to be. Occasionally it will scratch like a Spotted Towhee, with a double-footed backward kick, but such scratchings are rather feeble and infrequent.

There are signs that California Towhees are not only bold but downright cheeky. One gardener related planting seeds in spring as California Towhees looked on, and fearing pilferage he carefully smoothed over the soil to disguise the planting sites—but as soon as he moved off, the towhees moved in and immediately dug up every one.

The winter home of the California Towhee is the same as its summer home: a few acres of brush or chaparral along the Pacific Coast, often including some suburban areas. Mates stick close together throughout the year. Indeed, if the male and female become separated by as little as 20 feet, they start to call and move closer together again. Territorial defense is relaxed in winter, with the towhees merely chasing intruders away and singing infrequently. They will even abandon their territories temporarily and mix peacefully with flocks of various sparrow species.

Towhees are almost completely vegetarian in winter, eating grain, weed seeds, and grass seeds. At feeders these ground foragers eat seeds in the main, but this is partly because seeds are usually the only food available on the ground. If you also scatter crumbs of suet or bits of dried fruit, these birds are likely to be among the takers.

Key references: Bent 1968, Davis 1957, Leach 1927.

FeederWatch Findings

California Towhees are virtually identical to Canyon Towhees in their patterns at feeders. Both are faithful visitors through most of the winter and visit the majority of feeders within their core range (most often as pairs). They are more likely to visit feeders in suburban areas, but the numbers seen at one time are slightly higher at rural sites. California Towhees visit over two-thirds of feeders in their namesake state.

Favorite feeder foods: According to small samples, *mixed seed*, millet, milo, and water.

Infrequent choices: Small samples indicate sampling of black-oil sunflower, cracked corn, suet, and peanut butter mixes.

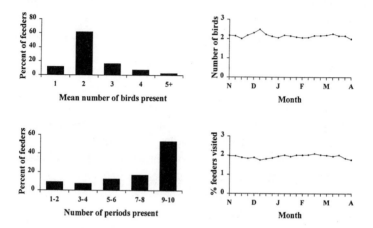

California Towhee: percent of feeders visited

Abundance at feeders

American Tree Sparrow

Spizella arborea

Amerrican Tree Sparrows are relatively uncommon visitors at feeders. Flocks prefer to forage in fields and pasture with few shrubs or trees, belying the species' name. They are "bad-weather birds" that usually ignore feeders unless the weather turns severely cold or stormy.

As major consumers of weed seeds, American Tree Sparrows can be regarded as farmers' friends. One study in Iowa estimated that these sparrows remove 875 tons of such seeds from the state annually: about one-half from grasses and one-half from ragweed, lamb's quarters, and other herbaceous weeds. The seeds consumed can be freshly fallen or be leftovers from the previous year. Perhaps as a way of discovering older seeds, the sparrows scratch the ground frequently as they forage, even when plenty of seed is still visible on the surface. American Tree Sparrows spend the winter in regions where snow might be expected to cover food supplies—but seed continues to drop from plants throughout the winter, generating a constant rain of fresh supplies on top of each fall of snow. Moreover, American Tree Sparrows will go after seeds still attached to plants, jumping up to peck at seed heads or landing on them to feed, even hovering next to old flower heads and striking them with the wings to knock seeds off.

At feeders, as in the wild, American Tree Sparrows are generalists and will sample any small seeds that are available. Water is an attractant in dry areas. (In cold regions they eat snow to get needed water.) But the best attractant of all is a weedy garden left untilled until spring, which allows you to be a lazy—and guilt-free—gardener.

Flocks of American Tree Sparrows appear to the casual observer as permanent bands, but studies have shown that individuals move freely from group to group. Loosely constructed flocks move continuously as the birds forage, spending only a few minutes in a spot even though there may still be plenty of food there. After five to ten minutes of feeding, the birds may do other things for fifteen or twenty minutes before starting to look for food again. At night the flocks split up and go to roost individually (although there are reports of several roosting together in a snow cavity when conditions are severe).

American Tree Sparrows cannot go without food for even one winter day because they do not store a lot of fat. This may account for their coming to feeders in bad weather when other, fatter species might instead sit out the storm in shelter. American Tree Sparrows do have capacious crops, however, which allow them to pack in up to a thousand small seeds at one time. They can then retreat to a safe place for leisurely digestion.

This species breeds where the northern forest meets the tundra, so we only see the American Tree Sparrow at feeders during migration and in winter. It is one of the few sparrows wintering in the United States that does not reach as far as the Gulf Coast. Possibly it is avoiding Chipping Sparrows, which winter to their south, but it is not known whether the two species actively exclude each other.

If you live at the southern edge of the winter range of American Tree Sparrows, you are probably hosting more females at your feeder than males, as the females tend to migrate farther. Whatever the mix, the birds you see may return year after year to winter in the same area. In one case the same sparrow returned eight years in a row.

Key references: Brooks 1985, Gaines 1989, Graul 1967, Naugler 1993, Ohmart and Smith 1970, Stuebe and Ketterson 1982, Root 1988.

FeederWatch Findings

American Tree Sparrows are reported at three times as many sites in the coldest part of the winter as in the fall, and in twice the numbers. In keeping with this trend, many feeders only record the species a few times during the winter. Nonetheless, a substantial proportion of feeder sites host American Tree Sparrows on a weekly basis. The likelihood of seeing this species is much lower in cities than in suburbs or rural areas. Usually only a few individuals are attracted at a time, even though wild flocks may be large. The mapped gap in Nebraska and South Dakota is an artifact of poor coverage there; in fact, Nebraska is a center of winter abundance.

Favorite feeder foods: *Mixed seed,* millet, cracked corn.

Infrequent choices: Canary seed, sunflower (any type), niger, peanut butter mixes, baked goods, water.

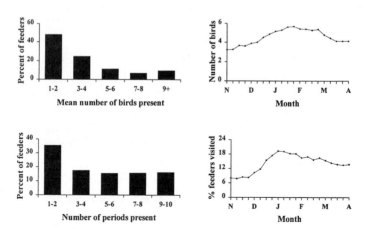

American Tree Sparrow: percent of feeders visited

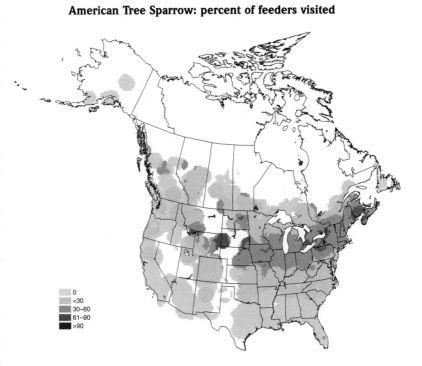

0
<30
30–60
61–90
>90

Abundance at feeders

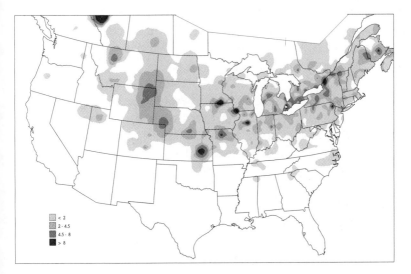

< 2
2 - 4.5
4.5 - 8
> 8

Chipping Sparrow

Spizella passerina

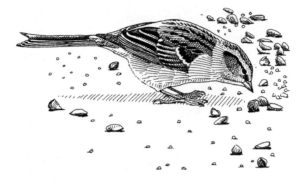

"Chippies" are almost wholly migratory, wintering across a narrow band of the southern United States and in Mexico. Their winter range is conspicuously separate from the more northern one occupied by American Tree Sparrows, with which this bird is often confused by beginning feeder watchers.

On its winter range the Chipping Sparrow prefers areas of pine, oak scrub habitat, or a mix of the two. Chippies are also common in residential areas, where they eat seeds of lawn and garden pest plants, such as crabgrass, ragweed, purslane, and chickweed. This habit, combined with a tame and confiding nature, makes these little sparrows popular backyard visitors.

Winter flocks of up to fifty Chipping Sparrows may perch high in pine trees while resting between feeding bouts; then they fly one by one to field margins below to feed. Eventually all fly up to the trees again before moving on to a new spot. In open areas, flocks often "roll" across a field: Individuals stop to peck or scratch lightly for seeds (usually in a patch smaller than a dinner plate), then fly over the flock to land at the advancing edge for another feeding stop. Often Chippies will be joined by other species in mixed flocks that include bluebirds, cardinals, and warblers as well as other sparrows.

Extensive research on Chipping Sparrows in Arizona has shed light on their frenetic winter survival schedule. Each bird must eat a seed every few seconds, day in and day out, and over the course of a winter, each sparrow probably consumes about 2¼ pounds of seeds. This may not sound like much, but it amounts to 160 times the bird's body weight.

Since each seed requires one to three seconds for husking, Chipping Sparrows concentrate on types that are easy to open. Most of the preferred seeds weigh 1 milligram or less, but the commercial millet offered at feeders weighs about 5 milligrams. How do they manage these? It turns out that millet has a loose husk (probably selected during domestication for easy threshing), which can be removed by a Chipping Sparrow in about one second.

Fortunately for sparrow survival, weed seeds are usually very abundant, and during an average winter in the Arizona studies mentioned above, all sparrow species combined consumed less than a third of the seeds available. However, in poor crop years that follow low rainfall in the previous summer or fall, larger sparrow species also turn to small weed seeds; and in these years as much as 80% of the total crop may be consumed. Populations of all species may decline as a result.

Chipping Sparrows come readily to feeders, but they are not bold when other species are present. Food should be scattered widely to afford them access. Some larger seeds are eaten, including cracked corn, but the sparrows probably only take small, broken pieces.

Key references: Allaire and Fisher 1975, Dunning and Brown 1982, Hebrard 1978, Pulliam 1980, 1985, Pulliam and Dunning 1987.

FeederWatch Findings

The map for Chipping Sparrows probably includes some American Tree Sparrows, with which it is sometimes confused, but northern records may indeed depict Chipping Sparrow migrants seen in spring. The percent of feeders visited rises steeply in this season as migrants head north. Lack of sparrows on the map for West Texas results from poor FeederWatch coverage there; in fact, Chippies are common in that region. Chipping Sparrows often visit feeders alone, but flocks of ten or more are not uncommon, especially at rural sites and in the coldest parts of the winter. They are not season-long visitors at most feeders.

Favorite feeder foods: *Mixed seed,* millet. Small samples suggest that hulled sunflower and canary seed are also favored foods.

Infrequent choices: Black-oil and striped sunflower, cracked corn, niger, suet, bird puddings, water. Small samples indicate occasional choice of milo and popped corn.

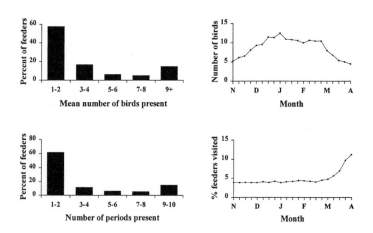

Chipping Sparrow: percent of feeders visited

0
<30
30–60
61–90
>90

Abundance at feeders

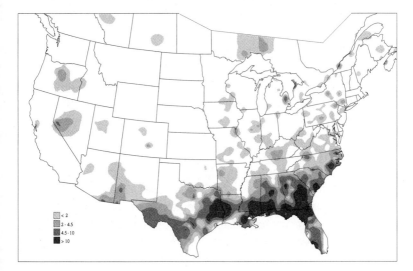

< 2
2 - 4.5
4.5 - 10
> 10

Field Sparrow

Spizella pusilla

The Field Sparrow's white eye ring and pink bill give it a look of innocence, and this is backed up by the bird's general manner. These peaceful sparrows are seldom aggressive to other species or even to each other—at least once the breeding season is over. They may sometimes join other species in winter, including Chipping Sparrows, warblers, cardinals, and bluebirds, but Field Sparrows are more retiring than certain other sparrows and often prefer to keep to themselves.

Field Sparrows suffer from the cold and some may die when temperatures drop below 5°F. They therefore behave as many humans do in winter: They migrate to a warmer climate. Migration empties the breeding range north of an imaginary line extending approximately from Massachusetts to Kansas, while birds from mid-latitude states either move shorter distances or simply stay put. The migrants appear to journey rather slowly, spending several days or even weeks in a given area before moving on. It is not known whether individuals return to the same wintering spot each year.

Field Sparrows do not hold territories in winter but gather into small flocks that are evidently poorly coordinated in their activities. However, there has been very little study of Field Sparrow social behavior, so there may be some structure to the winter flocks of which we are unaware, such as dominance hierarchies. One known feature of flocks is that individuals, regardless of flock size, maintain distances from other birds at least the width of a person's spread hand, and this individual distance becomes larger when a flock visits a high-quality food patch. Even though Field Sparrows prefer to forage near cover, they will move farther into the open if that is required to maintain individual distance. Perhaps this personal spacing is the key to lack of squabbling within flocks.

Field Sparrows might better be named Old Field Sparrows because they prefer abandoned fields overgrown with brush or with a margin of woodland. Their favorite winter foods are the tiny seeds of grasses and weeds that are also eaten by many other small sparrow species. However, Field Sparrows also use somewhat larger seeds that average about the size and weight of millet. They hop along, pecking at visible food on the ground, or perch on bushes while reaching for seeds on adjacent food plants. They will also land on a seed head to bend it to the ground, where feeding can be accomplished more easily.

If Field Sparrows are visiting your feeder, you may be able to attract more by scattering seed widely. Although these birds visit raised feeders on occasion, more often they concentrate on cleaning up spilled and broken seeds on the ground underneath feeders.

Key references: Allaire and Fisher 1975, Carey et al. 1994, Fretwell 1968, Olson and Kendeigh 1980, Pearson 1991.

FeederWatch Findings

The Field Sparrow is not a very common feeder visitor, either in number of sites visited (usually under a fifth of feeders in any state) or frequency of sighting during the winter (usually less than half the winter). Field Sparrows visit more feeders in midwinter and in spring, while abundance declines slightly throughout the winter.

Favorite feeder foods: *Mixed seed,* cracked corn, and probably (according to small samples) millet.

Infrequent choices: Striped and black-oil sunflower, water. Small samples indicate canary seed and milo are also acceptable foods.

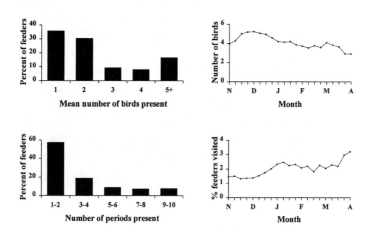

Field Sparrow: percent of feeders visited

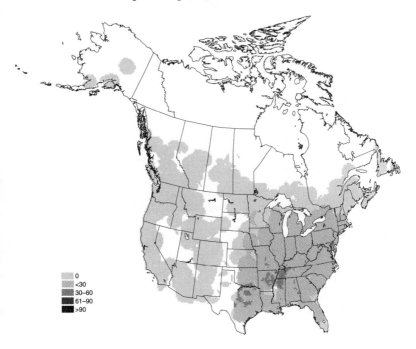

0
<30
30–60
61–90
>90

Abundance at feeders

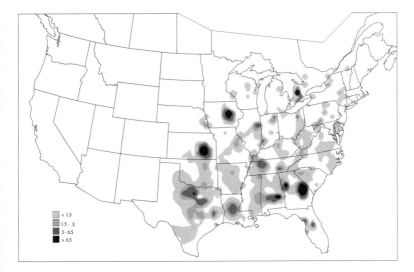

< 1.5
1.5 · 3
3 · 6.5
> 6.5

Fox Sparrow

Passerella iliaca

The Fox Sparrow is named for its rufous plumage. Although the extent of redness varies considerably among the eighteen described subspecies, with western birds showing more gray or dark brown, nearly all have "fox"-colored rumps, tails, and wings. In summer these large, rather plump, sparrows sing a lovely song. Unfortunately most of us never hear it because Fox Sparrows nest in the far north, and we only see them as migrants or during the winter.

Fox Sparrows are two-footed scratchers like towhees. Their main foraging method consists of clearing away leaf litter to expose hidden food, a process that sometimes sends showers of dirt flying up to 20 inches. Light spring snows are scratched away with as much vigor as leaves are. Feeder owners sometimes remark on the stereotypy of this scratching behavior, as some Fox Sparrows scratch even where seeds are in full view. However, a foraging Fox Sparrow does watch the ground as it scratches and stops once something edible has been turned up. If you see one scratching more than five times without a break the site is probably unprofitable, and the bird will likely move elsewhere very soon.

The seeds that Fox Sparrows eat are on the small side, considering the size of the bird, but are still slightly larger than seeds preferred by other sparrow species. At feeders Fox Sparrows often ignore sunflower seeds and go after millet or cracked corn instead. They eat a wider variety of other foods in winter than most of their fellow sparrow species, consuming insects when encountered (mostly millipedes and ground beetles) and lots of dried berries. This "meat and vegetable" diet allows Fox Sparrows to accumulate enough fat to tide them over temporary food shortages, although mortality can be high if snow covers their food sources for long periods.

In the eastern part of their range, Fox Sparrows overwinter in moist deciduous forests and swampy areas along rivers. In the West they are more often found in coniferous forest, but their habitats also include rather arid areas of savannah and chaparral or city parks and gardens where there are dense, low-growing shrubs and vines. Whatever the habitat type, the wary Fox Sparrow usually hides in dense cover. This is important for daytime concealment and protection as well as for roosting, and at night several birds may gather together to perch a few feet off the ground amidst thick vegetation.

Social behavior of Fox Sparrows is evidently quite fluid. While flocks of fifty may form on migration, the birds must spread out on reaching their destination because only two to four individuals can normally be found together in the wintering area. They do not appear to defend winter territories, but they can be intolerant toward one another and may even fight if under stress (such as during snowstorms). In interactions with other species, the Fox Sparrow can be described as sociable but shy. For example, flocks of White-crowned and Golden-crowned Sparrows in California often have a Fox Sparrow or two in tow, but the latter normally run for cover if chased, even by smaller species.

Key references: Bent 1968, Hailman 1976, Linsdale 1928.

FeederWatch Findings

Fox sparrows overwinter in California and the southern United States, but most feeder sightings are of spring migrants. Three times as many feeders are visited in spring as in fall, and most feeders report Fox Sparrows present for only a few weeks. Typically these sparrows are seen in ones or twos, but abundance in the West is notably higher than in the East.

Favorite feeder foods: *Mixed seed, millet,* cracked corn, and (according to small samples) probably milo, as well.

Infrequent choices: Sunflower (any type), niger, suet, water. According to small samples, canary seed and whole corn may also be eaten.

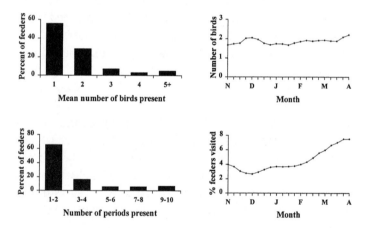

Fox Sparrow: percent of feeders visited

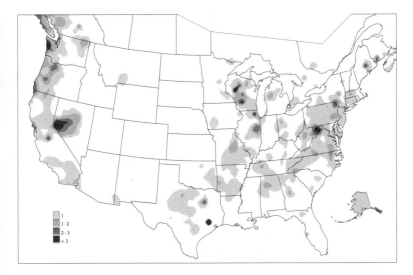

	0
	<30
	30–60
	61–90
	>90

Abundance at feeders

	1
	1 - 2
	2 - 3
	> 3

Song Sparrow

Melospiza melodia

The Song Sparrow is a successful, widespread generalist. It has only minimal habitat needs, and these can be found almost anywhere: a few shrubs, some song perches, and a source of open water in winter. Nonetheless, Song Sparrows have adapted extensively to quite local conditions. Thirty-one subspecies have been recognized, more than for any other North American bird.

Northern-nesting populations of Song Sparrows are partially migratory, with females moving farther south than males. A seemingly stable population at your feeder may actually be an ever-changing combination of year-round residents, wintering birds from farther north, and returning local breeders that spent the winter farther south. Males who choose not to migrate continue to defend their territory on and off through the winter (although they spread their activities over a larger area than in the summer). The flocks that gather at favored feeding sites during cold or snowy conditions are probably made up largely of juveniles and migrants.

The course of a Song Sparrow's life is strongly influenced by dominance relationships. The slightly larger males are dominant to females, and sparrows hatched early in the spring dominate later-hatched juveniles through the first winter. These macho juveniles are also the ones most likely to carve out breeding territories for themselves. Territorial males are by far the heaviest users of any feeders (or other concentrated food sources) located on their turf, and probably as a result they are better able to survive the harsh winters that cause occasional roller-coaster fluctuations in population size. Knowing the importance of hierarchies to Song Sparrows, we can better appreciate their pugnacious nature at feeders. They are aggressive toward other species as well as their own and quite capable of dominating slightly larger birds, such as White-throated Sparrows.

A foraging Song Sparrow spends most of its time on the ground, searching for grain or weed and grass seeds by scratching at the soil or clearing away light snow. Small, easily opened seeds are chosen over harder ones, even if the latter have higher energy content. To maintain energy balance on a day when temperatures fall to freezing, a Song Sparrow must eat eighty-five to four thousand seeds per hour (depending on seed size), so it not surprising that ease of husking is an important consideration in food choice. Song Sparrows are better able than some other ground feeders to survive in snowy climates, as they will readily take to trees in search of insects or other foods—and this behavioral plasticity can be observed at feeders, where Song Sparrows will visit platform and raised feeders of various designs.

Song Sparrows rely on cover for defense, so adding shrubbery or a brush pile to your yard will increase your chances of attracting this species to feeders. Song Sparrows venture into the open to forage if necessary, but in so doing they are more vulnerable to hawk predation than are sparrow species that forage in flocks.

Key references: Arcese and Smith 1985, DeGraff 1989, Knapton and Krebs 1976, Morrison 1984, Nice 1937, 1943, Rogers et al. 1991, Smith et al. 1980, Wagner and Gauthreaux 1990, Watts 1990, Willson and Harmeson 1973.

FeederWatch Findings

Song Sparrows are a widespread feeder species, and gaps on the maps largely reflect lack of coverage. The high numbers shown in northern Nebraska are also an anomaly based on scant data. Song Sparrows visit some sites only a few times but others throughout the winter. Many feeders, especially in the East, only attract these sparrows during spring migration. These birds are usually seen in ones or twos, with larger flocks more likely to occur at rural and suburban feeders than in urban areas.

Favorite feeder foods: *Mixed seed,* millet.

Infrequent choices: Sunflower (all types), safflower, corn (whole or cracked), milo, wheat, niger, hulled peanuts or hearts, peanut butter mixes, bird puddings, baked goods, sugar water, water. Small samples also show occasional choice of canary seed and popped corn.

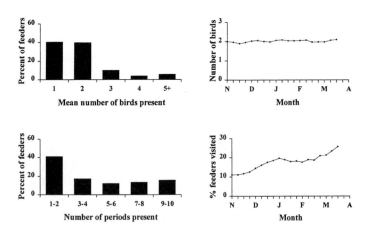

Song Sparrow: percent of feeders visited

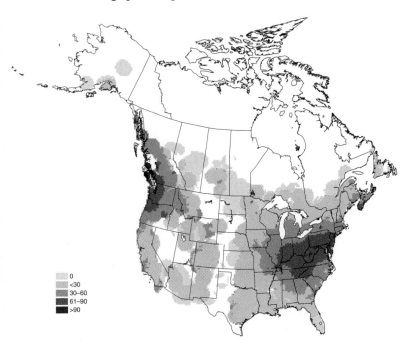

0
<30
30–60
61–90
>90

Abundance at feeders

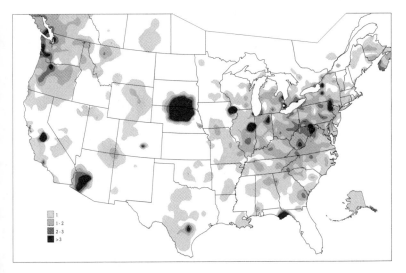

1
1 - 2
2 - 3
>3

White-throated Sparrow
Zonotrichia albicollis

White-throats come in two varieties: those with white stripes over the crown and those with tan stripes. In most birds such a plumage difference would be a sign of age or sex, but in White-throats it is a genetic polymorphism. Youngsters of both types can be raised in the same family and the color pattern is retained for life. One of the most intriguing aspects of the responsible gene is that it affects behavior as well as plumage color. For example, the white-striped birds tend to be more aggressive and sing more often, and the males prefer to mate with tan-striped females. Nonetheless, crown color has no effect on reproductive success or dominance status in winter. All evidence suggests that the two genes are stable in their frequency—that is, the species is not in transition from one type to the other.

While most White-throats migrate, a few birds remain at their breeding sites, thus helping to make this sparrow one of the more widespread at feeders (along with Song Sparrows and Dark-eyed

Juncos). Wintering territories are established and maintained year after year. These territories often overlap broadly, and individuals frequently join into loose flocks when foraging. This seems to imply tolerance and lack of aggression—but there is actually a well-defined dominance hierarchy.

Dominance in White-throated Sparrows is based primarily on sex and age: Males rank above females, and older birds dominate younger ones. Each individual establishes a rank within its own age/sex class through aggressive interactions during the first winter. Once the social order is set it lasts for life, and there is little occasion for further aggression. You can make a good guess at which overwintering individuals are dominant because the highest-ranking birds within each age and sex grouping are the ones that sing the most.

White-throats occupying dominant positions gain benefits from their exalted status: They get first access to food regardless of who found it first, and they can spend more time feeding, so they accumulate more body fat—which in turn increases chances of survival. They also get to feed closer to cover, which probably protects them from predation. So much do White-throats value shrubbery that they stay close by cover to feed even when food is more abundant farther away.

A foraging White-throat spends most of its time kicking aside leaf litter to search for small seeds, but it may also pick seeds directly from grass and weed stems. Perhaps this behavioral flexibility explains why they are more willing to visit raised feeders than are many other ground-feeding birds. White-throats usually feed peacefully at feeders with other species—except that they are bossed about by the smaller but more strongly territorial Song Sparrows.

Key references: Bent 1968, Knapton et al. 1984, Piper 1990a, 1990b, Piper and Wiley 1989, 1990a, 1990b, Pulliam and Enders 1971, Schneider 1984, Wagner and Gauthreaux 1990, Watt et al. 1984, Wiley 1991, Wiley et al. 1993.

FeederWatch Findings

White-throated Sparrows are among the more faithful sparrows at feeders as the winter progresses (although not as regular as Dark-eyed Juncos). Slightly more feeders are visited in the coldest months, and at the same time abundance nearly doubles. The map shows White-throats in West Coast states, where they do occur occasionally, but probably some of these records include errors of identification or data recording.

Favorite feeder foods: *Mixed seed,* millet.

Infrequent choices: Sunflower (all types), safflower, whole or cracked corn, milo, niger, hulled peanuts or hearts, peanut butter mixes, baked goods, water, and (according to small samples) canary seed.

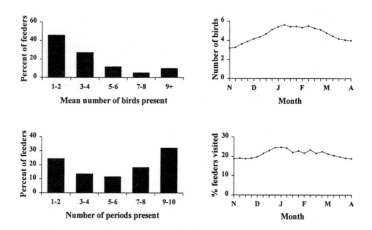

White-throated Sparrow: percent of feeders visited

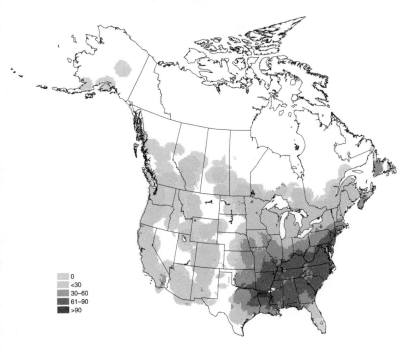

0
<30
30–60
61–90
>90

Abundance at feeders

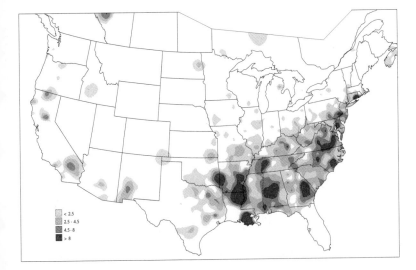

< 2.5
2.5 - 4.5
4.5 - 8
> 8

Harris's Sparrow

Zonotrichia querula

H arris's Sparrows nest in northern Canada (and are that country's only endemic songbird). We therefore see them at feeders only during migration or winter, by which time the solid black bibs of summer have molted to a mottled patch. Research has shown that the size and blackness of the breast patch signals the age and sex of the bird—and its personal dominance ranking. The more heavily marked adult males generally dominate adult females, who in turn lord it over young males. Juvenile females hold the lowliest positions.

Dominance hierarchies are thought to reduce fighting because each individual "knows its place." Harris's Sparrows often form flocks of unacquainted individuals during migration, and by using plumage as a badge of rank, there is no need for a stranger to squabble with others before inserting itself into the correct hierarchical slot. One look and it knows whether the neighboring bird is a prince or a peon.

Studies of White-crowned Sparrows have shown that this

species also bases dominance on plumage brightness, but in White-crowns looks are all that counts: You can dye a bird's feathers and instantly change its rank. Harris's Sparrows differ in that they behave as befits their status. A researcher who dyed dull birds darker and bleached blacker males pale discovered that each Harris's Sparrow continued to behave submissively or aggressively according to its original dominance rank. The newly dull, for example, continued to act like tyrants, and when confronted by others they reacted with a fight instead of giving way as dull birds normally would.

Dominant individuals gain assured access to the best feeding sites—and probably command the most sheltered roost sites, as well. The latter hypothesis was proposed after birds with darker breast patches were observed on frigid mornings with less frost on their tails than subordinates.

Studies of banded birds have shown that Harris's Sparrows are very regular in their migration and wintering routes. During the leisurely fall migration, individuals typically stay at a given feeder for about a week before moving on, though sometimes lingering as much as a month. The same birds may turn up briefly at the same feeders on spring migration (which is much faster than the fall journey). Within the wintering ground in the central United States, most Harris's Sparrows settle onto specific wintering sites and return to them year after year. Despite this evidence of strong site fidelity, it is notable that a few Harris's Sparrows regularly wander off track. Occasional stragglers have been reported visiting feeders in nearly every state and province.

Although these sparrows readily come to feeders in residential areas, they normally do so only in severe weather, usually preferring more wooded and brushy habitats than suburbia offers. Harris's Sparrows feed mainly on the ground but like to be near tall trees where they can shelter and rest. They find some food in trees and shrubs, as well, adding fruits and insects to the main foodstuffs of weed seeds and grain. This broad diet is reflected at feeders, where Harris's Sparrows sample many foods, and these sparrows are reported to be among the few species that readily eat milo.

Key references: Bent 1968, Bridgewater 1966, Harkins 1937, Norment and Shackleton 1993, Pray 1950, Rohwer 1975, 1977, Watt 1986.

FeederWatch Findings

The winter range of the Harris's Sparrow is quite narrow, as shown on the maps despite lack of FeederWatch coverage in a strip that cuts through the western edge of the wintering range. Vagrants are fairly regular outside this range and are particularly likely to turn up at feeders. Although many of the feeder sightings are of migrants, this species does remain throughout the winter at about one-quarter of all sites that report it. It is usually seen in small groups of two to five birds, with the larger numbers occurring in midwinter.

Favorite feeder foods: *Mixed seed,* water, and probably (according to small samples) striped sunflower.

Infrequent choices: Black-oil sunflower. The few feeders offering millet and cracked corn also reported these as occasional choices by Harris's Sparrows.

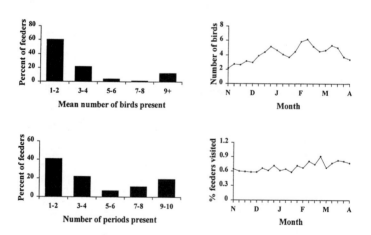

Harris's Sparrow: percent of feeders visited

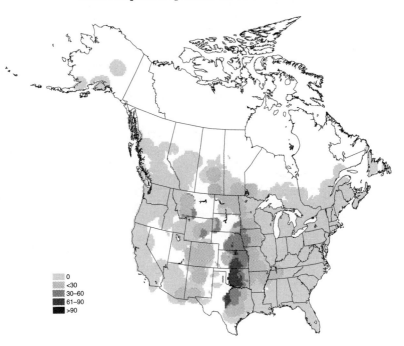

0
<30
30–60
61–90
>90

Abundance at feeders

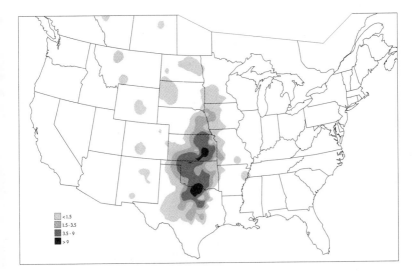

<1.5
1.5 - 3.5
3.5 - 9
> 9

White-crowned Sparrow

Zonotrichia leucophrys

White-crowned Sparrows are a sort of guinea pig of the wild bird world, as they are frequently the study species of choice for research on migration, flocking behavior, dominance, and song. Part of the reason for their popularity with scientists is that White-crowns are divided into numerous geographic races, which sing different dialects and migrate different distances. This diversity allows many interesting comparative studies to be done using a single species.

For example, the White-crowns that breed in southern California do not migrate. Juveniles rove about in small groups during their first winter, but once they have set up territories, they remain on them year-round forever after. Among migratory White-crowns there is a contrasting social order. These birds join into larger winter flocks and establish a communal territory. Within this area each individual may have favorite foraging and roosting sites—a sort of miniterritory within the larger one—but the flock as a whole is definitely a cohesive group that returns each winter to the same area and seldom mixes with neighboring assemblages.

As in many flocking species, social order is maintained in the

White-crowned Sparrow through a dominance hierarchy. Males have brighter plumage (whiter whites and blacker blacks) and are dominant over females. Juveniles also have relatively low status. Exalted rank appears to be based entirely on looks rather than accomplishment: Experimenters wielding paintbrushes have brightened the plumage of duller-colored birds and discovered that changelings gain an automatic increase in dominance. Recognition of status based on plumage evidently helps reduce any need to fight to establish rank. White-crowns seem to avoid aggressive interactions through other means, as well, such as keeping a minimum distance from other sparrows at all times and facing in the same direction as nearby birds while foraging (thus avoiding face-to-face meetings that might lead to squabbles).

Low levels of aggression among flock members probably contributes to more rapid food consumption by all parties, as each bird can concentrate on eating instead of social interaction. White-crowned Sparrows do not accumulate sufficient fat reserves to let them sit out a winter storm in shelter for more than a day, so there may be a premium on behavior conducive to efficient food gathering.

As a ground forager, the White-crowned Sparrow must literally scratch for a living. It prefers small seeds, especially of grass and weeds, and eats insects or other seeds when available. Millet, which is favored at feeders, is much larger than the wild seeds chosen by White-crowns, but agricultural plant breeding has produced a millet that is easy to husk, making it available to the many sparrow species that normally ignore such "large" seeds.

Most White-crown visits to feeders occur early or late in the day—the times when birds are most anxious to break their overnight fast or stock up in anticipation of the next one. A migrating sparrow that has discovered a feeder will often pause in its journey for several days to fatten up before moving on. There is a good chance that the same individual will repeat the stopover in subsequent years, just as vacationing humans develop favorite restaurant stops when they make regular trips.

Key references: Barrentine 1990, Blanchard 1941, Cherry 1982, Cortopassi and Mewaldt 1965, DeWoskin 1980, Fugle et al. 1984, Ketterson and King 1977, Mewaldt 1976, Pulliam 1985, Zink and Watt 1987.

FeederWatch Findings

The White-crowned Sparrow is a feeder species primarily in the West, where incoming migrants join resident populations for the winter. It is common in Nevada, Utah and West Texas, despite gaps in the maps (which result from lack of FeederWatch coverage). In the East, feeders record White-crowns less frequently, in many cases only during spring migration. The proportion of feeders visited is lowest in rural areas. Overall, about a fifth of feeder sites that host the species maintain a small flock of White-crowns all season long.

Favorite feeder foods: *Mixed seed, millet,* cracked corn. Small samples show that milo, wheat, and hulled peanuts are also frequent choices.

Infrequent choices: Sunflower (any type), safflower, niger, suet, peanut butter mixes, bird puddings, fresh fruit, water. According to small samples, whole corn, peanut hearts, and baked goods may also be acceptable.

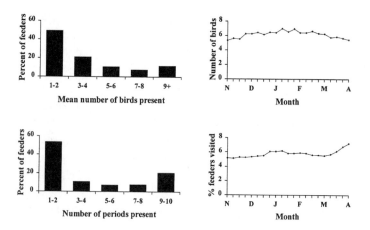

White-crowned Sparrow: percent of feeders visited

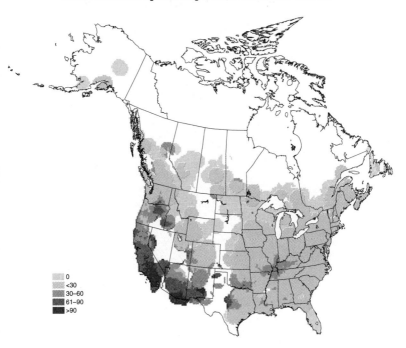

0
<30
30–60
61–90
>90

Abundance at feeders

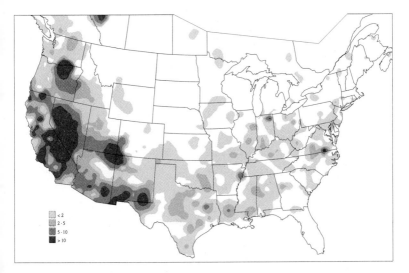

< 2
2 - 5
5 - 10
> 10

Golden-crowned Sparrow

Zonotrichia atricapilla

We often think of Golden-crowned Sparrows as California birds, even though their breeding range is in British Columbia and Alaska, because they live in California eight months of the year and leave only briefly to raise their young. You can even hear Golden-crowns singing in winter, although song production slackens off in midseason and lacks the incessant vigor typical of the breeding grounds. The plaintive spring song of three whistled notes in descending tones has earned this sparrow the nickname "Weary Willie."

The wintering range of Golden-crowned Sparrows is restricted to a narrow strip along the West Coast where coastal rains stimulate a flush of new plant growth in autumn. These sparrows are uniquely dependent on green plant foods throughout the winter and frequently sport green beaks, stained by the juices of their most recent meal. Their liking for sprouts and buds makes Golden-crowns unpopular to gardeners because the birds can inflict damage on ornamental trees, annual flowers, newly seeded lawns, or carefully tended vegetables. Although residential developments are not prime Golden-crown habitat (they prefer open brushland), suburbia will attract them as long as there is a supply of food, water, and protective shrubbery. Feeders may serve as an additional attractant, but perhaps they also distract the backyard visitors from raiding gardens by providing a ready source of alternate foods.

Golden-crowns are evidently vulnerable to predation, as they are slow to emerge from cover (compared to other sparrow species) and quick to return there when frightened. A specialized escape behavior may also reflect predator avoidance: Golden-crowns resting in shrubbery will not flush en masse as many other species do when disturbed but rather move off inconspicuously in small groups, flying at low level to another patch of cover nearby.

This species forms winter flocks of about twenty-five birds (sometimes three times that number) that collectively hold a territory of 15 to 20 acres. There is little interchange of individuals between flocks, and each bird has a strong tendency to return to the same territory the following year. However, other species are not excluded, and very commonly flocks of Golden-crowned and White-crowned Sparrows will mingle.

Golden-crowns are somewhat quarrelsome among themselves but appear to have many social mechanisms for reducing aggression. One researcher unexpectedly discovered that individuals using a large feeding tray returned repeatedly to the very same spot on the feeder, even when few other birds were present. Just to see what would happen, he turned the tray 180°. About half the sparrows in the flock continued to land on the same spot relative to surroundings (for example, always on the south west corner); the other half, however, used the same *specific* spots on the feeder as before—even though those spots were now in different positions (imagine marking an *X* on the feeder, and the bird landing on that *X* no matter how the feeder is turned). These behaviors suggest an importance to "knowing one's place" as a means of reducing the frequency of aggressive interaction, whether that place is a certain spot relative to surroundings or a specific spot on a feeder. The sparrows in this study also maintained a fairly uniform individual distance, and adjacent birds showed a marked tendency to point their heads in the same direction—additional ways to avoid confrontations.

Key references: Bent 1968, Davis 1973, Pearson 1979, Price 1931, Pulliam and Mills 1977.

FeederWatch Findings

Golden-crowned Sparrows are very steady visitors to feeders through the winter. Over half of the feeders within the main range report at least one visit. While fewer rural sites are visited than are suburban or urban feeders, flock sizes in the more built-up areas are about two-thirds of those in the countryside.

Favorite feeder foods: *Mixed seed,* millet, cracked corn, bird puddings, and probably (according to small samples) milo and peanut butter mixes.
Infrequent choices: Black-oil sunflower, niger, suet, popped corn. Small samples show that striped and hulled sunflower, canary seed, peanut hearts, and fresh fruit may also be accepted.

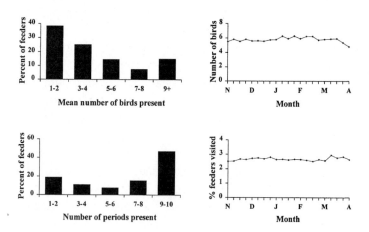

Golden-crowned Sparrow: percent of feeders visited

0
<30
30–60
61–90
>90

Abundance at feeders

< 3
3 - 5.5
5.5 - 9.5
> 9.5

Dark-eyed Junco

Junco hyemalis

"Snowbirds," as juncos are known to many a layman, have earned their informal name on two counts. Not only are they more likely to visit feeders during snowy periods, but their very return from far-northern breeding areas is a signal that colder weather is close behind. Juncos are sighted at more feeders across North America than any other species, visiting over 80% of sites—a greater number than are visited by all species of chickadees combined or by all species of jays.

The sociable junco spends its winter in a flock with a few to thirty or more others, who remain together throughout the season. Within the main flock there are smaller groups of regular buddies. In severe weather these smaller units may temporarily go their own way.

Each flock is internally organized through having a dominance hierarchy, with adult males at the top, then young males, followed by adult females, and finally young females. Sometimes, however, rankings are based more on "who you know" than "who you are." If two flocks merge, the particular pals of the most dominant male tend to gain exalted status within the joined flock—a sort of coat-tail effect among juncos. Constant status testing goes on, and you can often observe aggressive interactions involving lunges at other birds and flicking of the tail to briefly expose the white outer tail feathers. Such activities are especially common in the morning and at dusk, when feeding activity is most intense.

The advantage of dominance to those birds at the top is obvious in that they get to feed in the center of a food patch and spend less time looking around for predators, thereby taking in more food and accumulating more body fat than subordinates. But do subordinates gain any benefits from this social structure? It turns out that under good food conditions subordinates survive just as well as dominants, although their survival is lower than that of dominants when food-finding conditions are poor. On the other hand, a junco living on its own might have even greater difficulty finding food and certainly would be more vulnerable to predation. Probably it is better to be a lowly member of a successful flock than it is to live alone.

Some juncos are resident, others move from high to low altitudes in winter, and others migrate. When migrants mix with residents, they are usually subordinate to the local birds. Female migrants head farther south than males, perhaps in part because they are subordinate to just about everybody and therefore seek to avoid competition. Up to 70% of juncos wintering in parts of the southern United States are females. Males overwintering in cold regions suffer higher mortality than if they, too, went farther south—but this disadvantage is balanced by their ability to arrive first on the northern breeding grounds and obtain prime breeding territories before others arrive.

A typical junco requires the daily energy intake of hundreds or thousands of seeds (depending on their size), and because most feeder owners do not see their seed supplies depleted at anything like that rate, we must suppose that juncos prefer natural foods. Juncos rely heavily on small seeds in the wild but will also try out much larger seeds at feeders (especially cracked corn or hulled sunflower). Each individual has its own food preferences, depending on which seeds it is able to open most economically with its particular bill shape.

Key references: Baker and Fox 1978, Balph 1977a, Cristol 1995, Fretwell 1969, Goldman 1980, Goldstein and Baker 1984, Gottfried and Franks 1975, Ketterson 1979, Ketterson and Nolan 1982, 1983, Millikan et al. 1985, Pulliam 1985, Sabine 1959, Wiedemann and Rabenold 1987.

FeederWatch Findings

The relatively inconspicuous Dark-eyed Junco holds the record for being recorded at the highest proportion of feeders in North America, visiting nearly all sites within its range at least once. Gaps on the maps are a result of low FeederWatch coverage in those areas. However, abundance is generally higher in western states as well as being nearly twice as high at rural as at urban feeders. Typical flock size is about six, rising in midwinter to about nine. Most feeders that see juncos at all report them present for the entire winter.

Favorite feeder foods: *Mixed seed,* millet, hulled sunflower, cracked corn.

Infrequent choices: Canary seed, striped or black-oil sunflower, safflower, whole corn, milo, wheat, niger, hulled peanuts or hearts, oats, canola, suet, peanut butter mixes, bird puddings, baked goods, water.

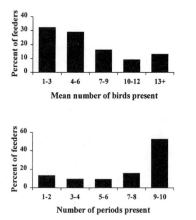

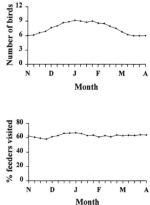

Dark-eyed Junco: percent of feeders visited

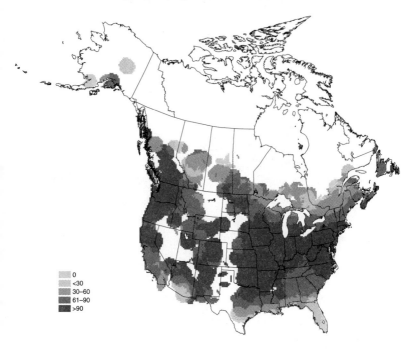

0
<30
30–60
61–90
>90

Abundance at feeders

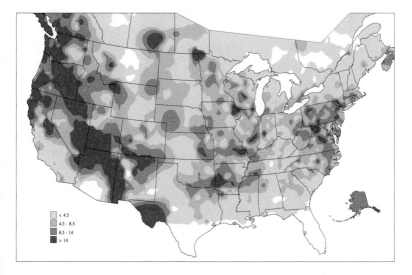

< 4.5
4.5 · 8.5
8.5 · 14
> 14

Northern Cardinal

Cardinalis cardinalis

The "Redbird" is among the most striking of winter visitors to feeders. It is far from being the most bold, however, and often prefers to visit in the semidarkness of dawn or dusk, nervously flicking the tail or crest and repeatedly giving the chip call denoting mild alarm. Flocking evidently generates a more relaxed atmosphere. In southern areas where populations are most dense, flocks of fifty or more may visit feeders, treating homeowners to colorful carpets of calm cardinals.

Northern populations of cardinals are partially migratory (that is, some individuals depart for warmer climes, and others tough out the winter where they bred), while cardinals breeding at more southern latitudes are resident throughout the year. Winter flocks consist largely of young of the year (subordinate to adults of both sexes) and some adults (perhaps migrants far from their summer homes). Meanwhile, resident adults relax their territorial behavior in winter, expanding their areas of activity to overlap broadly with the ranges of neighboring pairs. But their assertiveness is not abandoned altogether, and bright, sunny weather can stimulate males to sing at any time of winter. There is no finer antidote to a deep freeze than seeing a brilliant red cardinal perched conspicuously in full sunlight atop a snow-covered tree, broadcasting his distinctive territorial song at full volume.

Northern Cardinals are so named because their closest relatives are more tropical. Over the past one hundred years they have become even more "northern," expanding their range to the north and west. Juveniles disperse up to 50 miles from their birthplaces, often moving along wooded river courses, and this short-distance dispersal is sufficient for slow range expansion as long as conditions are suitable in newly invaded areas. Bird feeding is thought to have played a role in allowing cardinals to live farther north, although ameliorating climate has probably contributed, as well.

Illustrations of cardinals often show them perched on feeders. In fact, they prefer foraging on the ground or in short vegetation, preferably underneath plenty of woody cover. Most of their diet consists of grain, weed seeds, and grass seeds, supplemented with fruits plucked from low bushes. Despite possessing massive beaks, cardinals prefer seeds that are scarcely larger than the seeds chosen by large sparrows. When plenty of food is available, cardinals select seeds that are easy to open, regardless of energy content. However, these birds can evidently recognize nutrition when they have to because in cold conditions they switch to seeds that offer the most energetic return per unit of time to crack them open. Cardinals are among the few birds that readily eat safflower seeds at feeders, and sunflower is, of course, a staple.

Key references: Beddall 1963, Dow 1969, 1970, Dow and Scott 1971, Laskey 1944, Pulliam and Enders 1971, Ritchison and Omer 1990, White et al. 1996, Willson and Harmeson 1973.

FeederWatch Findings

The Northern Cardinal is a common feeder species that is usually present all winter long, dropping in to nearly all feeders within their main wintering range. While Blue Jays are more abundant at northern feeders (probably in response to colder weather), Cardinals are more abundant at southern ones (probably as a simple result of larger populations there). Some southern feeder owners report flocks of more than fifty cardinals at a time, although the vast majority of feeder owners see fewer than five at once (and usually only one or two). Chances of seeing several at a time increase in midwinter. Rural sites are visited a little less often than feeders elsewhere, but when they are, flock sizes tend to be larger. The mapped gap in West Texas is an artifact of low coverage there. While Cardinals do occur in Arizona, some records there may include misidentified Pyrrhuloxias.

Favorite feeder foods: *Striped and black-oil sunflower,* hulled sunflower, mixed seed, safflower.

Infrequent choices: Millet, canary seed, corn (whole or cracked), milo, wheat, peanuts (any form), pet food, peanut butter mixes, bird puddings, fresh fruit, baked goods, water, and (according to small samples) canola.

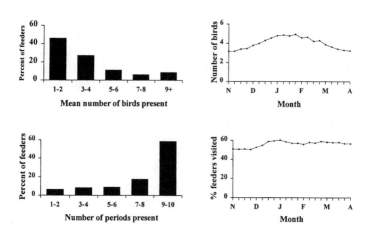

Northern Cardinal: percent of feeders visited

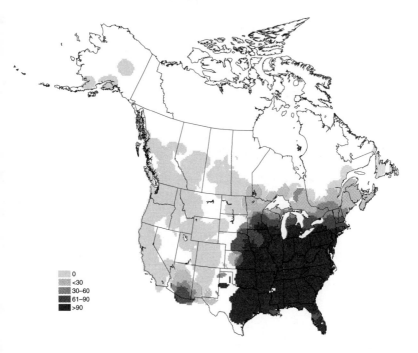

0
<30
30–60
61–90
>90

Abundance at feeders

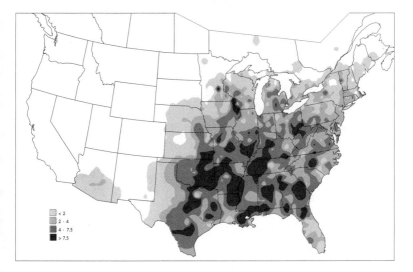

< 2
2 - 4
4 - 7.5
> 7.5

Pyrrhuloxia

Cardinalis sinuatus

Pyrrhuloxia is a name combining words meaning "fire" and "crosswise," the latter referring to the bird's beak. The top part of the bill is strongly decurved over the heavy lower portion, giving a parrotlike appearance. Frequent movement of the crest seems to animate the Pyrrhuloxia's face, making it more expressive (to human eyes) than its rather wooden cousin, the Northern Cardinal.

The Pyrrhuloxia is confined to the American Southwest, where its range overlaps with that of the more widespread Northern Cardinal, and the interactions of these closely related species have been the subject of study. Within this range both species often roost together, and they feed together (relatively peacefully) as they forage on the ground. Both species form winter flocks, with Pyrrhuloxias being more gregarious and wandering a little farther from summer territories. The songs of Pyrrhuloxias and Northern Cardinals are also very similar (aside from call notes), although Pyrrhuloxias are less likely than Northern Cardinals to repeat the same phrase several times in a row. Also, female Pyrrhuloxias rarely sing, whereas Northern Cardinal mates sing duets together. Despite their similarities, Pyrrhuloxias and Northern Cardinals do not defend territories against one another, suggesting that they are not competing for the same resource base of food and shelter.

Mesquite thicket is an important feature of Pyrrhuloxia habitat, to the extent that nearly half of a typical breeding territory consists of this vegetation. The thick bushes are used for winter roosting, and the mesquite bean is an important winter food, while the dense cover afforded by the thorny scrub probably serves as protection from predators. Pyrrhuloxias are not strong flyers, so startled birds rely on nearby cover, which they reach with an undulating flap-and-glide flight. These birds will venture into agricultural hedgerows, however, and are readily attracted to residential areas.

After Pyrrhuloxia breeding territories break down in autumn, the birds join into loose flocks with somewhat fluid memberships. Although these flocks wander a bit, Pyrrhuloxias basically remain in the same area year-round. The largest winter flocks are found at sites where food is concentrated, such as at feeders, where Pyrrhuloxias favor sunflower and cracked corn. Reports in the literature also mention these birds eating millet, milo, and halved fruits, such as apples or tomatoes.

Key references: Bent 1968, Dennis 1991, Gould 1961.

FeederWatch Findings

Pyrrhuloxias are frequent feeder visitors within their regionally restricted range. They are especially common in West Texas, where FeederWatch data are lacking. Feeders that report the species are split between those that attract it only a couple of times, usually in midwinter, and those that have Pyrrhuloxias on a near-weekly basis. Normally only one or two birds are seen at once, and some of the reports of larger numbers may erroneously include Northern Cardinals.

Favorite feeder foods: According to small samples, mixed seed, black-oil sunflower, cracked corn, water.

Infrequent choices: Small samples suggest that striped sunflower and milo may occasionally be eaten.

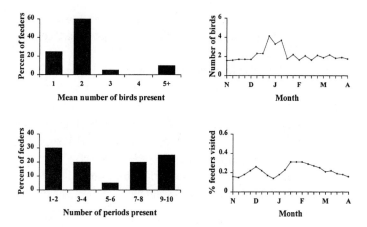

Pyrrhuloxia: percent of feeders visited

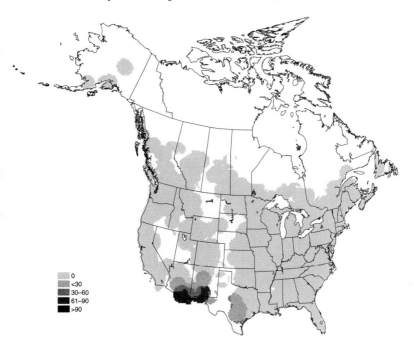

0
<30
30–60
61–90
>90

Abundance at feeders

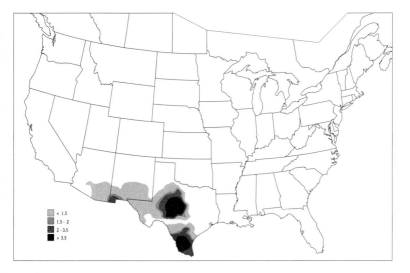

< 1.5
1.5 - 2
2 - 3.5
> 3.5

Red-winged Blackbird

Agelaius phoeniceus

Red-winged Blackbirds like more open country than is generally found near feeders, so flocks visiting residential areas are quite nervous and rarely settle in for a long stay. At northern feeders the largest numbers of blackbirds turn up during migration. Indeed, the arrival of hordes of Red-wings in late winter is one of the first signs of spring.

The polygynous Red-wing is also something of a misogynist in winter. Flocks are often partially segregated by sex, whether foraging or at a roost, and females winter slightly farther south—mechanisms that may help females avoid competition with the slightly larger males. Females also eat a somewhat different diet, consuming more weed seeds and less waste corn than males, but it is not clear whether they do this because they have different tastes or because males control the access to more favored foods.

Much of the winter food intake of both sexes consists of waste grain left behind in fields following mechanical harvesting. This modern supplement to the winter diet may have led to increase in Red-wing populations, contributing to damage that they inflict on newly ripening corn, sunflower, and rice and on mature crops.

Red-wings frequently join grackles and other blackbird species while foraging or roosting. However, the Red-wings always maintain some flock integrity, banding together (with birds of a feather) in smaller flocks within the larger ones. This tendency for separation may even be noticeable at feeders when several species visit at the same time.

Within the Red-wing flocks themselves there are further subdivisions, this time based on dominance rankings. Adult males outrank young ones, forcing juveniles at roosts to accept exposed sleeping sites while they themselves occupy the choice perches in denser cover. Submissive males deflect attacks from dominant males by flattening feathers over their colored shoulder patches, which would otherwise stimulate dominants to become aggressive.

Communal roosting is a conspicuous phenomenon of winter behavior in Red-wings. In the southeastern United States there can be ten or more roosts each winter that each contain over a million birds, and of course there are many more of smaller dimensions. Roosts are only temporary aggregations, changing markedly in size and composition through the winter. On average a Red-wing will spend only four nights at a particular site before moving on. It will then move to a new site, typically 3 to 6 miles from the previous one, although some individuals may move five times that distance. During the day the blackbirds spread out from the roost site to forage in nearby fields. Some will commute as far as 50 miles from the current roost site.

Studies of captive birds have shown that Red-wing feeding behavior is strongly influenced by fellow foragers. If one bird sees another eating very rapidly, it is stimulated to feed faster, too, even though it may not be particularly hungry. In addition, a Red-wing will carefully watch companions that are sampling a new food, closely observing their reaction before deciding whether to sample the novel meal itself.

At feeders Red-wings will eventually try out a wide variety of seeds, but they do not seem to care much for suet or peanut butter.

Key references: Clark et al. 1986, Crase and Dehaven 1978, Dolbeer 1978, 1982, Dolbeer et al. 1978, Hanson and Rohwer 1986, Heisterberg et al. 1984, Mason and Reidinger 1981, Mason et al. 1984, Meanley 1965, Mott 1984, Robertson et al. 1978, Searcy 1979, Weatherhead and Hoysak 1984.

FeederWatch Findings

During spring migration, the proportion of North American feeders that are visited by Red-winged Blackbirds rises from under 5% to nearly 30%. Gaps on the maps are largely due to lack of FeederWatch coverage. Although few feeders host Red-wings all winter, flocks at these sites can be large: over ten at rural and suburban feeders (about half that at urban sites).

Favorite feeder foods: Mixed seed, millet, striped sunflower, cracked corn, and probably (according to small samples) milo.

Infrequent choices: Hulled and black-oil sunflower, safflower, whole corn, hulled peanuts or hearts, suet, bird puddings, fresh fruit, baked goods, water, and (based on small samples) wheat and oats.

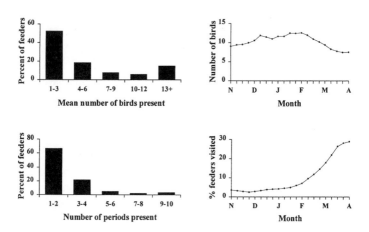

Red-winged Blackbird: percent of feeders visited

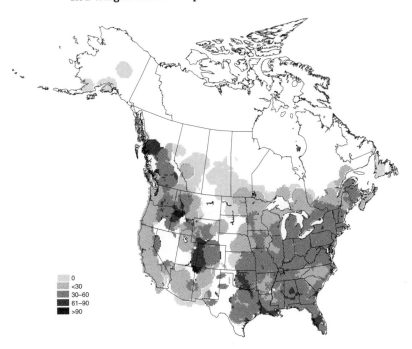

	0
	<30
	30–60
	61–90
	>90

Abundance at feeders

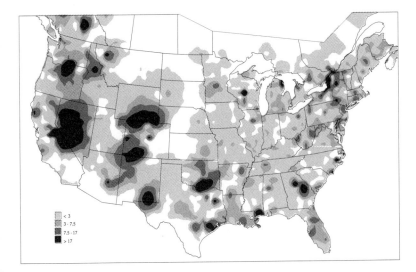

	< 3
	3 - 7.5
	7.5 - 17
	> 17

Eastern Meadowlark

Sturnella magna

Meadowlarks are not regular visitors to residential areas, preferring as they do the wide expanses of grassland or agricultural fields; but when snow covers the ground, meadowlarks may join sparrows and starlings at feeders. Repeat visitors can become bold enough to leave the ground and visit raised feeders for offerings.

One indication that meadowlarks visiting feeders do so only in desperation is the occasional eyewitness account of meadowlarks killing and consuming other birds at feeders. This should not totally surprise us, as meadowlarks are members of the blackbird family. Blackbirds as a group have broad diets that normally include some small vertebrates and scavenged corpses, and meadowlarks will readily join other scavengers feeding on roadkill when heavy snow has buried other foods.

Male Eastern Meadowlarks are especially likely to get caught in late spring snowstorms because they are very early migrants, preceding females to the breeding grounds. Indeed, their rather wistful song is one of our harbingers of spring. Its sweet sound is aggressive, announcing establishment of territory and preparing the way for the polygynous breeding that will soon follow.

Many blackbird species cause crop damage, but meadowlarks are generally welcomed by farmers—despite the birds' taste for sprouting corn—because the bulk of the meadowlark's summer diet is made up of insects, including many that are harmful to agriculture. The fall diet shifts to wild seeds; in winter, to waste grain. Foraging meadowlarks stalk through grass, picking seeds and insects from the ground or off plants, occasionally scratching away surface litter with the feet or digging with the bill. To loosen the soil, a lark pokes its closed bill into the ground and then opens it to pry open a hole, in the same manner as grackles and starlings.

A meadowlark in flight is reminiscent of a quail, mixing rapid, shallow wing beats with short, stiff-winged glides. The bright yellow front of the Eastern Meadowlark makes it conspicuous when it is flying or sitting on a song perch, but on the ground it is surprisingly well camouflaged.

Meadowlarks from the northern part of the breeding range migrate south for the winter. Migrant flocks frequently number in the hundreds, and loosely organized aggregations of thirty or forty persist throughout the winter. A flock may spread so widely across pastures and fields that it appears each individual is acting independently, but when a few birds fly off, additional small groups soon follow along behind.

Meadowlarks benefited from a vast range expansion as agriculture spread across North America, even though they were hunted widely by early settlers for food. In recent decades populations both of Eastern and Western Meadowlarks have declined steadily. The declines should perhaps be expected, given known change in farmland type and distribution, yet meadowlarks are still among the more abundant birds of open country.

Key references: Bell 1990, Bent 1958, Lanyon 1994, Waters 1990.

FeederWatch Findings

Eastern Meadowlarks are very uncommon feeder visitors, essentially never present all winter long. They are especially scarce at urban feeders. Chances of visitation increase in spring as migrants head north. When meadowlarks do appear, their numbers are quite variable, but typically one to five individuals will visit at one time.

Favorite feeder foods: Small samples indicate that black-oil sunflower is the most common food selection.

Infrequent choices: According to small samples, mixed seed, cracked corn, and water.

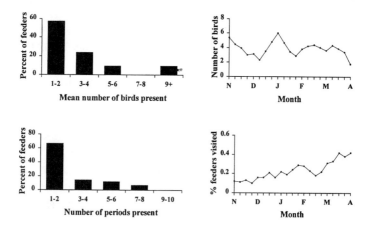

Eastern Meadowlark: percent of feeders visited

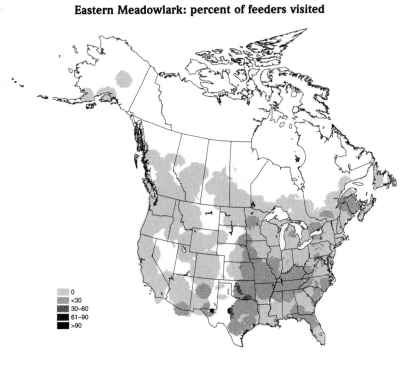

0
<30
30–60
61–90
>90

Abundance at feeders

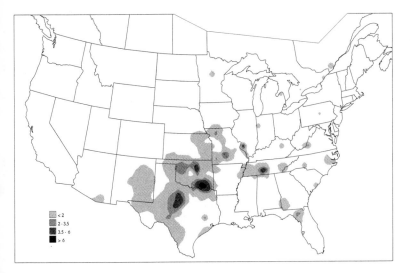

< 2
2 - 3.5
3.5 - 6
> 6

Brewer's Blackbird

Euphagus cyanocephalus

The winter habits of Brewer's Blackbirds are not nearly as well known as those of such other blackbird species as grackles, cowbirds, and Red-wings. Though a common and familiar bird within its range, the Brewer's Blackbird neither concentrates in huge flocks nor causes extensive agricultural damage, so it has attracted much less attention from researchers.

Like many other blackbirds, the Brewer's breed in wet places in loose colonies of five to ten pairs (sometimes as many as one hundred) and often practice polygyny. In winter they frequent farmland and towns, and both the wintering and breeding ranges have expanded during this century into suitable new habitat provided by agriculture and irrigation. Despite their comfort level with towns, however (and a liking for bread and cracked corn), Brewer's Blackbirds are rather sporadic visitors to feeders.

Brewer's Blackbirds from northern parts of the breeding range migrate. Especially large numbers are reported from southern Texas in spring and fall, which suggests that a big proportion of the population moves into Mexico for the winter. Females migrate farther south than males and are therefore the most likely to enjoy winter vacations south of the border.

Compared to related species, Brewer's Blackbirds are veritable loners. While migrants and residents do form roving flocks of one hundred to one thousand birds and occasionally join huge agglomerations of other blackbirds, the Brewer's flocks are nearly always the smallest of the constituent species. Even after tagging along to the site of a large mixed-blackbird roost, Brewer's Blackbirds are likely to move off to nearby fields or thick vegetation to roost by themselves.

Foraging Brewer's Blackbirds usually walk rather than run, jerking their heads as they move forward en masse. Laggards fly to the front of the crowd before starting again to forage, causing the flock to appear as if it is rolling across a field. Flocks can be found on pastures or mowed lawns, or striding boldly among parked cars or picnic areas to scavenge food. About a third of the winter diet consists of insects, often including such agricultural pests as grasshoppers, crickets, and harmful larvae. Weed seeds, particularly wild oats, make up another large portion, which perhaps predisposes these blackbirds to feeding on waste grain in fields of cultivated oats and other crops.

Some feeder owners have been startled to see Brewer's Blackbirds dipping bread or popped corn into water prior to eating it. This behavior, which is also known in Common Grackles, evidently softens the food for easier swallowing.

Key references: Bent 1958, Crase and Dehaven 1978, Meanley 1965, Stepney 1975.

FeederWatch Findings

Like other blackbirds, the Brewer's Blackbird is most likely to visit feeders during spring migration. Although the winter range is in the southern and western United States, these early migrants can reach northern feeders before the winter bird-feeding season comes to a close. Despite visiting most feeders in spring, flock sizes are largest in fall.

Favorite feeder foods: *Mixed seed,* and, based on small samples, cracked corn.

Infrequent choices: Water and (according to small samples) striped and black-oil sunflower and hulled peanuts.

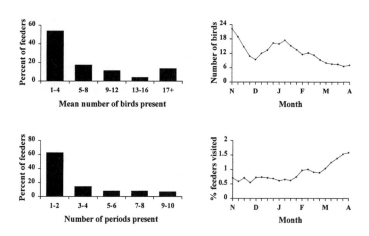

Brewer's Blackbird: percent of feeders visited

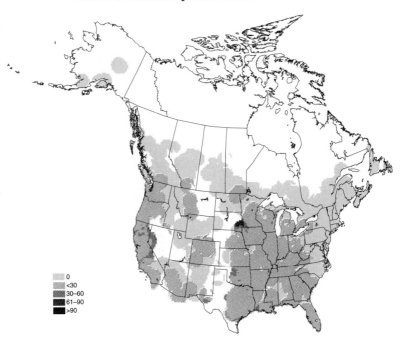

0
<30
30–60
61–90
>90

Abundance at feeders

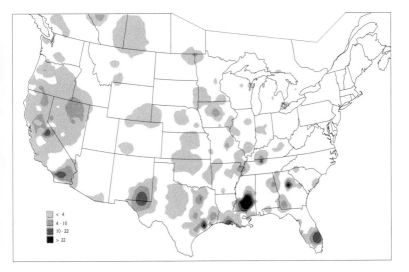

< 4
4 - 10
10 - 22
> 22

319

Common Grackle

Quiscalus quiscula

Of all the blackbirds that visit feeders, Common Grackles are among the most interesting to observe—and may cause the most problems. Large numbers of these wily, investigative birds sometimes settle in for a day at a time, intimidating other species and eating huge quantities of food. In springtime, males visiting feeders frequently display aggression, facing one another and stretching the bill skyward—a posture characteristic of other blackbird species, as well.

Almost any food will be welcome to a grackle, from fish, meat, and fowl to vegetable matter. These birds have been reported catching and eating small fish, all manner of crustaceans, small snakes, frogs and mice, and even other birds. Feeder owners are occasionally horrified to see grackles kill smaller birds and eat their brains. On the plus side, grackles relish beetles and savor many of the destructive sorts, such as Japanese beetles and rosebugs.

However, the vast majority of a grackle's diet during the winter is not meat but grain left in the fields after mechanical harvesting. Prior to human settlement of North America, chestnuts, beech-nuts, and acorns may have been the grackle's winter staples, and acorns are still important foods. Grackles hold these nuts in the bill close to the face and squeeze hard to crack them open—a testimonial to strong jaw muscles. Acorns and dried corn may also be "sawed" into smaller pieces, using the sharp keel of a horny plate on the bill as the operative tool.

Laboratory studies have shown that grackles can learn whether to sample or avoid new foods simply by watching the reactions of other grackles that try those foods first. This learning ability is evident in other aspects of grackle behavior, too. Some individuals figure out that by following robins, they will get chances to steal worms. Grackles in some areas soak foodstuffs in water prior to consumption, and as this habit is not universal, it, too, is probably learned. The dipping serves to soften stale bread and popped corn but seems to have no purpose when performed indiscriminantly, as it may be on such food as peanuts. This suggests that even if grackles do learn readily, they are not particularly insightful.

On the wintering grounds grackles gather in woodlots each evening in small to truly huge roosts, joining forces with several other species in numbers that can top a million birds. Daytime sees the roosts spreading out to forage in nearby fields, and when evening falls again, individual birds may move to different sites to roost with a new set of companions.

Most northern-nesting grackles migrate south for the winter, the males traveling less far than females—but only by 60 or so miles on average. Grackles of both sexes are quite early migrants, with males heading north a little earlier than females, and populations are sometimes hard hit by late-spring snowstorms.

Key references: Bent 1958, Beecher 1951, Caccamise et al. 1983, Cummings and Cummings 1989, Dolbeer 1982, Dolbeer et al. 1978, Darden 1974, Heisterberg et al. 1984, Mason et al. 1984, Roseberry 1962, Skaggs 1983, Wible 1975.

FeederWatch Findings

Common Grackles visit very few feeders before early February. As migratory movements start up, the proportion of feeders visited soars, and flock sizes at individual feeders drop off. This species is less likely to visit feeders in rural areas, where natural foods are probably in greater supply. Common Grackles are not common in West Texas (where FeederWatch coverage is lacking) but do occur in more northern portions of the central United States.

Favorite feeder foods: *Mixed seed,* sunflower (any type) cracked corn, water, and (according to small samples) pet food.

Infrequent choices: Millet, canary seed, safflower, whole corn, milo, wheat, peanuts (any form), suet, peanut butter mixes, bird puddings, fruit (fresh or dried), baked goods, sugar water, and (based on small samples) oats, meat scraps, and popped corn.

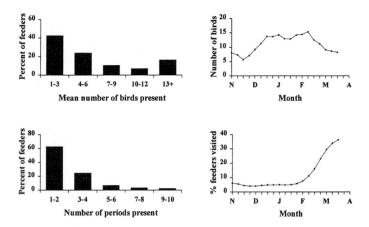

Common Grackle: percent of feeders visited

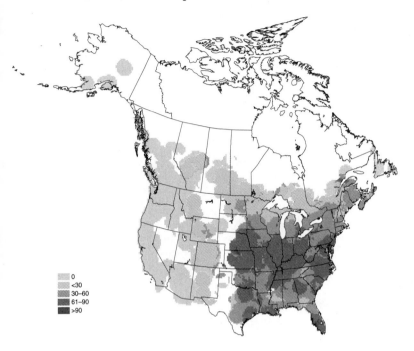

0
<30
30–60
61–90
>90

Abundance at feeders

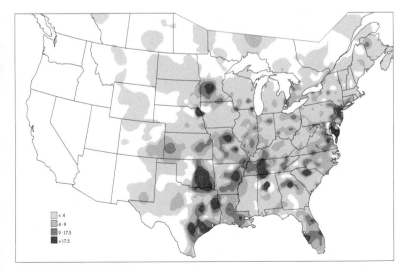

< 4
4 - 9
9 - 17.5
>17.5

Great-tailed Grackle

Quiscalus mexicanus

The "great tail" of the Great-tailed Grackle is a feature of the male only. The female, overall, is about one-quarter smaller than the male, and the difference in size and appearance between the sexes is so noticeable that some people call each sex by a different common name. Research on the blackbird family has demonstrated a positive correlation between sexual size difference and the degree of polygyny during nesting, and Great-tails certainly fit this pattern. They nest in colonies sometimes numbering in the thousands and are highly polygynous. Larger body size evidently helps males compete in the breeding season, but it carries a cost, as well: Males have an annual survival rate only 80% that of females. In monogamous blackbirds with equal-sized sexes, males survive as well or even better than females.

Great-tailed Grackles are common residents of towns in Central America and have recently expanded their southern United States range farther north and west. They are found in nearly every habitat except forest, and it matters little whether the locality is wet or dry overall, as long as there is at least some open water present. Foraging sites cover a broad range of open areas, including grassy lawns, streets, mangroves, beaches, and agricultural fields.

Great-tailed Grackle diets are as varied as their habitat tolerances, including grain, seeds, insects and small vertebrates. Grackles will rob the nests of other birds and eat any adults they can catch. They have also been seen wading into streams to snap up minnows, flying low to pick food from the water surface, and even doing a version of plunge-diving. Grackles are quick to take advantage of human activities to obtain food, following plows in fields, frequenting garbage piles, and, of course, visiting feeders.

The Great-tailed Grackle's manner is energetic and busy. The bird walks almost continuously, staring at the ground and pausing only momentarily to check for danger. The bill is used to probe the soil or to flip over shells, stones, leaves, paper, and anything else that might hide something edible. Males do more probing with their bills than do females and may have a slightly different diet overall.

Great-tailed Grackles roost together at night and evidently are not terribly fussy about sleeping places because they choose sites from marsh vegetation to palm trees in town plazas. It is hard to ignore the noise of such a roost; although some notes are attractive, others have been described as "nerve-shattering" and "best heard from a distance." (One call sounds like air squeaking out of a leaky balloon.)

Roost sites are sometimes shared with other kinds of blackbirds and with starlings, but during the daytime the grackles usually remain separate from other species. Flocks, frequently segregated by sex, disperse up to several miles from the roost site to forage. All members of a flock may act together in mobbing predators, but when both sexes are represented, the task is taken on more often by males than by females.

Key references: Bent 1958, Johnson et al. 1980, Searcy and Yasukawa 1981, Selander and Giller 1961, Smith 1977.

FeederWatch Findings

The Great-tailed Grackle is not a widespread feeder species, but it does appear at about a fifth of feeders in the south central United States, usually only a few times per winter. It is widespread in Texas, where our maps reflect a gap in FeederWatch coverage. This largely resident species has a smaller spring surge in feeder visitation than more migratory blackbirds. Rural feeder owners are far less likely to report these grackles than suburban or (especially) urban dwellers. Numbers visiting at one time vary widely but average about five.

Favorite feeder foods: The few data available indicate frequent choice of *mixed seed,* black-oil sunflower, and *water.*

Infrequent choices: According to small sample sizes, striped sunflower and whole and cracked corn.

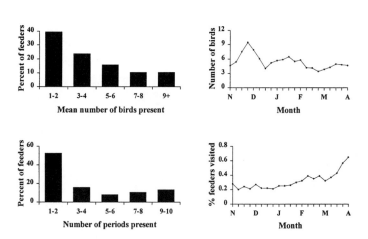

Great-tailed Grackle: percent of feeders visited

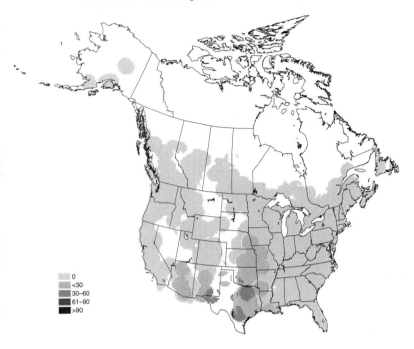

Abundance at feeders

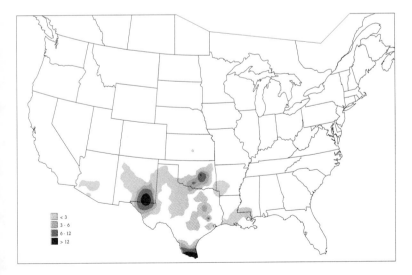

Brown-headed Cowbird

Molothrus ater

The latin name for Brown-headed Cowbird (*Molothrus*) means either parasite or vagabond, and both meanings apply to this bird's habits. Cowbirds do not raise their own young but instead lay up to forty eggs a year in the nests of other species. Perhaps this trait evolved out of necessity because cowbirds historically roamed the prairies with nomadic bison herds and did not stay in one place long enough to raise young. "Buffalo birds," as they were then called, relied on the insects that were stirred up by thousands of hooves. Later on, cowbirds switched to cattle, thereby earning their current common name. Though hardly dependent on the association today, cowbirds will still concentrate at cattle yards in winter and can eat into the profits of any farmer so unwise as to scatter cattle feed on the ground instead of placing it in troughs.

Some people do not like hosting cowbirds at their feeders because of the potential negative impact of this species on songbird reproduction. Clearing forests for agriculture allowed cowbirds to extend their range and begin to parasitize naive species that had not evolved any defenses. If you wish to exclude cowbirds from your feeder, avoid offering small seeds and cracked corn and use tube feeders (on which cowbirds are loathe to perch). Such measures may rarely be necessary, however, as cowbirds are not common visitors to feeders, anyway (relative to their overall numbers). They prefer instead to forage at sites with much more open habitat than is typical of residential areas. Moreover, cowbird populations have declined steadily over recent decades in much of the central and eastern United States, perhaps as a result of forest regeneration.

Cowbirds from southern regions are nonmigratory, while northern birds head south for the winter to join them. Migratory males travel just as far south as females, in contrast to the situation in many other blackbird species. But male cowbirds do start north earlier in spring than females; they are among the first spring returnees to northern regions, and their appearance at feeders in still frostbound regions is a signal of winter's waning.

Once on the wintering grounds, migrant Brown-headed Cowbirds from many different breeding populations mix together in unstructured flocks whose composition changes from day to day. That males are dominant over females can be deduced from the fact that males are most frequently found at the best food sources, but cowbirds are a little unusual among birds in that juvenile males have higher status than adults.

Subordinate individuals are more likely to die during cold snaps, probably because they are at a disadvantage in competing for food. Less aggressive cowbirds are also more likely to sleep on the periphery of a roost, in positions most vulnerable to predation. Dominant birds jockey for central positions each evening as they fly to communal roost sites—a jostling that sometimes results in impressive aerial displays. Huge "megaroosts" form in some southern states, and up to 300,000 cowbirds have been recorded joining other blackbird species in a single one of these massive agglomerations.

Key references: Dolbeer 1982, Dolbeer and Smith 1985, Dolbeer et al. 1978, Glahn and Otis 1986, Johnson et al. 1980, Lowther 1993, Robertson et al. 1978.

FeederWatch Findings

As with other blackbirds, the Brown-headed Cowbird visits few feeders before spring migration, at which time sightings rise rapidly. At the few sites that host cowbirds throughout the winter, flock sizes peak in late fall. Flock size varies a lot, but most feeders average only a few birds at a time.

Favorite feeder foods: *Mixed seed,* millet, cracked corn, and probably (based on data from a few feeders) pet food.

Infrequent choices: Sunflower (any type), safflower, hulled peanuts, suet, bird puddings, water. Small samples indicate occasional choice also of canary seed, milo, dried fruit, and oats.

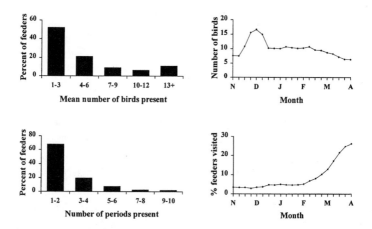

Brown-headed Cowbird: percent of feeders visited

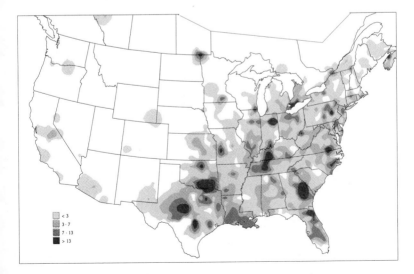

0
<30
30–60
61–90
>90

Abundance at feeders

< 3
3 · 7
7 · 13
> 13

331

Gray-crowned Rosy-Finch, Black Rosy-Finch, and Brown-capped Rosy-Finch

Leucosticte tephrocotis, L. atrata, and L. australis

Rosy-Finches come in several forms that are so distinct, they were once considered separate species—and in fact, they recently regained these separate statuses. At the time our data were gathered, however, all forms were collectively known as Rosy Finch. We were unable to separate the data after the fact because the different species sometimes overlap in winter, so we cover them here under a single account.

In winter the montane forms of rosy finches migrate down slope from high altitudes to relatively snow-free areas. Most move only a few hundred miles (sometimes farther in the Black Rosy-Finch), but heavy snowfall will force the finches farther afield. Under stormy conditions, residential neighborhoods may suddenly be invaded by rosy finches in the thousands.

Rosy finches are seldom seen alone in winter but rather in roving flocks that typically contain twenty-five to fifty birds. They forage on the ground, seeking the small weed seeds that make up to 99% of their diet, using vigorous sideways swipes of the bill to toss aside snow and soil and uncover seeds below the surface. The action of one individual taking flight triggers others into swirling upward and following after the leader in a compact group. Possibly this flocking habit helps finches to locate widely scattered patches of food. Rosy finches banded at one study site were later found feeding at another location 25 miles away, suggesting that the winter foraging range of a flock could be on the order of 500 square miles.

Each evening, foraging groups coalesce into flocks of up to a thousand individuals going off to roost at traditional sites that are used repeatedly by the same birds, night to night and year to year. Roost sites nearly always have shelter overhead and include caves, mine shafts, wells, buildings, and even old Cliff Swallow nests. Rosy finches tend to retire long before sunset, and once settled they may refuse to be scared off from their chosen bivouacs. Besides providing protection from predators, roost sites can be considerably warmer than outside; the temperature in one cave roost was nearly 54°F higher than out in the open. Cozy shelter may be especially important to winter survival, as rosy finches do not have exceptional fat stores and do not save energy by lowering body temperature at night.

When rosy finches move out of their montane and arctic habitats to spend the winter in more populated areas, they appear to tolerate humans well. These birds are uncommonly tame and have been reported entering buildings and even cars (although they prefer open country). They visit feeders readily, at least in rural areas, and like other seed-dependent species, rosy finches like to drink water and have a fondness for salt. They evidently remember where food is regularly available and return to such sites year after year.

Feeder owners may notice that males often outnumber females by severalfold. Skewed sex ratios in many other species indicate that the sexes separate in winter or migrate different distances, but in the case of rosy finches the imbalance appears permanent, persisting throughout the year. Females do have lower first-year survival than males—for unknown reasons—but there may also be other causes for this imbalance.

Key references: Behle 1973, Clemens 1989, French 1959, Hendricks 1981, King and Wales 1964, Leffingwell and Leffingwell 1931, Shaw 1936, Shreve 1980, Swenson et al. 1988.

FeederWatch Findings

Rosy finches are mainly montane, and while they winter at lower altitudes, they prefer open country and are casual in towns (almost never being seen at urban feeders). They usually are irregular visitors, as opposed to winter long, but visit up to a third of feeders in some states at least once, especially in spring. Numbers are quite variable, and though typically seen at feeders in small flocks, thirty or more may come to feeders in the coldest months. The winter range is broader than suggested by the maps, including parts of Nevada and Utah where FeederWatch coverage is low.

Favorite feeder foods: Data available from a small number of feeders indicate that *black-oil sunflower*, mixed seed, and *water* are chosen frequently.

Infrequent choices: Cracked corn, millet.

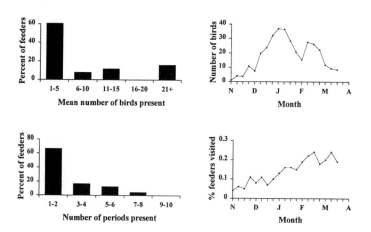

Gray-crowned, Black, and Brown-capped Rosy-Finch: percent of feeders visited

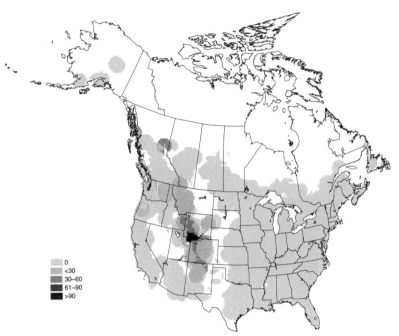

- 0
- <30
- 30–60
- 61–90
- >90

Abundance at feeders

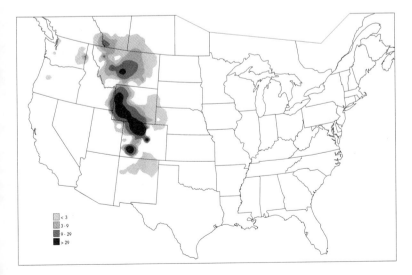

- < 3
- 3 - 9
- 9 - 29
- > 29

Pine Grosbeak

Pinicola enucleator

The Pine Grosbeak is completely unlike its flashy cousin, the Evening Grosbeak. The latter is brightly colored, pugnacious, voracious, loves bird feeders, and is wary. The Pine Grosbeak is uncommon at feeders, much less noisy, and quite tame. Newfoundlanders sometimes call it "the Mope" because it sits around so quietly. However, if you get close to a flock, you'll hear a constant conversation of barely audible, musical "toots."

Pine Grosbeaks rarely seek out feeders, even during southward irruptions in years when natural food supplies are low. The most likely place to see them is in the northern areas where they live year-round, but even then they are not abundant visitors at feeders. These grosbeaks apparently prefer natural foods, which include a wide variety of tree seeds (birches to conifers), fruits (such as crabapple and mountain ash), and buds (maple, elm, and birch, among others). Spruce buds are sometimes the major food source, probably in years when tree seeds are scarce or of lower-than-average nutritional quality. As long as a flock is undisturbed, it may settle down to a long feeding session on buds before moving on. In a pinch, Pine Grosbeaks will eat grass and weed seeds, or even waste grain, but seeds are clearly not their favorite food.

When Pine Grosbeaks do deign to descend to feeders, they are easily bullied by Evening Grosbeaks and may defer visits to afternoon, by which time Evening Grosbeaks have usually departed. There are casual observations that Pine Grosbeaks decrease in years when Evening Grosbeak numbers are high, both at feeders and in the wild, although no direct causation has been proposed. Evening Grosbeaks thrive during outbreaks of spruce budworm, and spruce buds are sometimes an important source of food for Pine Grosbeaks, so perhaps any alternation between the species results from different responses to that important northern forest pest.

Well-adapted to its northern climate, the Pine Grosbeak wears a heavy coat of down under its rose-tinged gray contour feathers—so heavy that the birds look quite rotund. These grosbeaks can be seen feeding contentedly in open, windy habitat even when temperatures fall below -31°F, long after other species have sought shelter, and sometimes they bathe in soft snow. Pine Grosbeaks are not totally immune to cold, however. They fill their crops for overnight ingestion before retiring to heavy cover for nocturnal roosting, and apparently roost in very close contact with one another—a hypothesis formed when a researcher captured some grosbeaks in winter that were adorned with droppings on their heads and backs.

Little is known of the Pine Grosbeak's social behavior in winter, possibly because human researchers prefer to study them in warmer weather. The grosbeaks are known to travel in groups of five to ten birds, sometimes twenty, with occasional flocks of up to one hundred, but the larger numbers may only represent temporary associations of smaller flocks at sites with especially abundant food. Small flocks are marked by such peaceful coexistence among members as to suggest that the individuals know one another well. Chances are these groups are made up of one or several families that stay together all winter.

Key references: Cade 1952, Dunn 1989, Pittaway 1989, Pulliainen 1974.

FeederWatch Findings

Pine Grosbeaks will sometimes visit week after week. They are much more likely to be reported at rural and suburban feeders than at urban sites. The proportion of feeders visited increases to late winter, then drops off markedly in February and March, at which time flock size also declines.

Favorite feeder foods: *Black-oil and striped sunflower,* water. Small samples show that hulled sunflower is also acceptable.

Infrequent choices: Mixed seed, suet. A few feeders that offered fresh fruit reported infrequent selection of this food, as well.

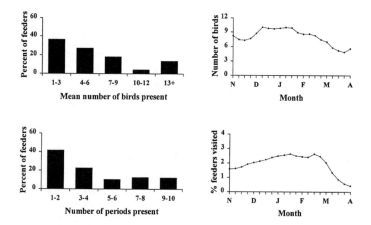

Pine Grosbeak: percent of feeders visited

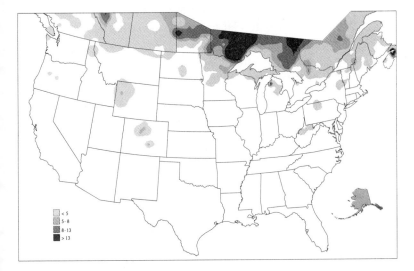

0
<30
30–60
61–90
>90

Abundance at feeders

< 5
5 - 8
8 - 13
> 13

Purple Finch

Carpodacus purpureus

Purple Finches were once kept as caged birds because of their pleasing song. They can also be quite nice to look at. Yearling males retain the brown coloring of their youth and thus resemble females, but adult males sport more vivid yellow, orange, or purple-red plumage. Lemony-yellow variants are fairly common in these and many other finches, a genetically based condition known as xanthochroism.

A Purple Finch's broad diet includes seeds from weeds and a wide variety of deciduous trees. Insects are added as summer foods. Purple Finches like to eat leaf and flower buds, sometimes making themselves unpopular with orchard owners, but defenders feel that fruit trees actually suffer little damage and may even benefit from avian pruning.

Bird banding has been an important tool in tracking the winter movements of Purple Finches. Results show that these birds are faithful to their breeding area but are nomadic in winter. Like other birds that eat tree seeds, Purple Finches disperse widely in winters when seed crops are poor. Their broad diet causes emigrations to be relatively infrequent and unspectacular, but occasionally there are Purple Finch "superinvasions." The factors causing these are not well understood. Few Purple Finches live more than three to four years, so most individuals never take part in one of these major emigrations. Once on a wintering site, Purple Finches may retreat to deep shelter in cold weather, then suddenly reappear in residential areas on warm spring days—fooling us into thinking that migration has occurred.

Purple Finches are year-round visitors to feeders, where they consume large quantities of sunflower seed. Sources of salt can also prove attractive. The preferred feeder type is a tray raised high off the ground—even as high as second-story level—though nearly any type of feeder is acceptable.

Observant feeder owners may notice their Purple Finches expressing dominance with a "head-forward" threat display, holding the body horizontally and gaping the bill at an antagonist. Surprisingly, dull-colored Purple Finches often supplant brightly colored ones, as is also true of House Finches. Normally in birds with dominance hierarchies it is the more highly colored males who take precedence. One hypothesis suggested for House Finches (but perhaps applicable to this species, as well) is that males who defer to females are advertising their superiority: Any bird that can afford to defer to others in the harshest part of the year must have excellent foraging abilities.

The Purple Finch was once a much more common breeder in the northeastern United States than it is today, and some researchers have speculated that competition with the rapidly increasing House Finch was a causal factor. Purple Finches lose altercations with these immigrants and try to avoid confronting them. However, the decline of Purple Finches in New England took place long before House Finches ever appeared on the scene, and the decline also occurred in parts of the range where House Finches are absent. Habitat change appears a more likely cause.

Key references: Bent 1968, Bock and Lepthien 1976, Fraser 1985, Isted 1985, Hill 1990, Popp 1987a, Shedd 1990, Smith and Balda 1979, Yunick 1978, 1983a,b.

FeederWatch Findings

While some Purple Finches remain in northern areas for the winter, abundance is higher at feeders in the southern half of the United States, and the number of feeders visited in the north increases as spring migration begins. Usually four to six birds visit feeders together in a flock. This finch is present in all habitats but is less likely to be seen at urban feeders (as well as in smaller numbers).

Favorite feeder foods: *Black-oil sunflower,* striped and hulled sunflower.

Infrequent choices: Mixed seed, millet, canary seed, safflower, cracked corn, niger, peanut hearts, peanut butter mixes, bird puddings, fresh fruit, water. According to small samples, meat scraps and popped corn may also be eaten on occasion.

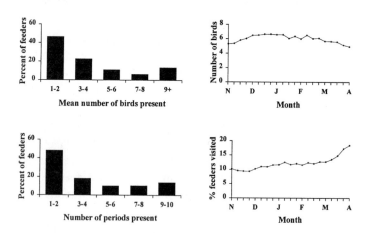

Purple Finch: percent of feeders visited

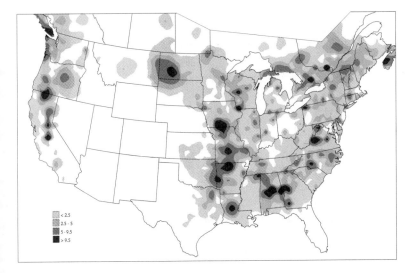

Abundance at feeders

Cassin's Finch

Carpodacus cassinii

Among the *Carpodacus* finches (Cassin's, House, and Purple), Cassin's Finch is the least known. It is fairly nomadic, like the Purple Finch, and is much less associated with man than the House Finch.

Cassin's Finches breed in high-elevation open-coniferous forests, often in loose colonies. Some populations return to the same site year after year, whereas others breed once or twice and then move elsewhere. The deciding factor in summer site fidelity is probably regularity of food supply. Staminate (male) tree buds make up a large part of the spring diet, and the quality of buds at a given breeding site may not be sufficient to sustain finch reproduction every year.

In late summer, families join into small foraging groups and later move to lower elevations for the winter, where they join into flocks as large as five thousand individuals. However, winter flocks are typically closer to ten to thirty birds, perhaps consisting of those that bred near each other. Wild flocks are only loosely organized, though, with composition that can change daily.

Cassin's Finches maintain social order in winter through a dominance hierarchy. As in most species, adults dominate younger birds; but unlike the situation in most birds, the dull-colored adult females occupy ranks superior to those of the more brightly colored adult males. Female dominance is also known to occur in House and Purple Finches as well as in some other related species (for example, the Lesser Goldfinch), but the underlying causes are not well understood. One explanation suggested for the Cassin's Finch is that female dominance enhances winter survival; because female finches are often in short supply relative to males, it may ultimately be to the males' advantage to ensure that as many females survive the winter as possible. Where sex ratios are strongly skewed, young males (and perhaps some older ones) are unable to attract mates. If the sex ratio is more equal, all birds get to breed, even yearling males that have not yet attained their rosy-splashed adult plumage.

The winter diet of Cassin's Finch consists of conifer seeds supplemented with buds and berries. Much foraging takes place on the ground, where the finches can easily extract seeds from fallen and fully opened cones. While conifer seeds make wonderful foods when abundant, these trees are notorious for showing wide annual variation in quality and abundance of their cone crops—explaining why finches must roam widely in early winter to locate a good food source. Sometimes a few birds return to an area where there was plenty of food the year before, but most do not. Evidently Cassin's Finches are not always successful in finding a good wintering area because mortality rates differ widely among winters. Regular visits to feeders may reduce that toll. While average life expectancy is two to three years, one individual is known to have lived seven years.

Cassin's Finches may confound birders by mimicking the songs of other montane species, such as Evening Grosbeaks, Pine Siskins, or crossbills. These are all species that the Cassin's Finch may join in mixed foraging flocks.

Key references: Balph 1978, Hahn 1996, Mewaldt and King 1985, Samson 1976, 1977.

FeederWatch Findings

Like Purple Finches, the Cassin's Finch is more abundant at southern than northern feeders during the winter, and the number of sightings at northern feeders increases in spring. Flock size is fairly stable all season, averaging about six individuals. Cassin's Finches are most often seen at rural feeders. These birds are common in Nevada and Utah, and gaps on the maps result from lack of FeederWatch coverage there.

Favorite feeder foods: *Black-oil sunflower,* water. A few feeders offering millet report it is also chosen frequently.

Infrequent choices: Cracked corn and (according to small samples) mixed seed, niger, peanut butter mixes, and bird puddings.

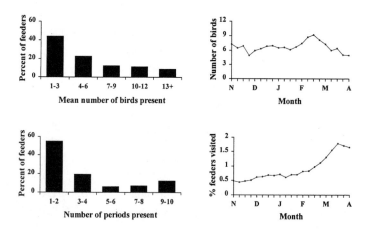

Cassin's Finch: percent of feeders visited

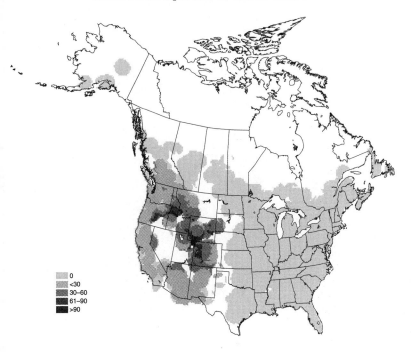

Abundance at feeders

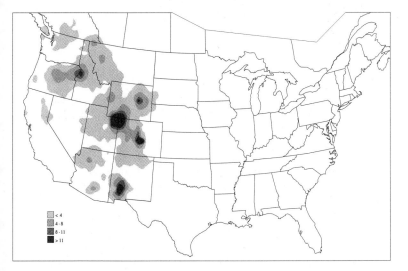

House Finch

Carpodacus mexicanus

This familiar, sweetly singing bird of the West was only introduced to easterners fairly recently. Pet dealers who were threatened
with prosecution for illegally selling the birds as caged songsters
responded in 1940 by freeing their captives on New York's Long
Island, and House Finches have since become established through
all of eastern North America.

Eastern birds have already evolved different characteristics than
their western ancestors. They have a larger bill, making it easier to
handle bigger seeds (including sunflower)—possibly an indication
that widespread bird feeding contributed to range expansion. Eastern
House Finches have also become partially migratory, whereas the
ancestral stock is resident. Females tend to migrate the farthest, as
is the case in many other species, which explains the predominance
of colorful finches at northern feeders and of brown individuals at
feeders farther south.

As House Finch numbers increased in the East, populations of
another suburban species, the House Sparrow, declined. A link was
suspected, but a recent review of all available evidence suggested

that the explosive expansion of House Finch range was not respon-sible. Sparrows decreased in many regions before House Finches arrived there, and House Sparrows are in any case dominant to House Finches in aggressive encounters.

Male House Finches come in all shades from gray or yellow through orange tints to bright crimson. The coloration comes from the carotenoid pigments found in some wild foods (but not in commercial birdseed). A male more brightly colored than average may therefore mark himself as a good forager who is able to find sources of high-quality natural foods. Juvenile and yearling males have less colorful plumage than older birds, though they are still distinguished by a touch of red. Dullness in young males is an advantage in winter because older males defer to brown birds at feeders, but in springtime the more vivid, experienced males are the ones first chosen as mates.

Juveniles learn something about which foods to choose or avoid during the relatively short period they are dependent on par-ents. This was demonstrated through an experiment in which adults were trained to avoid oats by treating the grain with a distasteful chemical. Youngsters subsequently raised by those adults copied their parents' food choices, avoiding oats even though they were no longer treated with chemicals—and the aversion persisted after the birds became fully independent.

After family breakup, juvenile House Finches join flocks that can number in the hundreds where food is concentrated. Later in the fall these large groups break into smaller winter flocks. Flocking has advantages but also some hazards, one of which is susceptibili-ty to disease. House Finches seem particularly subject to avian pox. Although this disease causes visible tumors that sometimes lead to death, recovery is possible, and the disease is mainly self-limiting. In the 1990s an outbreak of a bacillus causing conjunctivitis (ooz-ing and crusted eyes) spread throughout the eastern population and may have played a role in ending the previously steady rise in House Finch numbers.

Flocks of House Finches may stay at feeders for long periods, often keeping other species waiting for a turn. They try out all kinds of feeders and eat a wide variety of foods, including sugar water. If they become a nuisance at your hummingbird feeders, try offering them an open dish "feeder" of their own. House Finches may drink

40% of their body weight daily during hot weather, so a water source will definitely be an attractant.

Key references: Avery 1996, Bartholomew and Cade 1956, Bennett 1990, Belthoff and Gauthreaux 1991, Bent 1968, Brown and Brown 1988, Dawson et al. 1983, Dennis 1986, McClure 1989, Hamilton and Novis 1994, Hill 1990, 1993, Kalinoski 1975, Mundinger and Hope 1982, Shedd 1990, Sprenkle and Blem 1984.

FeederWatch Findings

Feeder observers have documented the spread of eastern House Finches through the Midwest, where there is no longer a gap between them and western populations (although abundance is still low in the contact zone). Gaps in the distribution map result from lack of Feeder-Watch coverage rather than lack of birds. Flock sizes vary widely, averaging ten to fifteen in early January and becoming steadily smaller thereafter. Unlike the other "red" finches, Purple and Cassin's, the House Finch is very likely to be present at a feeder all winter long.

Favorite feeder foods: *Black-oil and hulled sunflower,* striped sunflower, mixed seed, safflower, niger, water.

Infrequent choices: Millet, canary seed, cracked corn, milo, wheat, hulled peanuts and hearts, oats, canola, suet, peanut butter mixes, bird puddings, fresh fruit, baked goods, sugar water, popped corn.

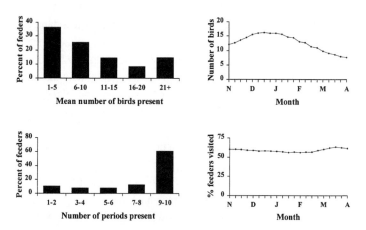

House Finch: percent of feeders visited

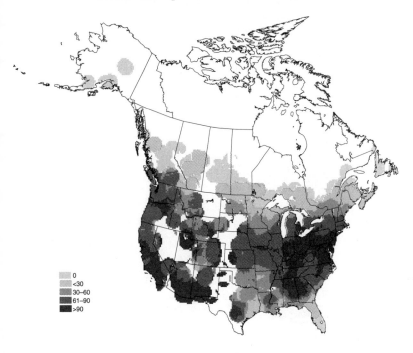

- 0
- <30
- 30–60
- 61–90
- >90

Abundance at feeders

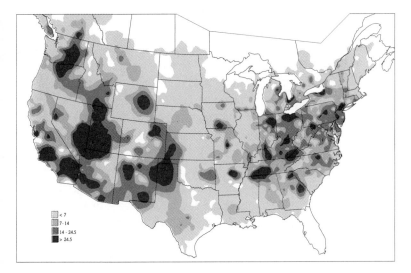

- < 7
- 7 - 14
- 14 - 24.5
- > 24.5

Common Redpoll and Hoary Redpoll

Carduelis flammea and C. hornemanni

The Common and Hoary Redpoll are combined here because so little is known about differences in their winter ecology. Maps and charts refer to Common Redpoll alone, but results are very similar for Hoaries. Previously treated as one species, Hoary and Common Redpolls are now thought to be separate, in part because they do not appear to hybridize where their breeding ranges overlap.

Redpolls breed in scrubby areas of the high arctic where they feed on the tiny seeds of birch and alder trees, which is the basis of their German name, *Birkenzeisig* ("Birch Siskin"). Birch trees vary from year to year in the quantity of seeds produced, with poor years following those of bumper crops. Redpolls respond by shifting their breeding sites each spring to the most suitable local areas, and by irrupting southward in winters when seed crops are low. Such irregular nomadic movements occur about once every two to three years, although the pattern is not wholly predictable.

A few redpolls always remain in the north, so irruptions are not very noticeable to people living close to the breeding range. Farther south, however, the variation is dramatic: Either there are no redpolls at all or there are multitudes. So great is the wandering tendency of redpolls that individuals have been caught in different winters at sites over 1,200 miles apart. It is not known whether cohesive flocks travel together or whether every individual goes its own way.

In the absence of birch seeds, redpolls eat everything from tiny weed seeds to pine nuts. At feeders both redpoll species select sunflower (preferably shelled) and niger but are willing to try novelties such as canola seed, and they also enjoy water and sources of salt. Just as redpolls in the wild forage anywhere from treetop to ground level, they will visit feeders hung high in trees or pick up fallen seeds below them. You may notice frequent aggression at your feeder, expressed as open-mouthed lunges at neighbors, but rarely severe fights. Males are dominant and the dominance hierarchy (once established) helps reduce ferocity of squabbling.

Redpolls are among the smallest birds to winter regularly in the far north. They do not accumulate much fat, but have other adaptations to cold weather, including good insulation, a high-energy food source, and remaining active at low-light intensities (a necessary adaptation if a bird is to find enough food in the very short winter days of the north). There are behavioral adaptations to cold, as well: Redpolls have been reported foraging in the cozy comfort of spaces underneath the snow and may also roost there to conserve heat.

The most distinctive anatomical adaptation to a severe climate is a small pouch on one side of the esophagus. A redpoll fills this pouch with unhusked seeds, then retreats to a warmer or less windy site to cough them up and hull them for final consumption. Though the pouch holds only enough seeds for about a quarter of one day's total energy requirements, this supplement is sufficient to ensure survival through a night of -81°F. Without this supply of midnight snack food, it is estimated that redpolls could survive temperatures of "only" -23°F.

Key references: Bock and Lepthien 1976, Brooks 1968, 1978, Cade 1953, Dilger 1960, Herremans 1989, Kennard 1976, Knox 1988, Larson and Bock 1986, Pulliainen et al. 1978, Smith 1979b, Troy 1983, White and West 1977.

FeederWatch Findings

Feeder findings for redpolls vary widely depending on whether or not it is an irruption year. The maps show averages over several years, including seasons of both short and long distance movements. Hoary Redpolls stay farther north than Commons. In general, the percent of feeders visited increases rapidly whenever redpolls begin to invade, and flock sizes also get larger, often reaching fifty or more. Numbers per feeder may continue to increase as more and more birds move into an invaded area. Abundance and length of stay vary strongly among localities from year to year, but once redpolls reach an area, they tend to be faithful visitors (except that Hoary Redpolls may be more likely to abandon feeders after a few visits). Redpolls tend to be most abundant and commonly seen at rural feeders. The food preferences of Common and Hoary Redpolls are essentially the same, although Hoaries are reported taking black-oil sunflower and canola more often than are Commons.

Favorite feeder foods: *Hulled sunflower, niger,* mixed seed, striped and black-oil sunflower, canola, water, and (according to small samples) canary seed.

Infrequent choices: Millet, cracked corn, suet, peanut butter mixes, bird puddings, baked goods, and (based on small samples) milo.

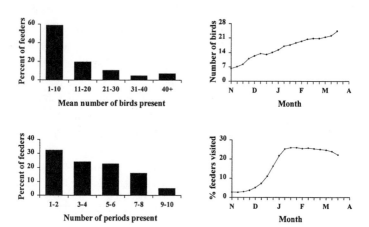

Common Redpoll: percent of feeders visited

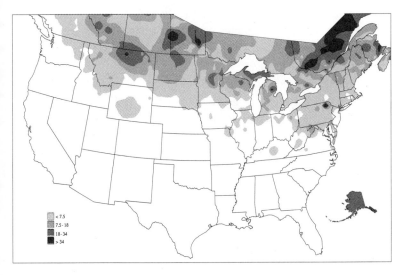

0
<30
30–60
61–90
>90

Abundance at feeders

< 7.5
7.5 - 18
18 - 34
> 34

Pine Siskin

Carduelis pinus

The Pine Siskin is a classic "boom-or-bust" species. It has a regular winter range, but every few years there is a large irruption to areas far beyond those boundaries. This is evidently caused by fluctuation in the abundance of tree seeds that are the main food source (especially pine and alder).

Trees with edible seeds face a dilemma: Mammals and insects like to eat these seeds as much as birds do, and if trees produce a predictable annual crop of seed, seed predators may become so dependent on the food source that no seeds survive to germinate. Many tree species solve this problem by generating huge seed crops every few years—called mast years—with poor crops in between. Seed predator populations decline when there are few seeds, so the next time there is a bonanza seed crop, there are fewer predators on hand to eat them. The Pine Siskin's countermove to this fluctuation in food supply is to move away in search of a better source when the local stores are low. In the past, heading into the unknown in hopes of finding a better food source could be pretty risky. Today, with feeders nearly everywhere, Pine Siskins can be sure of finding food in their travels.

Siskins are not only nomadic between winters—rarely returning to the same destinations twice—but also within a winter. The birds visiting your feeder today may not be the ones you saw a few days or weeks before. Examples come from a bird bander in North Dakota, whose marked birds were resighted later the same winter as far away as 450 miles. Another was recaptured three years later in Connecticut—2,000 miles to the east.

Weather evidently plays little role in Pine Siskin wanderings, as these birds are quite capable of withstanding a severe climate. At the onset of winter they become considerably more plump through accumulation of fat. Each bird can pack sufficient seeds into its distendable esophagus to support itself through five hours of rest at -4°F temperatures.

Siskins are social year-round, possibly even nesting in loose colonies and nearly always visiting feeders in the company of others. They are nonetheless pugnacious, and even casual observers will see frequent examples of aggression. A siskin leaning forward with its wings slightly spread and beak wide open is telling its companions to back off. The same display may be directed at other species, and these sometimes take more notice than fellow siskins, deferring their feeder visits until the siskins have departed. Despite this propensity for minor squabbling, siskins readily join flocks of other species for winter foraging.

Pine Siskins are especially attracted to feeders with niger seed or sunflower chips, and will readily accept black-oil sunflower seed, but they evidently have difficulty opening the large seeds of striped sunflower. If an Evening Grosbeak is eating these larger seeds, a siskin may take up a position near its head to pick up dropped particles—and will even defend the position vigorously against other siskins that try to barge in.

Siskins, crossbills, and other finches have been observed eating road salt and flaking mortar, and pecking at other sources of sodium and calcium. Perhaps they do this because tree seeds are relatively poor in elemental sodium, as are the granitic rocks of much of the boreal region where many of the finch species live. If you offer a source of salt at your feeder (see recipe in the Evening Grosbeak account), you may want to ensure that there is also a source of water nearby.

Key references: Balph and Balph 1979, Bennetts and Hutto 1985, Bock and Lepthien 1976, Bonta 1988, Dawson 1997, Fraser 1985, Tallman 1989.

FeederWatch Findings

Like redpolls, Pine Siskins are very unpredictable feeder visitors. In some years they irrupt as far southeast as Florida, as shown on the maps, but in other winters siskins remain in their northern and western breeding areas. Gaps in mapped distribution are an artifact of holes in FeederWatch coverage. Although rural feeders tend to attract larger flocks, the species is nearly as likely to visit feeders in urban areas as elsewhere. As long as siskins are present in your area, flocks are likely to visit feeders regularly.

Favorite feeder foods: *Hulled sunflower, niger,* black-oil sunflower, water.

Infrequent choices: Mixed seed, millet, canary seed, striped sunflower, safflower, cracked corn, milo, wheat, peanut hearts, suet, peanut butter mixes, bird puddings. Small samples indicate that canola may also be eaten.

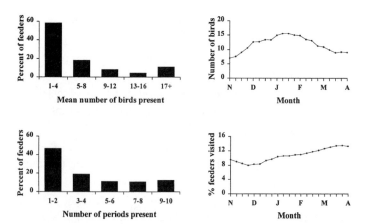

Pine Siskin: percent of feeders visited

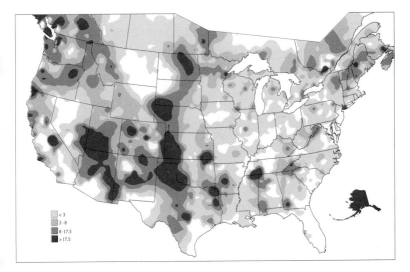

0
<30
30–60
61–90
>90

Abundance at feeders

< 3
3 - 8
8 - 17.5
> 17.5

Lesser Goldfinch

Carduelis psaltria

The southwestern United States must be goldfinch heaven, with three species occurring together: Lesser, Lawrence's, and American. The Pine Siskin (a close relative of goldfinches) also occurs in parts of this region. The only absent members of the genus *Carduelis* are the two redpoll species.

The Lesser Goldfinch is very poorly known in comparison to the well-studied American Goldfinch, although the two species appear similar in many regards. Lessers relish the seeds of composite flowers, particularly dandelions, and even delay breeding until the late-summer period, when the greatest number of composites go to seed. While most bird babies are fed on insects, infant goldfinches are stuffed with seed mash; only in summer do a few insects get added to their otherwise vegetarian diet. But Lesser Goldfinches eat a healthy variety of vegetables, including flowers, buds, maple keys, and the seeds of birch and alder. They are acrobatic foragers, often seen clinging to seed heads that are waving to and fro in the wind.

The Lesser Goldfinch lives in semiarid regions where brush and scattered trees dot an open landscape (whereas the American Goldfinch prefers damper areas). Despite this tolerance for dry terrain, Lessers are seldom found more than half a mile from water, and distribution of water sources may determine that of the birds, at least in the dry season. Indeed, water is among the best attractant to feeders. Like other birds that rely heavily on seeds year-round, these goldfinches need a lot to drink. They are also attracted to sources of salt, perhaps to obtain minerals lacking in seeds. Once Lesser Goldfinches have been lured to feeders, they consume the same sorts of seeds that are also favorites of American Goldfinches.

In squabbles over food sources, the female Lesser Goldfinch generally beats out the male. This is also true in the "red finches"— House, Cassin's, and Purple—but is opposite to the pattern of male dominance typical of such feeder species as sparrows and blackbirds.

Lesser Goldfinches from the eastern portion of the range are partially migratory, with some remaining resident and others withdrawing southward for the winter. It is not known whether there is any variation in social behavior of residents and migrants or among the plumage variants across the range (goldfinches with black backs from the eastern part of the range vs. westerners with green backs). We do know that Lesser Goldfinches are highly gregarious. As many as four hundred may flock together in winter, although flocks more commonly consist of twenty to thirty. The average number seen visiting feeders at one time is usually only one to three birds; a little less than the four to five typical of American Goldfinches in the same region. Both goldfinch species mingle in winter flocks and may also join Pine Siskins.

Key references: Bent 1968, Coutlee 1968.

FeederWatch Findings

Lesser Goldfinches are fairly uncommon and irregular visitors to feeders, appearing most often during spring migration. They are more common in West Texas in winter, and in Nevada and Utah as migrants, than is indicated by the maps. This species can be confused with the American Goldfinch in winter plumage, so our data may possibly overrepresent the abundance of Lesser Goldfinches. Most sites average fewer than five individuals at once.

Favorite feeder foods: The few data available indicate that water (and perhaps niger) are the main feeder attractants, but that mixed seed, black-oil sunflower, and hulled sunflower are also eaten.

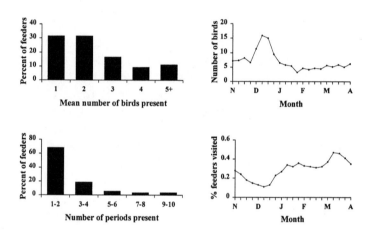

Lesser Goldfinch: percent of feeders visited

	0
	<30
	30–60
	61–90
	>90

Abundance at feeders

	< 2
	2 - 3
	> 3

American Goldfinch

Carduelis tristis

Amererican Goldfinch is a "southern" finch, at least in comparison to the redpolls and siskins that sometimes invade the United States in winter. Goldfinches are also far less nomadic. Though the distance they move varies from year to year—probably depending on food and weather conditions—the fact that there will be a migratory movement of some sort is quite predictable, as is the general direction. On average females move farther south than males.

Finding a goldfinch in winter is frequently as easy as locating a weedy field, especially one filled with composite flowers that have gone to seed. Only a tiny portion of the goldfinch's mainly vegetarian diet is made up of insects. When the ground is snow covered, these birds are more likely to be found eating the seeds of birch or alder trees. They will hang upside down to eat, but experiments with specially designed feeders have shown that they prefer to dine upright if possible.

Goldfinches are also known to prefer feeders hung above head height in trees, but if there is no choice available, they will accept just about any feeder design, at any height. They also feed readily on the ground. Although niger (thistle) is a particular favorite at feeders, goldfinches are quite capable of handling sunflower seeds—which are too large for many species of similar size. The seeds are held with the long axis parallel to the beak, whose cutting edges crack the husk. As with all birds that rely heavily on vegetable foods, goldfinches are attracted to water, but northerners need not feel obliged to maintain a source because goldfinches can get all the moisture they need from eating snow.

As one might expect in a species with a relatively southern distribution, goldfinches are not terribly well-adapted to winter cold. They rely more heavily on filling their crops each night than they do on accumulated fat reserves—a reliance that can lead to starvation when severe storms prevent feeding. Perhaps to ensure steady supplies, goldfinches sometimes move from agricultural areas to more suburban, feeder-rich areas for the winter, and the growth of the bird-feeding industry is thought to have contributed to a northward expansion of goldfinch wintering range in recent years.

Another strategy for getting through the winter involves keeping warm at night. Goldfinches roost in the most densely needled, leeward portions of conifers, and occasionally they will sleep in cavities under the snow. They also don winter clothes: The dull-green coat of feathers grown each fall has an especially dense layer of soft, plumaceous feathers to provide extra insulation. This strategy is possible because American Goldfinches wait until July and August to nest (when their favorite food of composite seeds is in peak supply), affording time for a second body molt in spring without an energetically expensive overlap of molt and reproduction. When goldfinches change into their brilliant sunshine-yellow garb, we know that warmer weather is not far away.

Goldfinches are social beings that usually forage in groups of a few birds to several hundred, sometimes including chickadees or sparrows. Each bird in the flock looks around for predators less often than when alone, and sharing the load of vigilance for predators means getting more time to concentrate on dinner. Dominant individuals within the flock fare even better. Adult males usually rank higher than females and juveniles, and the existence of a dominance hierarchy reduces the need for constant testing of neighbors. Hungry subordinates may nonetheless become assertive, so goldfinch flocks are not always entirely peaceful. Observant feeder owners can watch these finches jockeying for position with threat postures and aggressive calls. However, goldfinches are not particularly pushy toward other species. Though occasionally stealing food tidbits from larger finches at feeders, they usually give way to Pine Siskins and House Finches.

Key references: Buttemer 1985, Dawson and Marsh 1986, Dunn and Hussell 1991, Horn 1995, Middleton 1977, 1978, 1986, 1993, Popp 1987b, 1988, Prescott and Middleton 1990, Prescott et al. 1989.

FeederWatch Findings

American Goldfinches visit feeders in all habitats throughout most of the winter, but flock sizes are nearly twice as big at rural as at urban feeders. Flock size increases in the coldest months, reaching an average of ten birds per feeder in mid-January. Gaps in the maps are artifacts of low FeederWatch coverage, and the species is found all across the lower 48 states.

Favorite feeder foods: *Niger,* canary seed, black-oil and hulled sunflower, water.

Infrequent choices: Mixed seed, millet, striped sunflower, safflower, cracked corn, milo, wheat, peanuts in shell and hearts, canola, peanut butter mixes, bird puddings, baked goods, sugar water, popped corn.

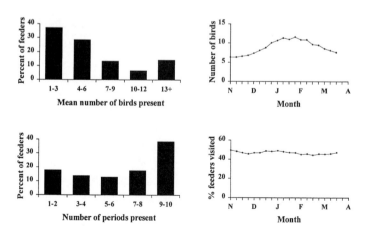

American Goldfinch: percent of feeders visited

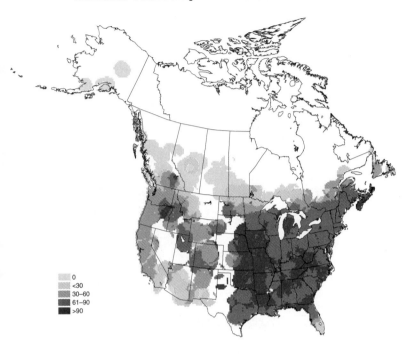

0
<30
30–60
61–90
>90

Abundance at feeders

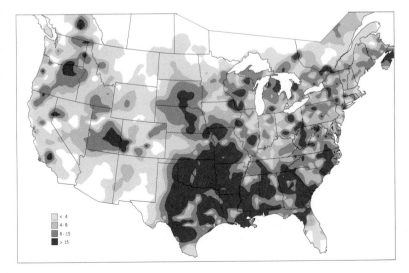

< 4
4 - 8
8 - 15
> 15

Evening Grosbeak

Coccothraustes vespertinus

Anyone who has entertained a large flock of "yellow bandits" knows how quickly they can empty feeders. About one hundred sunflower seeds are needed to meet the average daily energy requirements of a grosbeak, and one shocked observer saw a single bird down ninety-six seeds in less than five minutes. A flock of one hundred grosbeaks relying solely on sunflower could run through a fifty-pound bag of seed in eighteen days.

These birds are also large and quarrelsome—an intimidating combination that can keep other species away from feeders. One suggestion for limiting grosbeak food consumption while also providing for other birds is to offer a limited amount of food each morning (the time when grosbeaks do most of their feeding), then restock at noon after the grosbeak horde has cleaned out the feeder and moved on.

A different approach to giving other species a chance is to offer sunflower seeds in several different types of feeders. Grosbeaks strongly prefer feeding from open surfaces, especially elevated platforms. Dividing food into several widely spaced patches not only gives more access to other species but also to female grosbeaks, who are dominated by males to the extent of being excluded from a single food patch.

Evening Grosbeaks are nomadic rather than having a regular migration, roaming widely within a winter to find areas of abundant food. Few birds return to the same haunts the following year. Because females tend to move farther south than males—and males often return earlier to northern breeding grounds—females can make up to 70 to 80% of the flocks in some areas. A consequence of the Evening Grosbeak's roving nature is that birds visiting your feeder at different times of the day or throughout the winter may well involve different individuals.

Originally a species confined to the West, Evening Grosbeaks moved eastward across Canada in the first half of this century. The most likely explanation is that huge areas of favorable habitat were produced early in that period by extensive fires in eastern Canada. Outbreaks of spruce budworm (three this century) may also have figured in. Evening Grosbeaks are great consumers of budworm caterpillars and may play an important role in natural control of this serious forest pest. If an Evening Grosbeak was meeting all its energy requirements from budworm larvae alone, it would consume more than a thousand daily.

While insects are an important dietary supplement in summer, winter food consumption is nearly all seeds, including those of such deciduous trees as box elder, beech, and pin cherry. Other bird species also like to eat wild cherries, but only Evening Grosbeaks target the pits. The slippery seeds are held firmly with special protuberances on the "gross beak" and are simply crushed. So favored are cherry pits that Evening Grosbeaks sometimes seek out the pits voided by American Robins.

As with many finches whose diet is primarily vegetarian, Evening Grosbeaks are attracted to mineral sources. You can provide this at your feeder by mixing salt and fireplace ash into water, then pouring it over rotting wood (which serves as a base for crystals to form).

However, sunflower seeds in abundance are the main key to attracting grosbeaks.

Key references: Balph 1977b, Balph and Balph 1976, Balph and Lindahl 1978, Brunton 1994, Dennis 1986, Fraser 1985, Prescott 1991, Speirs 1972, Takekawa and Garton 1984.

FeederWatch Findings

The Evening Grosbeak is a fairly regular feeder visitor within its breeding areas (southern Canada and the Rockies) but is unpredictable in other regions, depending on the extent of wandering in a given winter. Usually they are absent from Nevada (where we have little FeederWatch data). Grosbeaks visit far more rural than urban or suburban feeders. Flock sizes are similar everywhere—typically fifteen—but numbers over one hundred are not uncommon.

Favorite feeder foods: *Striped and black-oil sunflower* (and probably hulled, as well), and water.

Infrequent choices: Mixed seed, millet, canary seed, cracked corn, peanut hearts, suet, bird puddings. Small samples suggest that safflower and milo may also be chosen occasionally.

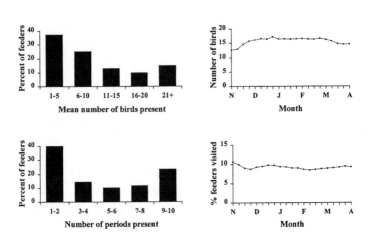

Evening Grosbeak: percent of feeders visited

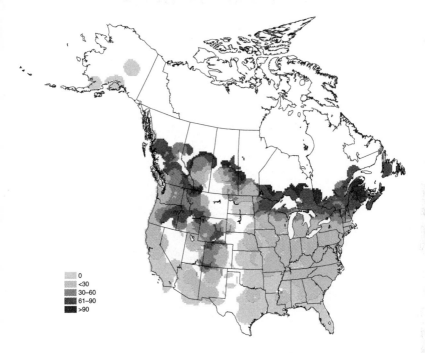

- 0
- <30
- 30–60
- 61–90
- >90

Abundance at feeders

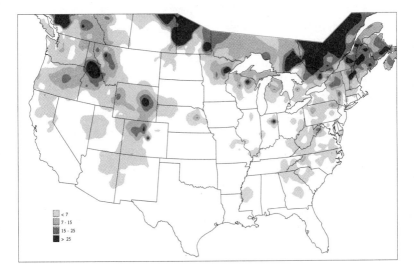

- < 7
- 7 - 15
- 15 - 25
- > 25

House Sparrow

Passer domesticus

It is hard to believe today that House Sparrows were introduced to North America on purpose. The aim was partly to control insect pests, but it was already well-known that this sparrow exploits human activity for food and shelter, so the subsequent spread of House Sparrows throughout the continent should not have been a surprise to anyone.

Urban sparrows concentrate where human population density and building complexity are greatest, and sparrow distribution can be correlated to the numbers of ventilation louvers, TV antennas, and bird feeders in a neighborhood. Commercial birdseed can dominate the diet of urban sparrows, but the total variety of foods eaten in cities may nonetheless be broader than in the countryside because most rural sparrows live on farms and subsist primarily on waste grain.

Seed from feeders makes up a larger proportion of the winter diet for male House Sparrows than it does for females because the dominant males monopolize concentrated food sources. While a group of sparrows does not maintain a linear dominance hierarchy, there is usually one top male, and females on average are subordinate. As a result, the ladies are more likely to forage separately from the bossy males.

Males are larger than females—one of the reasons they are dominant—and the average size of females is smaller in northern latitudes where winter is harshest. An explanation suggested by scientists is that larger females die more often than small ones in severe winter weather. Possibly smaller females are more obviously subordinate to males and therefore have better opportunities to forage free of male aggression. Also, small females may be able to find cosy and energy-saving roost sites that are too small for use by big males.

House Sparrows are essentially sedentary, with only minimal juvenile dispersal. In winter these birds form foraging flocks whose size is correlated to both the amount of food available and time of day (with feeding activity increasing in late afternoon). As flock size grows, however, so does the level of aggression. Birds in flocks of twenty-five fight twice as often as those in groups of ten. Each individual makes a decision to stay or leave the flock based on its feeding rate, so flock size stops increasing once fighting begins to interfere unduly with foraging efficiency.

Foraging in flocks must be highly beneficial, despite the drawbacks. As evidence, consider that a lone sparrow discovering a new food source is silent if there is only enough food for one bird. If the food is abundant, however, the discoverer makes *chirrup* calls that quickly recruit other House Sparrows. The benefit evidently comes from the protection against predation that is afforded by larger, more vigilant, flocks. Each bird spends less time looking up for danger and therefore forages more effectively. Efficient feeding may be especially important to House Sparrows because they are so "flighty." If one or two birds fly off, all the others follow—and alarms occur almost continuously.

If you have too many House Sparrows at your feeders for your liking, try avoiding small seed (although these birds have extremely broad tastes). Use hanging feeders or others with small perches, as House Sparrows prefer a broader platform to stand on.

Key references: Barnard 1980a,b,c, Caraco and Bayham 1982, Elgar 1986, Fleischer and Johnston 1984, Gavett and Wakeley 1986, Grubb and Greenwald 1982, Johnsen and Van Druff 1987, McGillivray and Murphy 1984, Summers-Smith 1963, Robbins 1973.

FeederWatch Findings

The resident House Sparrow, if present, is normally a consistent visitor from week to week. It is slightly less likely to visit rural sites but is equally abundant there. Flock size declines steadily throughout the winter, from an average of about fifteen to fewer than ten. The range extends across all of the United States, and gaps in the upper map indicate lack of FeederWatch coverage.

Favorite feeder foods: *Mixed seed,* millet, black-oil and hulled sunflower, cracked corn, milo, baked goods, water, popped corn, and (according to small samples) barley.

Infrequent choices: Canary seed, striped sunflower, safflower, whole corn, wheat, niger, hulled peanuts and hearts, canola, pet food, suet, peanut butter mixes, bird puddings, dried fruit, sugar water.

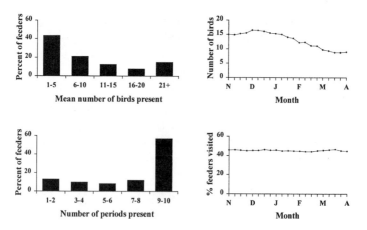

House Sparrow: percent of feeders visited

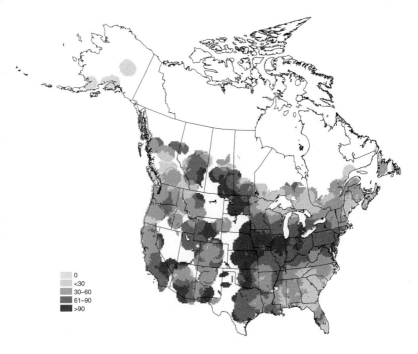

0
<30
30–60
61–90
>90

Abundance at feeders

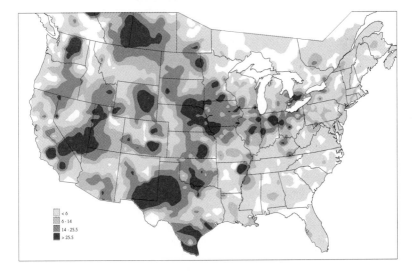

< 6
6 - 14
14 - 25.5
> 25.5

Appendix

About Project FeederWatch

Project FeederWatch is an ongoing winter survey of birds at feeders across North America. If you can identify the birds at your feeders, consider putting that knowledge to work by joining the thousands of volunteers who are already taking part.

As a FeederWatch participant, you can make an important contribution to bird science. For example, Project FeederWatch has documented the periodic southward "invasions" of northern species in more detail than any other survey. It has shown that counts at feeders accurately document distribution and relative abundance among geographic regions and can detect large population changes. FeederWatchers have contributed to special investigations on a broad range of topics, including food choice at feeders, numbers of birds striking windows, spread of a disease among House Finches, and migratory timing of Ruby-throated Hummingbirds.

Every two weeks from November to April you will note the numbers and kinds of birds visiting your feeders over a two-day period. (You do not have to watch your feeders continuously and can carry on with your normal activities.) You record information about the birds, the weather, and your backyard habitat on FeederWatch data forms, and then send them to the organizers at the end of the season.

Project FeederWatch is financed by moderate annual participants' fees, supplemented with corporate sponsorships, donations, and occasional grants. The survey is administered in the United States by the Cornell Laboratory of Ornithology and in Canada by Bird Studies Canada and is promoted by two other partners, the National Audubon Society and the Canadian Nature Federation.

As a FeederWatch participant, you receive the informative publication *BirdScope* (if you live in the United States) or *BirdWatch* (participants in Canada). These newsletters give you up-to-date results from FeederWatch, so you will know how scientists are putting your data to work. The newsletters also contain articles on other work of the Cornell Laboratory of Ornithology and Bird Studies Canada, including information on how to take part in other cooperative science projects.

Americans who wish to join Project FeederWatch should contact the Cornell Laboratory of Ornithology, 159 Sapsucker Woods Road, Ithaca, NY 14850 (Web site http://birdsource.cornell.edu/pfw). Canadians should contact the Bird Studies Canada, P.O. Box 160, Port Rowan, Ontario N0E 1M0 (Web site http://www.bsc-eoc.org/pfw.html).

Project FeederWatch Data Editing

FeederWatch participants record their data on computer-scannable forms or submit it electronically, allowing rapid compilation, editing, and analysis of results. Here we give a brief overview of the data-handling procedures that were used in preparing this book.

Each record consisted of the data for all species at one feeder site from one count period. A series of edits deleted entire records that had nonexistent or conflicting dates, state/province codes, or participant identification numbers. We also deleted records with "impossible" species (based on De Sante and Pyle's *Distributional Checklist of North American Birds,* making generous allowances for species that might be seen at feeders well outside their normal range). Another edit deleted records with improbably high numbers, defined separately for each species.

Because there is marked seasonal fluctuation in many species, a reasonable estimate of annual abundance requires that observations from each feeder come from all parts of the season. We therefore deleted all records for a feeder that, at the end of editing, did not meet the following criteria: at least five records for the year (out of a possible ten), with at least one each from weeks 1 to 3, 4 to 7, and 8 to 10.

We did not go back to original data sheets to attempt corrections, and our edits were basically arbitrary rules for cleaning up obvious errors quickly. An exception was made for records from states or provinces with data from fewer than thirty feeders in a given year. These records were flagged, and at each editing step we returned to the original data sheets to make as many corrections as possible—without second guessing—in an attempt to salvage the records.

Our editing procedures eliminated "orphan" records and deleted outlying data points that almost certainly represented errors of identification or data recording. However, there is no doubt that many less obvious errors remain in the data set, so caution is required in interpreting results for species that are easily mistaken for one another (for example, House Finch and Purple Finch).

On the other hand, we have a high degree of confidence in the skills of Project FeederWatch participants. For several years we asked participants to report species whose identity was uncertain in a special section of the data forms, and this very rarely revealed an inability to identify common species. Participants pay an annual fee to participate in the project and must cope with rather complicated data forms—both powerful deterrents to people with shaky identification skills. Lastly, we only analyzed data for the most widespread and common species, which few people are likely to mistake. Identification errors are more likely to occur in the approximately 250 species that have been reported much less commonly at feeders.

Literature Cited

Addison, E. M., R. D. Strickland, and D. J. H. Fraser. 1989. Gray Jays, *Perisoreus canadensis*, and Common Ravens, *Corvus corax*, as predators of winter ticks, *Dermacentor albipictus*. *Can. Field-Natur.* 103:406–408.

Allaire, P. N., and C. D. Fisher. 1975. Feeding ecology of three resident sympatric sparrows in eastern Texas. *Auk* 92:260–269.

Anderson, A. H., and A. Anderson. 1973. *The Cactus Wren.* Tucson: University of Arizona Press.

Anonymous. 1978. The living Christmas tree ornament. *Amer. Birds* 32:446.

Arcese, P., and J. N. M. Smith. 1985. Phenotypic correlates and ecological consequences of dominance in Song Sparrows. *J. Anim. Ecol.* 54:817–830.

Armstrong, E. R., and D. L. G. Noakes. 1983. Wintering biology of Mourning Doves, *Zenaida macroura*, in Ontario. *Can. Field-Natur.* 97:434–438.

Askins, R. A. 1993. Population trends in grassland, shrubland, and forest birds in eastern North America. Pp. 1–34 In *Current Ornithology* Vol. 11, D. M. Power, ed. New York: Plenum Press.

Austin, D. F. 1975. Bird flowers in the eastern United States. *Florida Scientist* 38:1–12.

Austin, G. T., and E. L. Smith. 1972. Winter foraging ecology of mixed insectivorous bird flocks in oak woodland in southern Arizona. *Condor.* 74:17–24.

Avery, M. L. 1996. Food avoidance by adult House Finches, *Carpodacus mexicanus*, affects seed preferences of offspring. *Anim. Behav.* 51:1279–1283.

Bailey, E. P. 1966. Abundance and activity of Starlings in winter in northern Utah. *Condor* 68:152–162.

Baker, M. C., and S. F. Fox. 1978. Dominance, survival, and enzyme polymorphism in Dark-eyed Juncos (*Junco hyemalis*). *Evolution* 32:697–711.

Baker, M. C., E. Stone, A. E. Miller Baker, R. J. Shelden, P. Skillicorn, and M. D. Mantych. 1988. Evidence against observational learning in storage and recovery of seeds by Black-capped Chickadees. *Auk* 105:492–497.

Balda, R. P., and G. C. Bateman. 1971. Flocking and annual cycle of the Piñon Jay, *Gymnorhinus cyanocephalus*. *Condor* 73:287–302.

Balda, R. P., G. C. Bateman, and G. F. Foster. 1972. Flocking associates of the Piñon Jay. *Wilson Bull.* 84:60–76.

Balda, R. P., and A. C. Kamil. 1989. A comparative study of cache recovery by three corvid species. *Anim. Behav.* 38:486–495.

Balph, M. H. 1977a. Winter social behaviour of Dark-eyed Juncos: communication, social organization, and ecological implications. *Anim. Behav.* 25:859–884.

Balph, M. H. 1977b. Sex differences in alarm responses of wintering Evening Grosbeaks. *Wilson Bull.* 89:325–327.

———. 1978. Some population trends among Cassin's Finches in northern Utah. *N. Amer. Bird Bander* 3:12–15.

Balph, M. H., and D. F. Balph. 1976. Some factors influencing observed sex ratios in a population of Evening Grosbeaks. *Bird-Banding* 47:340–344.

Balph, D. F., and M. H. Balph. 1979. Behavioral flexibility of Pine Siskins in mixed species foraging groups. *Condor* 81:211–212.

Balph, M. H. and A. M. Lindahl. 1978. Winter philopatry of Evening Grosbeaks in northern Utah. *N. Amer. Bird Bander* 3:149–151.

Barnard, C. J. 1980a. Factors affecting flock size mean and variance in a winter population of House Sparrows *Passer domesticus. Behaviour* 74:114–127.

———. 1980b. Flock feeding and time budgets in the House Sparrow (*Passer domesticus L.*). *Anim. Behav.* 28:295–309.

———. 1980c. Equilibrium flock size and factors affecting arrival and departure in feeding House Sparrows. *Anim. Behav.* 28:503–511.

Barrentine, C. D. 1990. Roost site tenacity in Gambel's White-crowned Sparrows. *N. Amer. Bird Bander* 15:134–135.

Bartholomew, G. A., and T. J. Cade. 1956. Water consumption of house finches. *Condor* 58:406–412.

Baumgartner, A. M. 1980. Hummingbird banding in Delaware County, Oklahoma. *Inland Bird Banding* 52:8–12.

Beddall, B. G. 1963. Range expansion of the Cardinal and other birds in the northeastern states. *Wilson Bull.* 75:140–158.

Beecher, W. J. 1951. Adaptations for food-getting in the American blackbirds. *Auk* 68:411–440.

Behle, W. H. 1973. Further notes on Rosy Finches wintering in Utah. *Wilson Bull.* 85:344–346.

Bell, P. M. 1990. Eastern Meadowlark predation on American Goldfinches. *Bull. Oklahoma Ornithol. Soc.* 23:20–22.

Belthoff, J. R. and S. A. Gauthreaux, Jr. 1991. Partial migration and differential winter distribution of House Finches in the eastern United States. *Condor* 93:374–382.

Bennett, W. A. 1990. Scale of investigation and the detection of competition: an example from the House Sparrow and House Finch introductions in North America. *Amer. Natur.* 135:725–747.

Bennetts, R. E., and R. L. Hutto. 1985. Attraction of social fringillids to mineral salts: an experimental study. *J. Field Ornithol.* 56:187–189.

Bent, A. C. 1932. Life histories of North American gallinaceous birds. *Bull. U.S. Nat. Mus.* 162.

———. 1937. Life histories of North American birds of prey (Part 1). *Bull. U.S. Nat. Mus.* 167.

———. 1940. Life histories of North American cuckoos, goatsuckers, hummingbirds, and their allies. *Bull. U.S. Nat. Mus.* 176.

———. 1948. Life histories of North American nuthatches, wrens, thrashers, and their allies. *Bull. U.S. Nat. Mus.* 195.

———. 1958. Life histories of North American blackbirds, orioles, tanagers, and allies. *Bull. U.S. Nat. Mus.* 211.

———. 1968. Life histories of North American cardinals, grosbeaks, buntings, towhees, finches, sparrows, and allies. *Bull. U.S. Nat. Mus.* 237 (3 parts).

Berner, T. O., and T. C. Grubb Jr. 1985. An experimental analysis of mixed-species flocking in birds of deciduous woodland. *Ecology* 66:1229–1236.

Berthold, P. 1976. *Der Seidenschwanz* Bombycilla garrulus *als frugivorer Ernährungsspezialist. Experientia* 32:1445.

Bertin, R. I. 1982. The Ruby-throated Hummingbird and its major food plants: ranges, flowering phenology, and migration. *Can. J. Zool.* 60:210–219.

Black, J. D. 1932. A winter robin roost in Arkansas. *Wilson Bull.* 19:13–19.

Blanchard, B. D. 1941. The White-crowned Sparrows (*Zonotrichia leucophrys*) of the Pacific seaboard: environment and annual cycle. *Univ. Calif. Publ. Zool.* 46:1–135.

Bock, C. E. 1969. Intra- vs. interspecific aggression in Pygmy Nuthatch flocks. *Ecology* 50:903–905.

———. 1982. Synchronous fluctuations in Christmas Bird Counts of Common Redpolls and Piñon Jays. *Auk* 99:382–383.

Bock, C. E., and L. W. Lepthien. 1975a. A Christmas count analysis of woodpecker abundance in the United States. *Wilson Bull.* 87:355–366.

———. 1975b. Distribution and abundance of the Black-billed Magpie (*Pica pica*) in North America. *Great Basin Naturalist* 35:269–272.

———. 1976. Synchronous eruptions of boreal seed-eating birds. *Amer. Natur.* 110:559–571.

Bonta, M. 1988. "Siskin Invasion." Brush Mountain Notebook. *Pennsylvania Birds* 2:126–127.

Botsford, L. W., T. C. Wainwright, J. T. Smith, S. Mastrup and D. F. Lott. 1988. Population dynamics of California Quail related to meteorological conditions. *J. Wildl. Manage.* 52:469–477.

Boughey, M. J. and N. S. Thompson. 1981. Song variety in the Brown Thrasher (*Toxostoma rufum*). *Zeit. Tierpsychol.* 56:47–58.

Boxall, P. C. 1982. Further observations of predation by Black-billed Magpies on small mammals. *J. Field Ornithol.* 53:172–173.

Brackbill, H. 1987. Duration of Tufted-Titmouse Carolina Chickadee pairings. *N. Amer. Bird Bander* 12:146.

Brawn, J. D., and F. B. Samson. 1983. Winter behavior of Tufted Titmice. *Wilson Bull.* 95:222–232.

Brennan, L. A., and M. L. Morrison. 1991. Long-term trends of chickadee populations in western North America. *Condor* 93:130–137.

Brewer, R., and D. F. Drewiske. 1980. Cedar Waxwings catching snowflakes. *Jack-Pine Warbler* 58:121.

Bridgewater, D. D. 1966. Winter movement and habitat use by Harris' Sparrow, *Zonotrichia querula* (Nuttall). *Proc. Oklahoma Acad. Sci.* 47:53–59.

Brittingham, M. C., and S. A. Temple. 1988. Impacts of supplemental feeding on survival rates of Black-capped Chickadees. *Ecology* 69:581–589.

———. 1989. Patterns of feeder use by Wisconsin birds: a survey of WSO members. *Passenger Pigeon* 51:321–324.

———. 1992a. Does winter bird feeding promote dependency? *J. Field Ornithol.* 63:190–194.

————. 1992b. Use of winter bird feeders by Black-capped Chickadees. *J. Wildl. Manage.* 56:103–110.

Brooks, E. W. 1985. Fidelity of an American Tree Sparrow to a wintering area. *J. Field Ornithol.* 56:406–407.

Brooks, W. S. 1968. Comparative adaptations of the Alaskan redpolls to the arctic environment. *Wilson Bull.* 80:253–280.

————. 1978. Triphasic feeding behavior and the esophageal diverticulum in redpolls. *Auk* 95:182–183.

Brown, J. L. 1963. Aggressiveness, dominance and social organization in the Steller Jay. *Condor* 65:460–484.

Brown, M. B., and C. R. Brown. 1988. Access to winter food resources by bright- versus dull-colored House Finches. *Condor* 90:729–731.

Brunton, D. F. 1994. The Evening Grosbeak in Ontario. Pp. 307–314 in *Ornithology in Ontario,* M. K. McNicholl and J. L. Cranmer-Byng, eds. Ontario Field Ornithol. Spec. Publ. 1. Whitby, Ontario: Hawk Owl Publishing.

Buitron, D., and G. L. Nuechterlein. 1985. Experiments on olfactory detection of food caches by Black-billed Magpies. *Condor* 87:92–95.

Bull, E. L., S. R. Peterson, and J. W. Thomas. 1986. *Resource Partitioning among Woodpeckers in Northern Oregon.* Research Note PNW–444. Portland, Ore.: U.S. Forest Service.

Bunch, K. G., and D. F. Tomback. 1986. Bolus recovery by Gray Jays: an experimental analysis. *Anim. Behav.* 34:754–762.

Burnell, K. L., and D. F. Tomback. 1985. Steller's Jays steal Gray Jay caches: field and laboratory observations. *Auk* 102:417–419.

Burtt, E. H., Jr., and J. P. Hailman. 1979. Effect of food availability on leaf-scratching by the Rufous-sided Towhee: test of a model. *Wilson Bull.* 91:123–126.

Buttemer, W. A. 1985. Energy relations of winter roost-site utilization by American goldfinches (*Carduelis tristis*). *Oecologia* 68:126–132.

Butts, W. K. 1931. A study of the chickadee and White-breasted Nuthatch by means of marked individuals. Part 3; the White-breasted Nuthatch. *Bird-Banding* 2:59–76.

Cabe, P. R. 1993. European Starling (*Sturnus vulgaris*). In *Birds of North America,* No. 48, A. Poole and F. Gill, eds. Philadelphia: Academy of Natural Sciences; Washington: American Ornithologists' Union.

Caccamise, D. F., L. A. Lyon, and J. Fischl. 1983. Seasonal patterns in roosting flocks of Starlings and Common Grackles. *Condor* 85:464–481.

Cade, T. J. 1952. The influence of food abundance on the over-wintering of Pine Grosbeaks at College, Alaska. *Condor* 54:363.

————. 1953. Sub-nival feeding of the Redpoll in interior Alaska: a possible adaptation to the northern winter. *Condor* 55:43–44.

Calder, W. A. 1993. Rufous Hummingbird (*Selophorus rufus*). In *Birds of North America,* no. 53, A. Poole and F. Gill, Eds. Philadelphia: Academy of Natural Sciences; Washington: American Ornithologists' Union.

Caldwell, L. D., and N. L. Cuthbert. 1987. Storm-induced weight loss in the American Robin. *Michigan Academician* 19:235–242.

Caraco, T., and M. C. Bayham. 1982. Some geometric aspects of House Sparrow flocks. *Anim. Behav.* 30:990–996.

Carey, M., D. E. Burhans and D. A. Nelson. 1994. Field Sparrow (*Spizella pusilla*). In *Birds of North America,* no. 103, A. Poole and F. Gill, eds. Philadelphia: Academy of Natural Sciences; Washington: American Ornithologists' Union.

Carothers, S. W. N. J. Sharber, and R. P. Balda. 1972. Steller's Jays prey on Gray-headed Juncos and a Pygmy Nuthatch during periods of heavy snow. *Wilson Bull.* 84:204–205.

Chamberlain-Auger, J. A., P. J. Auger and E. G. Strauss. 1990. Breeding biology of American Crows. *Wilson Bull.* 102:615–622.

Chaplin, S. B. 1974. Daily energetics of the Black-capped Chickadee, *Parus atricapillus,* in winter. *J. Comp. Physiol.* 89B:321–330.

———. 1982. The energetic significance of huddling behavior in Common Bushtits (*Psaltriparus minimus*). *Auk* 99:424–430.

Cherry, J. D. 1982. Fat deposition and length of stopover of migrant White-crowned Sparrows. *Auk* 99:725–732.

Cimprich, D. A. and T. C. Grubb. 1994. Consequences for Carolina Chickadees of foraging with Tufted Titmice in winter. *Ecology* 75:1615–1625.

Clark, L. 1991. Odor detection thresholds in Tree Swallows and Cedar Waxwings. *Auk* 108:177–180.

Clark, R. G., P. J. Weatherhead, H. Greenwood, and R. D. Titman. 1986. Numerical responses of Red-winged Blackbird *Agelaius phoeniceus* populations to changes in regional land-use patterns. *Can. J. Zool.* 64:1944–1950.

Clemens, D. T. 1989. Nocturnal hypothermia in Rosy Finches. *Condor* 91:739–741.

Collias, N. E., and R. D. Tabler. 1951. A field study of some grouping and dominance relations in Ring-necked Pheasants. *Condor* 53:265–275.

Confer, J. L., and P. Paicos. 1985. Downy Woodpecker predation at goldenrod galls. *J. Field Ornithol.* 56:56–64.

Connor, R. N. 1980. Foraging habitats of woodpeckers in southwestern Virginia. *J. Field Ornithol.* 51:119–127.

Conner, R. N. and C. S. Adkisson. 1976. Concentration of foraging Common Ravens along the Trans-Canada Highway. *Can. Field-Natur.* 90:496–497.

Connor, R. N., and J. C. Kroll. 1979. Food-storing by Yellow-bellied Sapsuckers. *Auk* 96:195.

Conner, R. N., and J. H. Williamson. 1987 (1984). Food storing by American Crows. Bull. *Texas Ornithol. Soc.* 17:13–14.

Cortopassi, A. J., and L. R. Mewaldt. 1965. The circumannual distribution of White-crowned Sparrows. *Bird-Banding* 36:141–169.

Coutlee, E. L. 1968. Comparative breeding behavior of Lesser and Lawrence's Goldfinches. *Condor* 70:228–242.

Cowie, R. J., and S. A. Hinsley. 1987. Breeding success of blue tits and great tits in suburban gardens. *Ardea* 75:81–90.

Cramp, S., ed. 1988. *Bombycilla garrulus* Bohemian Waxwing. Pp. 491–502 in *The Birds of the Western Palearctic,* Vol. V: Tyrant Flycatchers to Thrushes.

London: Oxford University Press.

Crase, F. T., and R. W. Dehaven. 1978. Food selection by five sympatric California blackbird species. *Calif. Fish and Game* 64:255–267.

Cristol, D. A. 1995. The coat-tail effect in merged flocks of dark-eyed juncos: social status depends on familiarity. *Anim. Behav.* 50:151–159.

Cruz, A., and D. W. Johnston. 1979. Occurrence and feeding ecology of the Common Flicker on Grand Cayman Island. *Condor* 81:370–375.

Cummings, B., and M. Cummings. 1989. Common Grackle consumes American Goldfinch. *Bull. Oklahoma Ornithol. Soc.* 22:29–30.

D'Agostino, G. M., L. E. Giovinazzo, and S. E. Eaton. 1981. The sentinel crow as an extension of parental care. *Wilson Bull.* 93:394–395.

Darden, T. 1974. Common Grackles preying on fish. *Wilson Bull.* 86:85–86.

Darley-Hill, S., and W. C. Johnson. 1981. Acorn dispersal by the Blue Jay (*Cyanocitta cristata*). *Oecologia* 50:231–232.

Davis, D. E., and M. L. Morrison. 1988 (1987). Changes in cyclic patterns of abundance in four avian species. *Amer. Birds* 41:1341–1343, 1345–1347.

Davis, J. 1957. Comparative foraging behavior of Spotted and Brown Towhees. *Auk* 74:129–166.

———. 1973. Habitat preferences and competition of wintering juncos and Golden-crowned Sparrows. *Ecology* 54:174–180.

Davison, V. E., and E. G. Sullivan. 1963. Mourning Doves' selection of food. *J. Wildl. Manage.* 217:373–383.

Dawson, W. R. 1997. Pine Siskin (*Carduelis pinus*). In *Birds of North America*, no. 280, A. Poole and F. Gill, eds. Philadelphia: Academy of Natural Sciences; Washington: American Ornithologists' Union.

Dawson, W. R., and R. L. Marsh. 1986. Winter fattening in the American Goldfinch *Carduelis tristis* and the possible role of temperature in its regulation. *Physiol. Zool.* 59:357–368.

Dawson, W. R., R. L. Marsh, W. A. Buttemer, and C. Carey. 1983. Seasonal and geographic variation of cold resistance in House Finches *Carpodacus mexicanus*. *Physiol. Zool.* 56:353–369.

DeGraff, R. M. 1989. Territory sizes of Song Sparrows, *Melospiza melodia*, in rural and suburban habitats. *Can. Field-Natur.* 103:43–47.

Dennis, J. V. 1981. *Beyond the Bird Feeder*. NY: Alfred A. Knopf.

———. 1986. *A Complete Guide to Bird Feeding*. NY: Alfred A. Knopf.

———. 1988. *Summer Bird Feeding*. Northbrook, Ill. :Audubon Workshop.

———. 1991. *A Guide to Western Bird Feeding*. Marietta, Oh.: Bird Watcher's Digest.

Derrickson, K. C. 1987. Yearly and situational changes in the estimate of repertoire size in Northern Mockingbirds (*Mimus polygottus*). *Auk* 104:198–207.

———. 1988. Variation in repertoire presentation in Northern Mockingbirds. *Condor* 90:592–606.

Derrickson, K. C., and R. Breitwisch. 1992. Northern Mockingbird (*Mimus polyglottis*). In *Birds of North America*, no. 7, A. Poole and F. Gill, eds. Philadelphia: Academy of Natural Sciences; Washington: American Ornithologists' Union.

DeSante, D., and P. Pyle. 1986. *Distributional Checklist of North American Birds.* Lee Vining, Calif.: Artemisia Press.

Desrochers, A., S. J. Hannon, and K. E. Nordin. 1988. Winter survival and territory acquisition in a northern population of Black-capped Chickadees. *Auk* 105:727–736.

DeWoskin, R. 1980. Heat exchange influence on foraging behavior of *Zonotrichia* flocks. *Ecology* 61:30–36.

Dìaz, J. A. and B. Asensio. 1991. Effects of group size and distance to protective cover on the vigilance behaviour of Black-billed Magpie *Pica pica. Bird Study* 38:38–41.

Dilger, W. C. 1960. Agonistic and social behavior of captive Redpolls. *Wilson Bull.* 72:114–132.

Dixon, K. L. 1949. Behavior of the Plain Titmouse. *Condor* 51:110–136.

———. 1954. Some ecological relations of chickadee and titmice in central California. *Condor* 56:113–124.

———. 1956. Territoriality and survival in the Plain Titmouse. *Condor* 58:169–182.

———. 1963. Some aspects of social organization in the Carolina Chickadee. *Proc. Internat. Ornithol. Congress* 13:140–258.

———. 1965. Dominance-subordination relationships in Mountain Chickadees. *Condor* 67:291–299.

———. 1986. Mountain Chickadee through the seasons. *Utah Birds* 1:65–69.

Dolbeer, R. A. 1978. Movement and migration patterns of Red-winged Blackbirds: a continental overview. *Bird-Banding* 49:17–34.

———. 1982. Migration patterns for age and sex classes of blackbirds and starlings. *J. Field Ornithol.* 53:28–46.

Dolbeer, R. A., and C. R. Smith. 1985. Sex-specific feeding habits of Brown-headed Cowbirds in northern Ohio in January. *Ohio J. Sci.* 85:104–107.

Dolbeer, R. A., P. P. Woronecki, A. R. Stickley Jr., and S. B. White. 1978. Agricultural impact of a winter population of blackbirds and starlings. *Wilson Bull.* 90:31–44.

Doughty, R. W. 1988. *The Mockingbird.* Austin: University of Texas Press.

Dow, D. D. 1965. The role of saliva in food storage by the Gray Jay. *Auk* 82:139–154.

———. 1969. Habitat utilization by cardinals in central and peripheral breeding populations. *Can. J. Zool.* 47:409–417.

———. 1970. Distribution and dispersal of the Cardinal, *Richmondena cardinalis*, in relation to vegetational cover and river systems. *Amer. Midland Natur.* 84:198–207.

Dow, D. D, and D. M. Scott. 1971. Dispersal and range expansion by the cardinal: an analysis of banding records. *Can. J. Zool.* 49:185–198.

Dunn, E. H. 1989. Are Pine Grosbeaks increasing at bird feeders in Ontario? *Ontario Birds* 7:87–91.

———. 1993. Bird mortality from striking residential windows in winter. *J.*

Field Ornithol. 64:302–309.

———. 1995. Bias in Christmas Bird Counts for species that visit feeders. *Wilson Bull.* 107:122–130.

Dunn, E. H., and J. A. T. Hussell. 1991. Goldfinch preferences for bird feeder location. *J. Field Ornithol.* 62:256–259.

Dunn, E. H., and D. L. Tessaglia. 1994. Predation of birds at feeders in winter. *J. Field Ornithol.* 65:8–16.

Dunning, J. B., Jr., and J. H. Brown. 1982. Summer rainfall and winter sparrow densities: a test of the food limitation hypothesis. *Auk* 99:123–129.

Ehrlich, P. R., and J. F. McLaughlin. 1988. Scrub Jay predation on starlings and swallows: attack and interspecific defense. *Condor* 90:503–505.

Eiserer, L. A. 1980. Effects of grass length and mowing on foraging behavior of the American Robin (*Turdus migratorius*). *Auk* 97:576–580.

Elgar, M. A. 1986. House Sparrows establish flocks by giving chirrup calls if the resource is divisible. *Anim. Behav.* 34:169–174.

Ellis, C. R., Jr., and A. W. Stokes. 1966. Vocalizations and behavior in captive Gambel Quail. *Condor* 68:72–80.

Emlen, J. T., Jr. 1939. Seasonal movements of a low-density valley quail population. *J. Wildl. Manage.* 3:118–130.

Engel, K. A., and L. S. Young. 1989. Spatial and temporal patterns in the diet of Common Ravens in southwestern Idaho. *Condor* 91:372–378.

Engel, K. A., L. S. Young, K. Steenhof, J. A. Roppe, and M. N. Kochert. 1992. Communal roosting of Common Ravens in southwestern Idaho. *Wilson Bull.* 104:105–121.

Ervin, S. 1977. Flock size, composition, and behavior in a population of Bushtits (*Psaltriparus minimus*) *Bird-Banding* 48:97–109.

Ewald, P. W. 1985. Influence of asymmetries in resource quality and age on aggression and dominance in Black-chinned Hummingbirds. *Anim. Behav.* 33:705–719.

Ewald, P. W., and R. J. Bransfield. 1987. Territory quality and territorial behavior in two sympatric species of hummingbirds. *Behav. Ecol. Sociobiol.* 20:285–293.

Farely, G. H. 1993. Observation of a Ruby-crowned Kinglet (*Regulus calendula*) roosting in a Verdin (*Auriparus flaviceps*) nest in winter. *Southwest. Naturalist* 38:72–73.

Farris, A. L., E. D. Klonglan, and R. C. Nomsen. 1977. *The Ring-necked Pheasant in Iowa.* Des Moines: Iowa Conservation Commission.

Ficken, M. S. 1981. Food finding in Black-capped Chickadees: altruistic communication? *Wilson Bull.* 93:393–394.

Ficken, M. S., and S. R. Witkin. 1977. Responses of Black-capped Chickadee flocks to predators. *Auk* 94:156–157.

Ficken, M. S., C. M. Weise, and J. A. Reinartz. 1987. A complex vocalization of the Black-capped Chickadee. II. Repertoires, dominance and dialects. *Condor* 89:500–509.

Ficken, M. S., C. M. Weise, and J. W. Popp. 1990. Dominance rank and resource access in winter flocks of Black-capped Chickadees. *Wilson Bull.* 102:623–633.

Ficken, M. S., M. A. McLaren and J. P. Hailman. 1996. Boreal Chickadee (*Parus hudsonicus*). In *Birds of North America,* no. 254, A. Poole and F. Gill, eds. Philadelphia: Academy of Natural Sciences; Washington: American Ornithologists' Union.

Filion, F. L., A. Jacquemot, and R. Reid. 1985. *The Importance of Wildlife to Canadians: An Executive Overview of the Recreational Economic Significance of Wildlife.* Environment Canada, Cat. No. CW66–76/1985E. Ottawa, Ont.: Canadian Wildlife Service.

Filion, F. L., E. DuWors, P. Boxall, P. Bouchard, R. Reid, P. A. Gray, A. Bath, A. Jacquemot, and G. Legare. 1993. *The Importance of Wildlife to Canadians: Highlights of the 1991 Survey.* Ottawa, Ont.: Canadian Wildlife Service, Environment Canada, Cat. No. CW66–103/1993E.

Fischer, D. H. 1980. Breeding biology of Curve-billed Thrashers and Long-billed Thrashers in southern Texas. *Condor* 82:392–397.

———. 1981a. Wintering ecology of thrashers in southern Texas. *Condor* 83:340–346.

———. 1981b. Winter time budgets of Brown Thrashers. *J. Field Ornithol.* 52:304–308.

Fleck, D. C. and D. F. Tomback. 1996. Tannin and protein in the diet of a food-hoarding granivore, the Western Scrub-Jay. *Condor* 98:474–482.

Fleischer, R. C., and R. F. Johnston. 1984. The relationships between winter climate and selection on body size of house sparrows. *Can. J. Zool.* 62:405–410.

Foster, W. L., and J. Tate Jr. 1966. The activities and coactions of animals at sapsucker trees. *Living Bird* 5:87–113.

Francis, W. J. 1976. Micrometeorology of a blackbird roost. *J. Wildl. Manage.* 40:132–136.

Franzreb, K. E. 1984. Foraging habits of Ruby-crowned and Golden-crowned Kinglets in an Arizona montane forest. *Condor* 86:139–145.

Franzreb, K. E. 1985. Foraging ecology of Brown Creepers in a mixed-coniferous forest. *J. Field Ornithol.* 56:9–16.

Fraser, D. 1985. Mammals, birds, and butterflies at sodium sources in northern Ontario forests. *Can. Field-Natur.* 99:365–367.

Frazier, A., and V. Nolan Jr. 1959. Communal roosting by the Eastern Bluebird in winter. *Bird-Banding* 30:219–226.

French, N. R. 1959. Life history of the black Rosy Finch. *Auk* 76:159–180.

Fretwell, S. 1968. Habitat distribution and survival in the Field Sparrow (*Spizella pusilla*). *Bird-Banding* 39:293–306.

Fretwell, S. D. 1969. Dominance behavior and winter habitat distribution in juncos (*Junco hyemalis*). *Bird-Banding* 40:1–25.

Fugle, G. N., S. I. Rothstein, C. W. Osenberg, and M. A. McGinley. 1984. Signals of status in wintering White-crowned Sparrows, *Zonotrichia leucophrys gambelii. Anim. Behav.* 32:86–93.

Gaddis, P. 1980. Mixed flocks, accipiters, and antipredator behavior. *Condor* 82:348–349.

Gaines, S. 1989. Comparisons of patch-use models for wintering American Tree Sparrows. *Auk* 106:118–123.

Gass, C. L., and K. P. Lertzman. 1980. Capricious mountain weather: a driving variable in hummingbird territorial dynamics. *Can. J. Zool.* 58:1964–1968.

Gass, C. L., G. Angehr, and J. Centa. 1976. Regulation of food supply by feeding territoriality in the rufous hummingbird. *Can. J. Zool.* 54:2046–2054.

Gavett, A. P., and J. S. Wakeley. 1986. Diets of House Sparrows in urban and rural habitats. *Wilson Bull.* 98:137–144.

Geis, A. D. 1980. *Relative Attractiveness of Different Foods at Wild Bird Feeders.* Washington, D.C.: United States Fish & Wildlife Service. Spec. Sci. Rept. Wildl. No. 233:1–11.

Genelly, R. E. 1955. Annual cycle in a population of California Quail. *Condor* 57:263–285.

George, M. W. 1980. Hummingbird foraging at *Malaviscus arboreus* var. *drummondi. Auk* 97:790–794.

George, W. G., and T. Kimmel. 1973. A slaughter of mice by Common Crows. *Auk* 94:782–783.

Gill, D. 1974. The Gray Jay as a predator of small mammals. *Can. Field-Natur.* 88:370–371.

Giraldeau, L. A., and L. Lefebvre. 1985. Individual feeding preferences in feral groups of Rock Doves. *Can. J. Zool.* 63:189–191.

Glahn, J. F., and D. L. Otis. 1986. Factors influencing blackbird and European Starling damage at livestock feeding operations. *J. Wildl. Manage.* 50:15–19.

Glase, J. C. 1973. Ecology of social organization in the Black-capped Chickadee. *Living Bird* 12:235–267.

Goldman, P. 1975. Hunting behavior of Eastern Bluebirds. *Auk* 92:798–801.

———. 1980. Flocking as a possible predatory defense in Dark-eyed Juncos. *Wilson Bull.* 92:88–95.

Goldsmith, T. H. 1980. Hummingbirds see near ultraviolet light. *Science* 207:786–788.

Goldstein, G. B., and M. C. Baker. 1984. Seed selection by juncos. *Wilson Bull.* 96:458–463.

Goodwin, D. 1976. *Crows of the World.* Ithaca, N.Y.: Cornell University Press.

Goodwin, S. H. 1905. Notes on the Bohemian Waxing. *Condor* 7:98–100.

Goslow, G. E., Jr. 1971. The attack and strike of some North American raptors. *Auk* 88:815–827.

Gottfried, B. M., and E. C. Franks. 1975. Habitat use and flock activity of Dark-eyed Juncos in winter. *Wilson Bull.* 87:374–383.

Gould, P. J. 1961. Territorial relationships between Cardinals and Pyrrhuloxias. *Condor* 63:246–256.

Graber, J. W., and R. R. Graber. 1979. Severe winter weather and bird populations in southern Illinois. *Wilson Bull.* 91:88–103.

———. 1983a. Expectable decline of forest bird population in severe and mild winters. *Wilson Bull.* 95:682–690.

———. 1983b. Feeding rates of warblers in spring. *Condor* 85:139–150.

Graul, W. D. 1967. Population movements of the Harris' Sparrow and Tree Sparrow in eastern Kansas. *Southwest Natur.* 12:303–310.

Greenlaw, J. S. 1996a. Eastern Towhee (*Pipilo erythrophthalmus*). In *Birds of North America,* no. 262, A. Poole and F. Gill, eds. Philadelphia: Academy of Natural Sciences; Washington: American Ornithologists' Union.

———. 1996b. Spotted Towhee (*Pipilo maculatus*). In *Birds of North America,* no. 263, A. Poole and F. Gill, eds. Philadelphia: Academy of Natural Sciences; Washington: American Ornithologists' Union.

Grinnell, J. 1903. Call notes of the Bush-tit. *Condor* 5:85–87.

Griscom, L. and A. Sprunt Jr. 1979. *The Warblers of America.* N.Y.: Garden City. Doubleday and Co. Inc.

Grossman, A. F., and G. C. West. 1977. Metabolic rate and temperature regulation of winter acclimatized Black-capped Chickadees *(Parus atricapillus)*, of interior Alaska. *Ornis Scand.* 8:127–138.

Grubb, T. C., Jr. 1977. Weather-dependent foraging behavior of some birds wintering in a deciduous woodland: horizontal adjustments. *Condor* 79:271–274.

———. 1978. Weather-dependent foraging rates of wintering woodland birds. *Auk* 95:370–376.

———. 1982. On sex-specific foraging behavior in the White-breasted Nuthatch. *J. Field Ornithol.* 53:305–314.

Grubb, T. C., Jr. and L. Greenwald. 1982. Sparrows and a brushpile: foraging responses to different combinations of predation risk and energy cost. *Anim. Behav.* 30:637–640.

Grubb, T. C. and V. V. Pravosudov. 1994. Tufted Titmouse (*Parus bicolor*). In *Birds of North America,* no. 86, A. Poole and F. Gill, eds. Philadelphia: Academy of Natural Sciences; Washington: American Ornithologists' Union.

Grubb, T. C., Jr., and T. A. Waite. 1987. Caching by Red-breasted Nuthatches. *Wilson Bull.* 99:696–699.

Gullion, G. W. 1960. The ecology of Gambel's quail in Nevada and the arid southwest. *Ecology* 41:518–536.

———. 1962. Organization and movements of coveys of a Gambel Quail population. *Condor* 64:402–415.

Güntert, M., D. B. Hay, and R. P. Balda. 1988. Communal roosting in the Pygmy Nuthatch: a winter survival strategy. *Proc. Internat. Ornithol. Congress* 19:1964–1972.

Gutiérrez, R. J., C. E. Braun, and T. P. Zapatka. 1975. Reproductive biology of the Band-tailed Pigeon in Colorado and New Mexico. *Auk* 92:665–677.

Haftorn, S. 1959. The proportion of spruce seeds removed by the tits in a Norwegian spruce forest in 1954–55. *Det Kgl. Norske Vidensk. Selsk. Forh.* 32:121–125.

Haftorn, S. 1974. Storage of surplus foods by the Boreal Chickadee, *Parus hudsonicus*, in Alaska, with some records on the Mountain Chickadee, *Parus gambeli*, in Colorado. *Ornis. Scand.* 5:145–161.

Haggerty, T. M. and E. S. Morton. 1995. Carolina Wren (*Thryothorus ludovicianus*). In *Birds of North America,* no. 188, A. Poole and F. Gill, eds. Philadelphia: Academy of Natural Sciences; Washington: American Ornithologists' Union.

Hahn, T. P. 1996. Cassin's Finch (*Carpodacus cassinii*). In *Birds of North America,* no. 240, A. Poole and F. Gill, eds. Philadelphia: Academy of Natural Sciences; Washington: American Ornithologists' Union.

Hailman, J. P. 1960. Hostile dancing and fall territory of a color-banded Mockingbird. *Condor* 62:464–468.

———. 1976. Leaf-scratching in White-crowned Sparrows and Fox Sparrows: test of a model. *Wilson Bull.* 88:354–356.

Ha, J. C, and P. N. Lehner. 1990. Notes on Gray Jay demographics in Colorado. *Wilson Bull.* 102:698–702.

Hamilton, T. R., and E. M. Novis. 1994. The migratory pattern of House Finch in eastern North America. *N. Amer. Bird Bander* 19:45–48.

Hampton, R. R. and D. F. Sherry. 1994. The effects of cache loss on choice of cache sites in Black-capped Chickadees. *Behav. Ecol.* 5:44–50.

Haney, J. C. 1981. The distribution and life history of the Brown-headed Nuthatch (*Sitta pusilla*) in Tennessee. *Migrant* 52:77–86.

Hanson, A. J., and S. Rohwer. 1986. Coverable badges and resource defense in birds. *Anim. Behav.* 34:69–76.

Harkins, C. E. 1937. Harris's Sparrow in its winter range. *Wilson Bull.* 49:286–292.

Harris-Haller, T. and S. W. Harris. 1991. Experiments with Allen's and Anna's Hummingbirds at sugar water feeders in spring. *Western Birds* 22:175–188.

Hayworth, A. M., and W. W. Weathers. 1984. Temperature regulation and climatic adaptation in Black-billed and Yellow-billed Magpies. *Condor* 86:19–26.

Hebrard, J. J. 1978. Habitat selection in two species of *Spizella*: a concurrent laboratory and field study. *Auk* 95:404–410.

Hedrick, L. D., and A. D. Woody. 1983. Northern Mockingbird kills Cedar Waxwing. *Wilson Bull.* 95:157–158.

Heinrich, B. 1988. Winter foraging at carcasses by three sympatric corvids, with emphasis on recruitment by the Raven, *Corvus corax. Behav. Ecol. Sociobiol.* 23:141–156.

Heisterberg, J. F., C. E. Knittle, O. E. Bray, D. F. Mott, and J. F. Besser. 1984. Movements of radio-instrumented blackbirds and European Starlings among winter roosts. *J. Wildl. Manage.* 48:203–209.

Hendricks, P. 1981. Observations on a winter roost of Rosy Finches in Montana. *J. Field Ornithol.* 52:235–236.

Hennessy, T. E., and L. Van Camp. 1963. Wintering mourning doves in northern Ohio. *J. Wildl. Manage.* 27:367–373.

Heppner, F. 1965. Sensory mechanism and environmental cues used by the American Robin in locating earthworms. *Condor* 67:247–256.

Herremans, M. 1989. Taxonomy and evolution in redpolls. *Ardea* 78:441–458.

Hertz, P. E., J. V. Remsen, and S. I. Jones. 1976. Ecological complementarity of three sympatric parids in a California Oak woodland. *Condor* 78:307–316.

Hess, P. 1989. Carolina Wrens at Pittsburgh, 1970–1988: persistence in a dangerous environment. *Pennsylvania Birds* 3:3–7.

Hickey, M. B., and M. C. Brittingham. 1991. Population dynamics of Blue Jays at a bird feeder. *Wilson Bull.* 103:401–414.

Hiebert, S. M. 1991. Seasonal differences in the response of Rufous Humming-birds to food restriction: body mass and the use of torpor. *Condor* 93:526–537.

Hill, B. G., and M. R. Lein. 1989. Territory overlap and habitat use of sympatric chickadees. *Auk* 106:259–268.

Hill, G. E. 1990. Female House Finches prefer colorful males: sexual selection for a condition-dependent trait. *Anim. Behav.* 40:563–572.

———. 1993. House Finch (*Carpodacus mexicanus*). In *Birds of North America,* no. 46. A. Poole and F. Gill, eds. Philadelphia: Academy of Natural Sciences; Washington: American Ornithologists' Union.

Hill, G. E., R. R. Sargent, and M. B. Sargent. 1998. Recent change in the winter distribution of Rufous Hummingbirds. *Auk* 115: 240–245.

Hill, R. W., D. J. Beaver, and J. H. Veghte. 1980. Body surface temperature and thermoregulation in the Black-capped Chickadee (*Parus atricapillus*). *Physiol. Zool.* 53:305–321.

Hitchcock, C. L., and D. F. Sherry. 1990. Long-term memory for cache sites in the Black-capped Chickadee. *Anim. Behav.* 40:701–712.

Homan, P. H. 1982. Distribution of the Ruby-crowned Kinglet in winter. *N. Amer. Bird Bander* 7:113.

Hooper, D. F. 1988. Boreal Chickadees feeding with Three-toed Woodpeckers. *Blue Jay* 46:85.

Horn, D. J. 1995. Perching orientation affects number of feeding attempts and seed consumption by the American Goldfinch (*Carduelis tristis*). *Ohio J. Sci.* 95:292–293.

Howard, W. E., and J. T. Emlen, Jr. 1942. Intercovey social relationships in the Valley Quail. *Wilson Bull.* 54:162–170.

Howell, T. R. 1953. Racial and sexual differences in migration in *Sphyrapicus varius. Auk* 70:118–126.

Ingold, J. L. and G. E. Wallace. 1994. Ruby-crowned Kinglet (*Regulus calendula*). In *Birds of North America,* no. 119, A. Poole and F. Gill, eds. Philadelphia: Academy of Natural Sciences; Washington: American Ornithologists' Union.

Isted, D. 1985. A xanthochroistic male Purple Finch. *Bull. Oklahoma Ornithol. Soc.* 18:31.

Jannsson, C., J. Ekman, and A. von Bromssen. 1981. Winter mortality and food supply in tits *Parus* spp. *Oikos* 37:313–322.

Johnsen, A. M. and L. W. Van Druff. 1987. Summer and winter distribution of introduced bird species and native bird species richness within a complex urban environment. Pp. 123–127 In *Integrating Man and Nature in the Metropolitan Environment,* L. W. Adams and D.L. Leedy, eds. Columbia, MD: National Institution for Urban Wildlife.

Johnsgard, P. A. 1973. *Grouse and Quails of North America,* Lincoln, Neb.: University of Nebraska Press.

Johnson, R. R. and L. T. Haight. 1996. Canyon Towhee (*Pipilo fuscus*). In *Birds of North America,* no. 264, A. Poole and F. Gill, eds. Philadelphia: Academy of Natural Sciences; Washington: American Ornithologists' Union.

Johnson, D. M., G. L. Stewart, M. Corley, R. Ghrist, J. Hagner, A. Ketterer, B. Mcdonnell, W. Newsom, E. Owen, and P. Samuels. 1980. Brown-headed Cowbird *Molothrus ater* mortality in an urban winter roost. *Auk* 97:299–320.

Johnson, W. C., and C. S. Adkisson. 1985. Dispersal of beech nuts by Blue Jays in fragmented landscapes. *Amer. Midland Natur.* 113:319–324.

Johnson, W. C. and T. Webb III. 1989. The role of Blue Jays (*Cyanocitta cristata* L.) in the postglacial dispersal of fagaceous trees in eastern North America. *J. Biogeogr.* 16:561–571.

Johnson, W. C., L. Thomas, and C. S. Adkisson. 1993. Dietary circumvention of acorn tannins by Blue Jays. *Oecologia* 94:159–164.

Johnston, R. F. 1992. Rock Dove (*Columba livia*). In *Birds of North America,* no. 13, A. Poole and F. Gill, eds. Philadelphia: Academy of Natural Sciences; Washington: American Ornithologists' Union.

Johnston, R. F., and S. G. Johnson. 1990. Reproductive ecology of feral pigeons. Pp. 237–252 In *Granivorous Birds in the Agricultural Landscape,* J. Pinowski and J. D. Summers-Smith, eds. Warsaw: Polish Scientific Publisher.

Jones, P. W. and T. M. Donovan. 1996. Hermit Thrush (*Catharus guttatus*). In *Birds of North America,* no. 261, A. Poole and F. Gill, eds. Philadelphia: Academy of Natural Sciences; Washington: American Ornithologists' Union.

Jung, R. E. 1992. Individual variation in fruit choice by American Robins (*Turdus migratorius*). *Auk* 109:98–111.

Kalinoski, R. 1975. Intra- and interspecific aggression in House Finches and House Sparrows. *Condor* 77:375–384.

Källender, H. 1981. The effects of the provision of food in winter on a population of the Great Tit *Parus major* and the Blue Tit *Parus caeruleus*. *Ornis. Scand.* 12:244–248.

Kattan, G., and C. Murcia. 1985. Hummingbird association with Acorn Woodpecker sap trees in Colombia. *Condor* 87:542–543.

Kautz, J. E., and C. E. Braun. 1981. Survival and recovery rates of band-tailed pigeons in Colorado. *J. Wildl. Manage.* 45:214–218.

Kennard, J. H. 1976. A biennial rhythm in the winter distribution of the Common Redpoll. *Bird-Banding* 47:231–237.

Kennedy, E. D. and D. W. White. 1997. Bewick's Wren (*Thryomanes bewickii*). In *Birds of North America,* no. 315, A. Poole and F. Gill, eds. Philadelphia: Academy of Natural Sciences; Washington: American Ornithologists' Union.

Kenward, R. E. 1978. Hawks and doves: factors affecting success and selection in goshawk attacks on woodpigeons. *J. Anim. Ecol.* 47:449–460.

Kessel, B. 1953. Distribution and migration of the European Starling in North America. *Condor* 55:49–67.

———. 1976. Winter activity patterns of Black-capped Chickadees in interior Alaska. *Wilson Bull.* 88:36–61.

Ketterson, E. D. 1979. Aggressive behavior in wintering Dark-eyed Juncos: determinants of dominance and their possible relation to geographic variation in sex ratio. *Wilson Bull.* 91:371–383.

Ketterson, E. D., and J. R. King. 1977. Metabolic and behavioral responses to fasting in the White-crowned Sparrow (*Zonotrichia leucophrys gambelii*). *Physiol. Zool.* 50:115–129.

Ketterson, E. D., and V. Nolan Jr. 1982. The role of migration and winter mortality in the life history of a temperate-zone migrant, the Dark-eyed Junco, as determined from demographic analyses of winter populations. *Auk* 99:243–259.

———. 1983. The evolution of differential bird migration. *Current Ornithol.* 1:357–402.

Kilham, L. 1956. Winter feeding on sap by sapsuckers. *Auk* 73:451–452.

———. 1959. Behavior and methods of communication of Pileated Woodpeckers. *Condor* 61:377–387.

———. 1961. Aggressiveness of migrant Myrtle Warblers towards woodpeckers and other birds. *Auk* 78:261.

———. 1963. Food storing of Red-bellied Woodpeckers. *Wilson Bull.* 75:227– 234.

———. 1964. The relations of breeding Yellow-bellied Sapsuckers to wounded branches and other trees. *Auk* 81:520–527.

———. 1965. Differences in feeding behavior of male and female Hairy Woodpeckers. *Wilson Bull.* 77:134–145.

———. 1970. Feeding behavior of Downy Woodpeckers: I. preferences for paper birch and sexual differences. *Auk* 87:544–556.

———. 1974. Covering of stores by White-breasted and Red-breasted Nuthatches. *Condor* 76:108–109.

———. 1975. Association of Red-breasted Nuthatches with chickadees in a hemlock cone year. *Auk* 92:160–162.

———. 1976. Winter foraging and associated behavior of Pileated Woodpeckers in Georgia and Florida. *Auk* 93:15–24.

———. 1988. Common Raven, *Corvus corax*, caching food in snow. *Can. Field-Natur.* 102:68.

King, J. R., and E. E. Wales Jr. 1964. Observations on migration, ecology, and population flux of wintering Rosy Finches. *Condor* 66:24–31.

Kingsolver, J. G., and T. L. Daniel. 1983. Mechanical determinants of nectar feeding strategy in hummingbirds energetics: tongue morphology and licking behavior. *Oecologia* 60:214–226.

Klein, B. C. 1988. Weather-dependent mixed-species flocking during the winter. *Auk* 105:583–584.

Klem, D. 1981. Avian predators hunting birds near windows. *Proc. Pennsylvania Acad. Sci.* 55:90–92.

Knapton, R. W. and J. R. Krebs. 1976. Dominance hierarchies in winter Song Sparrows. *Condor* 78:567–569.

Knapton, R. W., R. V. Cartar, and J. B. Falls. 1984. A comparison of breeding ecology and reproductive success between morphs of the White-throated Sparrow. *Wilson Bull.* 96:60–71.

Knopf, F. L., and B. A. Knopf. 1983. Flocking patterns of foraging American Crows in Oklahoma. *Wilson Bull.* 95:153–155.

Knox, A. G. 1988. The taxonomy of redpolls. *Ardea* 76:1–26.

Kodric-Brown, A., and J. H. Brown. 1978. Influence of economics, interspecific competition, and sexual dimorphism on territoriality of migrant Rufous Hummingbirds. *Ecology* 59:285–296.

Koenig, W. D., and M. K. Heck. 1988. Ability of two species of oak woodland birds to subsist on acorns. *Condor* 90:705–708.

Komers, P. E. 1989. Dominance relationships between juvenile and adult Black-Billed Magpies. *Anim. Behav.* 57:256–265.

Komers, P. E. and E. J. Komers. 1992. Juvenile male magpies dominate adults irrespective of size differences. *Can. J. Zool.* 70:815–819.

Krebs, J. R. 1973. Social learning and the significance of mixed-species flocks of chickadees (*Parus* spp.). *Can. J. Zool.* 51:1275–1288.

Kricher, J. C. 1981. Range expansion of the Tufted Titmouse (*Parus bicolor*), in Massachusetts. *Amer. Birds* 35:750–753.

Kroodsma, D. E. and L. D. Parker. 1977. Vocal virtuosity in the Brown Thrasher. *Auk* 94:783–785.

Lanyon, W. E. 1994. Western Meadowlark (*Sturna neglecta*). In *Birds of North America,* no. 104, A. Poole and F. Gill, eds. Philadelphia: Academy of Natural Sciences; Washington: American Ornithologists' Union.

Larson, D. L., and C. E. Bock. 1986. Eruptions of some North American boreal seed-eating birds, 1901–1980. *Ibis* 128:137–140.

Laskey, A. R. 1944. A study of the cardinal in Tennessee. *Wilson Bull.* 56:27–44.

Laurenzi, A. W., B. W. Anderson, and R. D. Ohmart. 1982. Wintering biology of Ruby-crowned Kinglets in the lower Colorado River valley. *Condor* 84:385–398.

Law, E. 1921. A feeding habit of the Varied Thrush. *Condor* 23:66.

Lawrence, L. de K. 1967. A comparative life-history of four species of woodpeckers. *Ornithol. Monogr.* 5:1–100.

Leach, F. A. 1927. Strange features in bird habits. *Condor* 29:233–238.

Lefebvre, L. 1985. Stability of flock composition in urban pigeons. *Auk* 102:886–888.

Leffingwell, D. J. and A. M. Leffingwell. 1931. Winter habits of the Hepburn Rosy Finch at Clarkston, Washington. *Condor* 33:140–150.

Leopold, A. S. 1977. *The California Quail.* Berkeley: University of California Press.

Leopold, A. S., and M. F. Dedon. 1983. Resident Mourning Doves in Berkeley, California. *J. Wildl. Manage.* 47:780–789.

Lepthien, L. W., and C. E. Bock. 1976. Winter abundance patterns of North American kinglets. *Wilson Bull.* 88:483–485.

Levey, D. J., and W. H. Karasov. 1989. Digestive responses of temperate birds switched to fruit or insect diets. *Auk* 106:675–686.

Ligon, J. D. 1978. Reproductive interdependence of Piñon Jays and piñon pines. *Ecol. Monogr.* 48:111–126.

Ligon, J. D, and D. J. Martin. 1974. Piñon seed assessment by the Piñon Jay,

Gymnorhinus cyanocephalus. Anim. Behav. 22:421–429.

Lima, S. L. 1985. Maximizing feeding efficiency and minimizing time exposed to predators: a trade-off in the Black-capped Chickadee *Parus atricapillus. Oecologia* 66:60–67.

Lima, S. L. and R. M. Lee III. 1993. Food caching and its possible origin in the Brown Creeper. *Condor* 95:483–484.

Lindström, A. 1989. Finch flock size and risk of hawk predation at a migratory stopover site. *Auk* 106:225–232.

Linsdale, J. M. 1928. Variations in the Fox Sparrow (*Passerella iliaca*) with reference to natural history and osteology. *Univ. Calif. Publ. Zool.* 30:251–392.

Logan, C. A. 1987. Fluctuations in fall and winter territory size in the Northern Mockingbird (*Mimus polyglottos*). *J. Field Ornithol.* 58:297–305.

Lowther, P. E. 1993. Brown-headed Cowbird (*Molothrus ater*). In *Birds of North America,* no. 47, A. Poole and F. Gill, eds. Philadelphia: Academy of Natural Sciences; Washington: American Ornithologists' Union.

Lucas, J. R., and L. R. Walter. 1991. When should chickadees hoard food? Theory and experimental results. *Anim. Behav.* 41: 579–601.

Lukes, R. 1980. Nature-wise. *Passenger Pigeon* 42:133–134.

MacArthur, R. H. 1958. Population ecology of some warblers of northeastern coniferous forests. *Ecology* 39:599–619.

Maccarone, A. D. and W. A. Montevecchi. 1986. Factors affecting food choice by Gray Jays. *Bird Behav.* 6:90–92.

Manolis, T. 1977. Foraging relationships of Mountain Chickadees and Pygmy Nuthatches. *Western Birds* 8:13–20.

March, G. L. and R. M. F. S. Sadlier. 1972. Studies of the Band-tailed Pigeon (*Columba fasciata*) in British Columbia; 2. Food resource and mineral gravelling activity. *Syesis* 5:279–284.

Marshall, J. T., Jr. 1960. Interrelations of Abert and Brown Towhees. *Condor* 62:49–64.

Martin, A. C., H. S. Zim, and A. L. Nelson. 1951. *American Wildlife and Plants.* New York: Dover Publications.

Martin, S. G. 1970. The agonistic behavior of Varied Thrushes (*Ixoreus naevius*) in winter assemblages. *Condor* 72:452–459.

Martinez del Rio, C., W. H. Karasov, and D. J. Levey. 1989. Physiological basis and ecological consequences of sugar preferences in Cedar Waxwings. *Auk* 106:64–71.

Marzluff, J. M., and R. P. Balda. 1988. The advantages of, and constraints forcing, mate fidelity in Pinyon Jays. *Auk* 105:286–295.

———. 1989. Causes and consequences of female-biased dispersal in a flock-living bird, the Pinyon Jay. *Ecology* 70:316–328.

Marzluff, J. M., and B. Heinrich. 1991. Foraging by Common Ravens in the presence and absence of territory holders: an experimental analysis of social foraging. *Anim. Behav.* 42:755–770.

Mason, J. R., and R. F. Reidinger Jr. 1981. Effects of social facilitation and observational learning on feeding behavior of the Red-winged Blackbird (*Agelaius phoeniceus). Auk* 98:778–784.

Mason, J. R., A. H. Arzt, and R. F. Reidinger. 1984. Comparative assessment of food preferences and aversions acquired by blackbirds via observational learning. *Auk* 101:796–803.

Matthysen, E., T. C. Grubb Jr., and D. Cimprich. 1991. Social control of sex-specific foraging behaviour in Downy Woodpeckers, *Picoides pubescens*. *Anim. Behav.* 42:512–517.

Maxson, S. J., and G.-A. D. Maxson. 1981. Commensal foraging between Hairy and Pileated Woodpeckers. *J. Field Ornithol.* 52:62–63.

Mayer, L., S. Lustick and B. Battersby. 1982. The importance of cavity roosting and hypothermia to energy balance of the winter acclimatized Carolina Chickadee. *Internat. J. Biometeorol.* 26:231–238.

McCallum, D. A. 1990. Variable cone crops, migration, and dynamics of a population of Mountain Chickadees (*Parus gambeli*). Pp. 103–116 in *Population Biology of Passerine Birds, an Integrated Approach,* vol. G-24, J. Blondel, A. Gosler, J. D. Lebreton, and R. McCleery, eds. Springer-Verlag, Heidelberg: NATO ASI Services.

McClure, H. E. 1989. Epizootic lesions of House Finches in Ventura County, California. *J. Field Ornithol.* 60:421–430.

McGillivray, W. B., and E. C. Murphy. 1984. Sexual differences in longevity of House Sparrows at Calgary, Alberta. *Wilson Bull.* 96:456–458.

McLaren, M. A. 1975. Breeding biology of the Boreal Chickadee. *Wilson Bull.* 87:344–354.

Meanley, B. 1965. The roosting behavior of the Red-winged Blackbird in the southern United States. *Wilson Bull.* 77:217–228.

Merritt, P. G. 1980. Group foraging by mockingbirds in a Florida strangler fig. *Auk* 97:869–872.

Mewaldt, L. R. 1976. Winter philopatry in White-crowned Sparrows (*Zonotrichia leucophrys*). *N. Amer. Bird Bander* 1:14–20.

Mewaldt, L. R., and J. R. King. 1985. Breeding site faithfulness, reproductive biology, and adult survivorship in an isolated population of Cassin's Finches. *Condor* 87:494–510.

Middleton, A. L. A. 1977. Increase in overwintering by the American Goldfinch, *Carduelis tristis*, in Ontario. *Can. Field-Natur.* 91:165–172.

———. 1978. The annual cycle of the American Goldfinch. *Condor* 80:401–406.

———. 1986. Seasonal changes in plumage structure and body composition of the American Goldfinch, *Carduelis tristis. Can. Field-Natur.* 100:545–549.

———. 1993. American Goldfinch (*Carduelis tristis*). In *Birds of North America,* no. 80, A. Poole and F. Gill, eds. Philadelphia: Academy of Natural Sciences; Washington: American Ornithologists' Union.

Miller, E. V. 1941. Behavior of the Bewick's Wren. *Condor* 43:81–99.

Miller, R. S. 1985. Why hummingbirds hover. *Auk* 102:722–726.

Miller, R. S., and R. E. Miller. 1971. The memory of hummingbirds. *Blue Jay* 29:29–30.

Miller, R. S., and R. W. Nero. 1983. Hummingbird-sapsucker associations in northern climates. *Can. J. Zool.* 61:1540–1546.

Miller, R. S., S. Tamm, G. D. Sutherland, and C. L. Gass. 1985. Cues for orientation in hummingbird foraging: color and position. *Can. J. Zool.* 63:18–21.

Millikan, G. C., P. Gaddis, and H. R. Pulliam. 1985. Interspecific dominance and the foraging behaviour of juncos. *Anim. Behav.* 33:428–435.

Minock, M. E. 1971. Social relationships among Mountain Chickadees *(Parus gambeli).* *Condor* 73:118–120.

———. 1972. Interspecific aggression between Black-capped and Mountain Chickadees at winter feeding stations. *Condor* 74:454–461.

Mirarchi, R. E. and T. S. Baskett. 1994. Mourning Dove *(Zenaida macroura).* In *Birds of North America,* no. 117, A. Poole and F. Gill, eds. Philadelphia: Academy of Natural Sciences; Washington: American Ornithologists' Union.

Moore, F. R. 1977. Flocking behaviour and territorial competitors. *Anim. Behav.* 25:1063–1065.

Moore, F. 1978. Interspecific aggression: toward whom should a mockingbird be aggressive? *Behav. Ecol. Sociobiol.* 3:173–176.

Morrison, M. L. 1984. Influence of sample size on discriminant function analysis of habitat use by birds. *J. Field Ornithol.* 55:330–355.

Morrison, M. L., and K. A. With. 1987. Interseasonal and intersexual resource partitioning in Hairy and White-headed Woodpeckers. *Auk* 104:225–233.

Morrison, M. L, and M. P. Yoder-Williams. 1984. Movements of Steller's Jays in western North America. *N. Amer. Bird Bander* 9:12–15.

Morse, D. H. 1967a. Foraging relationships of Brown–headed Nuthatches and Pine Warblers. *Ecology* 48:94–103.

———. 1967b. The use of tools by Brown-headed Nuthatches. *Wilson Bull.* 80:220–224.

———. 1970. Ecological aspects of some mixed-species foraging flocks of birds. *Ecol. Monogr.* 40:119–168.

———. 1971. Effects of the arrival of new species upon habitat utilization by two forest thrushes in Maine. *Wilson Bull.* 83:57–65.

———. 1972. Habitat utilization of the red-cockaded Woodpecker during the winter. *Auk* 89:429–435.

———. 1989. *American Warblers.* Cambridge, Mass: Harvard University Press.

Morton, E. S., and M. D. Shalter. 1977. Vocal response to predators in pair-bonded Carolina Wrens. *Condor* 79:222–227.

Mott, D. F. 1984. Research on winter roosting blackbirds and starlings in the southeastern United States. *Proc. Vertebrate Pest Conf.* 11:183–187.

Mountjoy, D. J., and R. J. Robertson. 1988. Why are waxwings "waxy"? Delayed plumage maturation in the Cedar Waxwing. *Auk* 105:61–69.

Mueller, A. J. 1992. Inca Dove *(Columbina inca).* In *Birds of North America,* no. 28, A. Poole and F. Gill, eds. Philadelphia: Academy of Natural Sciences; Washington: American Ornithologists' Union.

Mundinger, P. C., and S. Hope. 1982. Expansion of the winter range of the House Finch: 1947–1979. *Amer. Birds* 36:347–353.

Murton, R. K., R. J. P. Thearle, and J. Thompson. 1972. Ecological studies of the feral pigeon *Columba livia* var. I. Population, breeding biology and methods of control. *J. Appl. Ecol.* 9:835–874.

Musselman, T. E. 1941. Bluebird mortality in 1940. *Auk* 58:409–410.

Muzny, P. L. 1982. Goldfinches and waxwing drinking maple sap. *Bull. Oklahoma Ornithol. Soc.* 15:8.

Myton, B. A., and R. W. Ficken. 1967. Seed-size preference in chickadees and titmice in relation to ambient temperatures. *Wilson Bull.* 79:319–321.

Naugler, C. T. 1993. American Tree Sparrow (*Spizella arborea*). In *Birds of North America,* no. 37, A. Poole and F. Gill, eds. Philadelphia: Academy of Natural Sciences; Washington: American Ornithologists' Union.

Nesbitt, S. A., and W. M. Hetrick. 1976. Foods of the Pine Warbler and Brown-headed Nuthatch. *Florida Field Natur.* 4:28–33.

Nice, M. M. 1937. *Studies in the Life History of the Song Sparrow.* Part 1. Trans. Linnaean Society. New York: Dover Publications.

———. 1943. *Studies in the Life History of the Song Sparrow.* Part 2. Trans. Linnaean Society. New York: Dover Publications.

Noon, B. R. 1981. The distribution of an avian guild along a temperate elevational gradient: the importance and expression of competition. *Ecol. Monogr.* 51:105–124.

Norman, D. M., J. R. Mason and L. Clark. 1992. Capsaicin effects on consumption of food by Cedar Waxwings and House Finches. *Wilson Bull.* 104:549–551.

Norment, C. J. and S. A. Shackleton. 1993. Harris' Sparrow (*Zonotrichia querula*). In *Birds of North America,* no. 64, A. Poole and F. Gill, eds. Philadelphia: Academy of Natural Sciences; Washington: American Ornithologists' Union.

Norris, R. A. 1958. Comparative biosystematics and life history of the nuthatches, *Sitta pygmaea* and *Sitta pusilla. Univ. Calif. Publ. Zool.* 56:119–300.

O'Halloran, K. A., and R. N. Connor. 1987. Habitat used by Brown-headed Nuthatches. Bull. *Texas Ornithol. Soc.* 20:7–13.

Ohmart, R. D., and E. L. Smith. 1970. Use of sodium chloride solutions by the Brewer's Sparrow and Tree Sparrow. *Auk* 87:329–341.

Oliphant, M. 1991. An invasion of Steller's Jays into the Oklahoma Panhandle. Bull. *Oklahoma Ornithol. Soc.* 24:14–15.

Olson, J. B. and S. C. Kendeigh. 1980. Effect of season on the energetics, body composition, and cage activity of the Field Sparrow. *Auk* 97:704–720.

Orell, M. 1989. Population fluctuations and survival of Great Tits *Parus major* dependent on food supplied by man in winter. *Ibis* 131:112–127.

Ostry, M. E, T. H. Nicholls, and D.W. French. 1983. *Animal Vectors of Eastern Dwarf Mistletoe of Black Spruce.* Research Paper NC–232. St. Paul, Minn.: U.S. Forest Service.

Ouellet, H. 1970. Further observations on the food and predatory habits of the gray jay. *Can. J. Zool.* 48:327–330.

Palmer, R. S., ed. 1988. *Handbook of North American Birds,* vol. 4, Diurnal Raptors (Part I). New Haven: Yale University Press.

Parrish, J. R. 1988. Kleptoparasitism of insects by a Broad-tailed Hummingbird.

J. Field Ornithol. 59:128–129.

Peach, W. J., and J. A. Fowler. 1989. Movements of wing-tagged starlings *Sturnus vulgaris* from an urban communal roost in winter. *Bird Study* 36:16–22.

Pearson, O. P. 1979. Spacing and orientation among feeding Golden-crowned Sparrows. *Condor* 81:278–285.

Pearson, S. M. 1991. Food patches and the spacing of individual foragers. *Auk* 108:355–362.

Perrins, C. M., and T. R. Birkhead. 1980. The effect of Sparrowhawks on tit populations. *Ardea* 68:133–142.

Peters, W. D., and T. C. Grubb Jr. 1983. An experimental analysis of sex specific foraging in the Downy Woodpecker *Picoides pubescens. Ecology.* 64:1437–1443.

Petit, D. R., L. J. Petit, and K. E. Petit. 1989. Winter caching ecology of deciduous woodland birds and adaptations for protection of stored food. *Condor* 91:766–776.

Phelan, J. P. 1987. Some components of flocking behavior in the Rock Dove (*Columba livia*). *J. Field Ornithol.* 58:135–143.

Phillips, A. R. 1975. The migrations of Allen's and other hummingbirds. *Condor* 77:196–205.

Pietz, M. A. J., and P. J. Pietz. 1987. American Robin defends fruit resource against Cedar Waxwings. *J. Field Ornithol.* 58:442–444.

Pinkowski, B. C. 1977. Foraging behavior of the Eastern Bluebird. *Wilson Bull.* 89:404–414.

———. 1979. Effects of a severe winter on a breeding population of Eastern Bluebirds. *Jack-Pine Warbler* 57:8–12.

Piper, W. H. 1990a. Exposure to predators and access to food in wintering White-throated Sparrows *Zonotrichia albicollis. Behaviour* 112:284–298.

———. 1990b. Site tenacity and dominance in wintering White-throated Sparrows *Zonotrichia albicollis* (Passeriformes: Emberizidae). *Ethology* 85:114–122.

Piper, W. H., and R. H. Wiley. 1989. Correlates of dominance in wintering White-throated Sparrows: age, sex and location. *Anim. Behav.* 37:298–310.

———. 1990a. Correlates of range size in wintering White-throated Sparrows, *Zonotrichia albicollis. Anim. Behav.* 40:545–552.

———. 1990b. The relationship between social dominance, subcutaneous fat, and annual survival in wintering white-throated sparrows (*Zonotrichia albicollis*). *Behav. Ecol. Sociobiol.* 26:201–208.

Pittaway, R. 1989. Pine Grosbeaks using bird feeders. *Ontario Birds* 7:65–67.

Pitts, T. D. 1976. Fall and winter roosting habits of Carolina Chickadees. *Wilson Bull.* 88:603–610.

Place, A. R. and E. W. Stiles. 1992. Living off the wax of the land: bayberries and Yellow-rumped Warblers. *Auk* 109:334–345.

Popp, J. W. 1987a. Agonistic communication among wintering Purple Finches. *Wilson Bull.* 99:97–100.

————. 1987b. Resource value and dominance among American Goldfinches. *Bird Behav.* 7:73–77.

————. 1988. Scanning behavior of finches in mixed-species groups. *Condor* 90:510–512.

Pravosudov, V. V. and T. C. Grubb Jr. 1993. White-breasted Nuthatch (*Sitta carolinensis*). In *Birds of North America,* no. 54, A. Poole and F. Gill, eds. Philadelphia: Academy of Natural Sciences; Washington: American Ornithologists' Union.

Pray, R. H. 1950. History of a wintering Harris Sparrow at Berkeley, California. *Condor* 52:89–90.

Prescott, D. R. C. 1991. Winter distribution of age and sex classes in an irruptive migrant, the Evening Grosbeak (*Coccothraustes vespertinus*). *Condor* 93:694–700.

Prescott, D. R. C., and A. L. A. Middleton. 1990. Age and sex differences in winter distribution of American Goldfinches in eastern North America. *Ornis Scand.* 21:99–104.

Prescott, D. R. C., A. L. A. Middleton, and D. R. Lamble. 1989. Variations in age and sex ratios of wintering American Goldfinches trapped at baited stations. *J. Field Ornithol.* 60:340–349.

Price, J., D. Droege, and A. Price. 1995. *The Summer Atlas of North American Birds.* London: Academic Press.

Price, J. B. 1931. Some flocking habits of the crowned sparrows. *Condor* 33:238–242.

Pulliainen, E. 1974. Winter nutrition of the common crossbill (*Loxia curvirostra*) and the pine grosbeak *(Pinicola enucleator)* in northeastern Lapland in 1973. *Ann. Zool. Fennici* 11:204–206.

————. 1985. Body fat reserves and liver glycogen of the Waxwing *Bomby-cilla garrulus* overwintering in northern Finland. *Ornis Fennica* 62:27–28.

Pulliainen, E., T. Kallio, and A.-M. Hallaksela. 1978. Eating of wood by Parrot Crossbills, *Loxia pytyopsittacus*, and Redpolls, *Carduelis flammea. Aquilo Ser. Zool.* 18:23–27.

Pulliam, H. R. 1980. Do Chipping Sparrows forage optimally? *Ardea* 68:75–82.

————. 1985. Foraging efficiency, resource partitioning, and the coexistence of sparrow species. *Ecology* 66:1829–1836.

Pulliam, H. R., and J. B. Dunning. 1987. The influence of food supply on local density and diversity of sparrows. *Ecology* 68:1009–1014.

Pulliam, H. R., and F. A. Enders. 1971. The feeding ecology of five sympatric finch species. *Ecology* 52:557–566.

Pulliam, H. R., and G. S. Mills. 1977. The use of space by wintering sparrows. *Ecology* 58:1393–1399.

Racine, R. N., and N. S. Thompson. 1983. Social organization of wintering Blue Jays. *Behaviour* 87:237–255.

Ransom, W. R. 1950. Heavy winter mortality in Pacific Coast Varied Thrush. *Condor* 52:88.

Reebs, S. G. 1987. Roost characteristics and roosting behaviour of Black-billed

Magpies, *Pica pica*, in Edmonton, Alberta. *Can. Field-Natur.* 101:519–525.

Reebs, S. G., and D. A. Boag. 1987. Regurgitated pellets and late winter diet of Black-billed Magpies, *Pica pica*, in central Alberta. *Can. Field-Natur.* 101:108–110.

Reese, K. P., and J. A. Kadlec. 1984. Supplemental feeding: possible negative effects on Black-billed Magpies. *J. Wildl. Manage.* 48:608–610.

Reynolds, R. T., and E. C. Meslow. 1984. Partitioning of food and niche characteristics of coexisting *Accipiter* during breeding. *Auk* 101:761–779.

Ritchison, G., and M. K. Omer. 1990. Winter behavior of Northern Cardinals (*Cardinalis cardinalis*). Trans. *Kentucky Acad. Sci.* 51:145–153.

Robbins, C. S. 1973. Introduction, spread and present abundance of the House Sparrow in North America. *Ornithol. Monogr.* 14:3–9.

Robbins, C. S., D. Bystrak, and P. H. Geissler. 1986. *The Breeding Bird Survey: Its First Fifteen Years, 1965–1979.* Resource Publication 157. Washington, D.C.: U.S. Fish & Wildlife Service.

Roberts, W. A. 1988. Foraging and spatial memory in pigeons. *Proc. Internat. Ornith. Congress* 19:2083–2093.

Roberts, W. M. 1995. Hummingbird licking behavior and the energetics of nectar feeding. *Auk* 112: 456–463.

Robertson, P. B., and A. F. Schnapf. 1987. Pyramiding behavior of the Inca Dove: adaptive aspects of day-night differences. *Condor* 89:185–187.

Robertson, R. J., P. J. Weatherhead, F. J. S. Phelan, G. L. Holroyd, and N. Lester. 1978. On assessing the economic and ecological impact of winter blackbird flocks. *J. Wildl. Manage.* 42:53–60.

Rodgers, S. P. Jr. 1990. Predation of domestic fowl eggs by Red-bellied Woodpeckers. *Florida Field Natur.* 18:57–58.

Rogers, C. M., J. N. M. Smith, W. M. Hochachka, A. L. E. V. Cassidy, M. J. Taitt, P. Arcese, and D. Schluter. 1991. Spatial variation in winter survival of Song Sparrows *Melospiza melodia. Ornis Scand.* 22:387–395.

Rohwer, S. A. 1975. The social significance of avian winter plumage variability. *Evolution* 29:593–613.

———. 1977. Status signalling in Harris' Sparrow: some experiments in deception. *Behaviour* 61:107–129.

Root, R. B. 1964. Ecological interactions of the Chestnut-backed Chickadee following a range expansion. *Condor* 66:229–238.

———. 1969. Interspecific territoriality between Bewick's and House Wrens. *Auk* 86:125–127.

Root, T. L. 1988. *Atlas of Wintering North American Birds.* Chicago: University of Chicago Press.

Roseberry, J. L. 1962. Avian mortality in southern Illinois resulting from severe weather conditions. *Ecology* 43:739–740.

Roselaar, C. S. 1980. *Phasianus colchicus* Pheasant. In *The Birds of the Western Palearctic,* Vol. II: Hawks to Bustards, S. Cramp and K. E. L. Simmons, eds. London: Oxford University Press.

Rosenfield, R. N. and J. Bielefeldt. 1993. Cooper's Hawk (*Accipiter cooperii*).

In *Birds of North America,* no. 75, A. Poole and F. Gill, eds. Philadelphia: Academy of Natural Sciences; Washington: American Ornithologists' Union.

Roth, R. R. 1979. Foraging behavior of mockingbirds. The effect of too much grass. *Auk* 96:421–422.

Royall, W. C. Jr., and O. E. Bray. 1980. A study of radio-equipped flickers. N. Amer. *Bird Bander* 5:47–50.

Rusch, K. M., C. L. Pytte, and M. S. Ficken. 1996. Organization of agonistic vocalizations in Black-chinned Hummingbirds. *Condor* 98:557–566.

Russell, S. M. 1996. Anna's Hummingbird (*Calypte anna*). In *Birds of North America,* no. 226, A. Poole and F. Gill, eds. Philadelphia: Academy of Natural Sciences; Washington: American Ornithologists' Union.

Rutter, R. J. 1969. A contribution to the biology of the Gray Jay (*Perisoreus canadensis*). *Can. Field-Natur.* 83:300–316.

Sabine, W. S. 1959. The winter society of the Oregon Junco: intolerance, dominance, and the pecking order. *Condor* 61:110–135.

Sallabanks, R. 1993. Fruit defenders vs. fruit thieves: winter foraging behavior in American Robins. *J. Field Ornithol.* 64:42–48.

Samson, F. B. 1976. Territory, breeding density, and fall departure in Cassin's Finch. *Auk* 93:477–497.

———. 1977. Social dominance in winter flocks of Cassin's Finch. *Wilson Bull.* 89:57–66.

Samson, F. B., and S. J. Lewis. 1979. Experiments on population regulation in two North American parids. *Wilson Bull.* 91:222–233.

Sarno, R. J. 1989. A possible foraging relationship between Black-billed Magpies and American Kestrels. *Wilson Bull.* 101:507.

Sauer, J. R., J. E. Hines, G. Gough, I. Thomas, and B. G. Peterjohn. 1997. *The North American Breeding Bird Survey Results and Analysis.* Version 96.3. Laurel, Md.: Patuxent Wildlife Research Center.

Scarlett, T. L., and K. G. Smith. 1991. Acorn preference of urban Blue Jays (*Cyanocitta cristata*) during fall and spring in northwestern Arkansas. *Condor* 93:438–442.

Schardien, B. J., and J. A. Jackson. 1978. Extensive ground foraging by Pileated Woodpeckers in recently burned pine forests. *Mississippi Kite* 8:7–9.

Schneider, K. J. 1984. Dominance, predation, and optimal foraging in White-throated Sparrow flocks. *Ecology* 65:1820–1827.

Schwan, M. W., and D. D. Williams. 1978. Temperature regulation in the Common Raven of interior Alaska. *Comp. Biochem. Physiol.* 60:31–36.

Sealy, S. G. 1984. Capture and caching of flying carpenter ants by Pygmy Nuthatches. *Murrelet* 65:49–51.

Searcy, W. A. 1979. Morphological correlates of dominance in captive male Red-winged Blackbirds. *Condor* 81:417–420.

Searcy, W. A., and K. Yasukawa. 1981. Sexual size dimorphism and survival of male and female blackbirds (Icteridae). *Auk* 98:457–465.

Selander, R. K. and D. R. Giller. 1961. Analysis of sympatry of Great-tailed and Boat-tailed Grackles. *Condor* 63:29–86.

Shaw, W. T. 1936. Winter life and nesting studies of Hepburn's Rosy Finch in Washington State, Part I. Winter. *Auk* 53:9–16.

Shaw, W. W., and W. R. Mangun. 1984. *Nonconsumptive Use of Wildlife in the United States.* Washington, D.C.: U.S. Fish & Wildlife Service. Resource Publication 154.

Shedd, D. H. 1990. Aggressive interactions in wintering House Finches and Purple Finches. *Wilson Bull.* 102:174–178.

Sherry, D. 1984. Food storage by Black-capped Chickadees: memory for the location and contents of caches. *Anim. Behav.* 32:451–464.

Sherry, D. F. 1989. Food storing in the Paridae. *Wilson Bull.* 101:289–304.

Shreve, D. F. 1980. Differential mortality in the sexes of the Aleutian Gray-crowned Rosy Finch. *Amer. Midland Natur.* 104:193–197.

Shuman, T. W., R. J. Robel, A. D. Dayton, and J. L. Zimmerman. 1988. Apparent metabolizable energy content of foods used by Mourning Doves. *J. Wildl. Manage.* 52:481–483.

Siegfried, W. R., and L. G. Underhill. 1975. Flocking as an anti-predator strategy in doves. *Anim. Behav.* 23:504–508.

Skaggs, M. B. 1983. Murder at the bird banding station. *Redstart* 50:118.

Skeate, S. T. 1987. Interactions between birds and fruits in a northern Florida hammock community. *Ecology* 68:297–309.

Skorupa, J. P., and R. L. Hothem. 1985. Consumption of commercially-grown grapes by American Robins: a field evaluation of laboratory estimates. *J. Field Ornithol.* 56:369–378.

Skutch, A. F. 1991. *Life of the Pigeon.* Ithaca, N.Y.: Cornell University Press.

Smith, C. C., and R. P. Balda. 1979. Competition among insects, birds, and mammals for conifer seeds. *Amer. Zool.* 19:1065–1083.

Smith, J. N. M. 1977. Feeding rates, search paths, and surveillance for predators in Great-tailed Grackles. *Can. J. Zool.* 55:891–898.

Smith, J. N. M., R. D. Montgomerie, M. J. Taitt, and Y. Yom-Tov. 1980. A winter feeding experiment on an island Song Sparrow population. *Oecologia* 47:164–170.

Smith, K. G. 1979a. Migrational movements of Blue Jays west of the 100th meridian. *N. Amer. Bird Bander* 4:49–52.

———. 1979b. Common Redpolls using spruce seeds in northern Utah. *Wilson Bull.* 91:621–623.

———. 1986. Winter population dynamics of three species of mast-eating birds in the eastern United States. *Wilson Bull.* 98:407–418.

Smith, S. M. 1991. *The Black-capped Chickadee.* Ithaca, N.Y.: Comstock Publishing Associates, Cornell University Press.

———. 1992. Pairbond persistence and "divorce" in Black-capped Chickadees. *Wilson Bull.* 104:338–342.

———. 1993. Black-capped Chickadee (*Parus atricapillus*). In *Birds of North America,* no. 39, A. Poole and F. Gill, eds. Philadelphia: Academy of Natural Sciences; Washington: American Ornithologists' Union.

Smith, S. T. 1972. Communication and other social behavior in *Parus caroli-*

nensis. Publ. Nuttall Ornithol. Club. No. 11.

Southwick, E. E., and A. K. Southwick. 1980. Energetics of feeding on tree sap by Ruby-throated Hummingbirds in Michigan. *Amer. Midland Natur.* 104:328–334.

Speirs, J. M. 1972. Evening Grosbeak energetics. *Ontario Field Biol.* 26:16–19.

Sprenkle, J. M., and C. R. Blem. 1984. Metabolism and food selection of Eastern House Finches. *Wilson Bull.* 96:184–195.

Spring, L. W. 1965. Climbing and pecking adaptations in some North American woodpeckers. *Condor* 67:457–488.

Stallcup, P. L. 1968. Spatio-temporal relationships of nuthatches and woodpeckers in ponderosa pine forests of Colorado. *Ecology* 49:831–843.

Stallcup, R. 1991. Some thoughts on Anna's Hummingbirds and the ten-day cold snap in middle California. *Winging It* 3(2):7.

Stepney, P. H. R. 1975. Wintering distribution of Brewer's Blackbird: historical aspect, recent changes, and fluctuations. *Bird-Banding* 46:106–125.

Stewart, A. C., and M. G. Shepard. 1994. Steller's Jay invasion in southern Vancouver Island, British Columbia. *N. Amer. Bird-Bander* 19:90–95.

Stewart, P. A. 1980. Mockingbird's defense of a winter food source. *J. Field Ornithol.* 51:375.

Stiles, E. W. 1984. A fruit for all seasons. *Natural History* 93(8):42–53.

Stiles, F. G. 1976. Taste preferences, color preferences, and flower choice in hummingbirds. *Condor* 78:10–26.

Stone, E., and C. H. Trost. 1991. Predators, risks, and context for mobbing and alarm calls in Black-billed Magpies. *Anim. Behav.* 41:633–638.

Stoner, E. A. 1976. Cedar Waxwing recoveries. *N. Amer. Bird Bander* 1:171.

Storer, R. W. 1966. Sexual dimorphism and food habits in three North American accipiters. *Auk* 83:423–436.

Stotz, N. G. and R. P. Balda. 1995. Cache and recovery behavior of wild Pinyon Jays in northern Arizona. *Southwestern Naturalist* 40:180–184.

Stouffer, P. C., and D. F. Caccamise. 1991. Roosting and diurnal movements of radio-tagged American Crows. *Wilson Bull.* 103:387–400.

Strickland, D. 1991. Juvenile dispersal in Gray Jays: dominant brood member expels siblings from natal territory. *Can. J. Zool.* 69:2935–2945.

Strickland, D. and H. Ouellet. 1993. Gray Jay (*Perisoreus canadensis*). In *Birds of North America,* no. 40, A. Poole and F. Gill, eds. Philadelphia: Academy of Natural Sciences; Washington: American Ornithologists' Union.

Stuebe, M. M., and E. D. Ketterson. 1982. A study of fasting in Tree Sparrows (*Spizella arborea*) and Dark-eyed Juncos (*Junco hyemalis*): ecological implications. *Auk* 99:299–308.

Sturman, W. A. 1968. The foraging ecology of *Parus atricapillus* and *P. rufescens* in the breeding season, with comparisons with other species of *Parus. Condor* 70:309–322.

Sullivan, K. A. 1984. Information exploitation by Downy Woodpeckers in mixed-species flocks. *Behaviour* 91:294–311.

Sullivan, K. 1985. Selective alarm calling by Downy Woodpeckers in mixed-species flocks. *Auk* 102:184–187.

Summers, R. W., G. Westlake, and C. J. Feare. 1987. Differences in the ages, sexes, and physical condition of starlings at the centre and edges of roosts. *Ibis* 129:96–102.

Summers-Smith, D. 1963. *The House Sparrow.* London: Collins.

Sutherland, G. D., C. L. Gass, P. A. Thompson, and K. P. Lertzman. 1982. Feeding territoriality in migrant Rufous Hummingbirds: defense of Yellow-bellied Sapsucker (*Sphyrapicus varius*) feeding sites. *Can. J. Zool.* 60:2046–2050.

Swenson, J. E., K. C. Jensen, and J. E. Toepfer. 1988. Winter movements by Rosy Finches in Montana. *J. Field Ornithol.* 59:157–160.

Sydeman, W. J., and M. Güntert. 1983. Winter communal roosting in the Pygmy Nuthatch. In *Snag Habitat Management: Proceedings of the Symposium.* General Technology Report. RM–99, J. W. Davis, G. A. Goodwin, and R. A. Ockenfeis, Tech. Coord. Fort Collins, Colo: U.S. Forest Service.

Sydeman, W. J., M. Güntert, and R. P. Balda. 1988. Annual reproductive yield in the cooperative Pygmy Nuthatch (*Sitta pygmaea*). *Auk* 105:70–77.

Takekawa, J. Y., and E. O. Garton. 1984. How much is an Evening Grosbeak worth? *J. Forestry* 82:426–428.

Tallman, D. 1989. Siskin and other banding at two locations in Aberdeen, South Dakota: 1983–1987. *S. Dakota Bird Notes* 41:4–9.

Tamar, H., 1978. Indiana's Carolina Wrens and severe winters. *Indiana Audubon Quart.* 56:9–11.

Tate, J., Jr. 1973. Methods and annual sequence of foraging by the sapsucker. *Auk* 90:840–856.

Terres, J. K. 1981. Diseases of birds—how and why some birds die. *Amer. Birds* 35:255–260.

Terrill, S. B., and R. D. Ohmart. 1984. Facultative extension of fall migration by Yellow-rumped Warblers (*Dendroica coronata*). *Auk* 101:427–438.

Tooze, Z. J., and C. L. Gass. 1985. Responses of Rufous Hummingbirds to mid-day fasts. *Can. J. Zool.* 63:2249–2253.

Troy, D. M. 1983. Recaptures of Redpolls: movements of an irruptive species. *J. Field Ornithol.* 54:146–151.

Tweit, R. C. 1996. Curve-billed Thrasher (*Toxostoma curvirostre*). In *Birds of North America,* no. 235, A. Poole and F. Gill, eds. Philadelphia: Academy of Natural Sciences; Washington: American Ornithologists' Union.

U.S. Department of the Interior, Fish and Wildlife Service and U.S. Department of Commerce, Bureau of the Census. 1997. *1996 National Survey of Fishing, Hunting, and Wildlife-Associated Recreation.* Washington, D.C.: U.S. Government Printing Office.

U.S. Fish and Wildlife Service 1988. *1985 National Survey of Hunting, Fishing, and Wildlife-associated Recreation.* Washington, D.C.: U.S. Government Printing Office.

Van Balen, J. H. 1980. Population fluctuations of the Great Tit and feeding conditions in winter. *Ardea* 68:143–164.

Vander Wall, S. B. 1990. *Food Hoarding in Animals*. Chicago: University of Chicago Press.

Verbeek, N. A. M. 1972. Daily and annual time budget of the Yellow-billed Magpie. *Auk* 89:567–582.

Vines, G. 1981. A socio-ecology of Magpies *Pica pica*. *Ibis* 123:190–202.

Wagner, J. L. 1981. Seasonal change in guild structure; oak woodland insectivorous birds. *Ecology* 62:973–981.

Wagner, S. J., and S. A. Gauthreaux Jr. 1990. Correlates of dominance in intraspecific and interspecific interactions of Song Sparrows and White-throated Sparrows. *Anim. Behav.* 39:522–527.

Waite, T. A. 1987a. Dominance-specific vigilance in the Tufted Titmouse: effects of social context. *Condor* 89:932–935.

———. 1987b. Vigilance in the White-breasted Nuthatch: effects of dominance and sociality. *Auk* 104:429–434.

Waite, T. A., and T. C. Grubb Jr. 1988a. Copying of foraging locations in mixed-species flocks of temperate-deciduous woodland birds: an experimental study. *Condor* 90:132–140.

———. 1988b. Diurnal caching rhythm in captive White-breasted Nuthatches (*Sitta canadensis*). *Ornis Scand.* 19:68–70.

Wallace, R. A. 1974. Ecological and social implications of sexual dimorphism in five melanerpine woodpeckers. *Condor* 76:238–248.

Walsberg, G. E., and J. R. King. 1980. The thermoregulatory significance of the winter roost-sites selected by robins in eastern Washington. *Wilson Bull.* 92:33–39.

Waters, L. S. 1990. Meadowlarks prey on Pine Siskins and American Goldfinches. *Bull. Oklahoma Ornithol. Soc.* 23:7–8.

Watt, D. J. 1986. Relationship of plumage variability, size, and sex to social dominance in Harris' Sparrows. *Anim. Behav.* 34:16–27.

Watt, D. J., C. J. Ralph, and C. T. Atkinson. 1984. The role of plumage polymorphism in dominance relationships of the White-throated Sparrow. *Auk* 101:110–120.

Watts, B. D. 1990. Cover use and predator-related mortality in Song and Savannah Sparrows. *Auk* 107:775–778.

Weatherhead, P. J., and D. J. Hoysak. 1984. Dominance structuring of a Red-winged Blackbird roost. *Auk* 101:551–555.

Wells, J. V., K. V. Rosenberg, D. L. Tessaglia, and A. A. Dhondt. 1996. Population cycles in the Varied Thrush (*Ixoreus naevius*). *Can. J. Zool.* 74:2062–2069.

Westcott, P. W. 1969. Relationships among three species of jays wintering in southeastern Arizona. *Condor* 71:353–359.

Wheelwright, N. T. 1986. The diet of American Robins: an analysis of U.S. Biological Survey records. *Auk* 103:710–725.

———. 1988. Seasonal changes in food preferences of American Robins in captivity. *Auk* 105:374–378.

White, C. M., and G. C. West. 1977. The annual lipid cycle and feeding behavior of Alaskan redpolls. *Oecologia* 27:227–238.

White, D. H., C. B. Kepler, J. S. Hatfield, P. W. Sykes Jr., and J. T. Seginak. 1996. Habitat associations of birds in the Georgia Piedmont during winter. *J. Field Ornithol.* 67: 159–166.

Wible, M. W. 1975. Food washing by grackles. *Wilson Bull.* 87:282–283.

Widrlechner, M. P., and S. K. Dragula. 1984. Relation of cone-crop size to irruptions of four seed-eating birds in California. *Amer. Birds* 38:840–846.

Wiedenmann, R. N., and K. N. Rabenold. 1987. The effects of social dominance between two subspecies of Dark-eyed Juncos (*Junco hyemalis*). *Anim. Behav.* 35:856–864.

Wiley, R. H. 1991. Both high- and low-ranking White-throated Sparrows find novel locations of food. *Auk* 108:8–15.

Wiley, R. H., W. H. Piper, M. Archawaranon, and E. W. Thompson. 1993. Singing in relation to social dominance and testosterone in White-throated Sparrows. *Behaviour* 127:175–199.

Williams, H. W. 1969. Vocal behavior of adult California Quail. *Auk* 86:631–659.

Williams, J. B. 1975. Habitat utilization by four species of woodpeckers in a central Illinois woodland. *Amer. Midland Natur.* 93:354–367.

———. 1980. Foraging by Yellow-bellied Sapsuckers in central Illinois during spring migration. *Wilson Bull.* 92:519–523.

Williams, J. B., and G. O. Batzlie. 1979. Winter diet of a bark-foraging guild of birds. *Wilson Bull.* 91:126–131.

Williams, R. N., and R. C. Fleischer. 1989. Distributions and habitat associations of birds in Waikiki, Hawaii. *Pacific Science* 43:152–160.

Williamson, P., and L. Gray. 1975. Foraging behavior of the starling (*Sturnus vulgaris*) in Maryland. *Condor* 77:84–89.

Willimont, L. A., S. E. Senner, and L. J. Goodrich. 1988. Fall migration of Ruby-throated Hummingbirds in the northeastern United States. *Wilson Bull.* 100:482–488.

Willson, M. F., and J. C. Harmeson. 1973. Seed preferences and digestive efficiency of Cardinals and Song Sparrows. *Condor* 75:225–234.

Wilson, W. H., Jr. 1994. The distribution of wintering birds in central Maine: the interactive effects of landscape and bird feeders. *J. Field Ornithol.* 65:512–519.

Wiltschko, W., and R. P. Balda. 1989. Sun compass orientation in seed-caching Scrub Jays (*Aphelocoma coerulescens*). *J. Comp. Physiol.* 164:717–721.

Wilz, K. J., and V. Giampa. 1978. Habitat use by Yellow-rumped Warblers at the northern extremities of their winter range. *Wilson Bull.* 90:566–574.

With, K. A., and M. L. Morrison. 1990. Flock formation in two parids in relation to cyclical seed production in a pinyon-juniper woodland. *Auk* 107:522–532.

Witmer, M. C. 1996. Annual diet of Cedar Waxwings based on U.S. Biological Survey records (1885–1950) compared to diet of American Robins: contrasts in dietary patterns and natural history. *Auk* 113:414–430.

Witmer, M. C., D. J. Mountjoy, and L. Elliot. 1997. Cedar Waxwing (*Bombycilla cedrorum*). In *Birds of North America,* no. 309, A. Poole and F. Gill, eds. Philadelphia: Academy of Natural Sciences; Washington: American Ornithologists' Union.

Woodrey, M. S. 1990. Economics of caching versus immediate consumption by White-breasted Nuthatches: the effect of handling time. *Condor* 92:621–624.

———. 1991. Caching behavior in free-ranging White-breasted Nuthatches: the effects of social dominance. *Ornis Scand.* 22:160–166.

Woolfenden, G. 1962. Aggressive behavior by a wintering Myrtle Warbler. *Auk* 79:713–714.

Yarbrough, C. G. and D.W. Johnston. 1965. Lipid deposition in wintering and premigratory Myrtle Warblers. *Wilson Bull.* 77:175–191.

Yunick, R. P. 1978. The balance at the bird feeder. *N. Amer. Bird Bander* 3:48–51.

———. 1982. Some factors influencing feeder selection by Black-capped Chickadee and Red-breasted Nuthatches. *N. Amer. Bird Bander* 7:20–23.

———. 1983a. Winter site fidelity of some northern finches (Fringillidae). *J. Field. Ornithol.* 54:254–258.

———. 1983b. Age and sex determination of Purple Finches during the breeding season. *N. Amer. Bird Bander* 8:48–51.

———. 1984. An assessment of the irruptive status of the Boreal Chickadee in New York State. *J. Field Ornithol.* 55:31–37.

———. 1988. An assessment of the White-breasted Nuthatch and Red-breasted Nuthatch on recent New York State Christmas Counts. *Kingbird* 38:95–104.

Zink, R. M., and D. J. Watt. 1987. Allozymic correlates of dominance rank in sparrows. *Auk* 104:1–10.

Index